P9-AFD-307

Sixty Years of American Poetry

1-9-97

Expanded Edition

Wood Engravings by Barry Moser

Harry N. Abrams, Inc., Publishers

Sixty Years of American Poetry

CELEBRATING THE ANNIVERSARY OF THE ACADEMY OF AMERICAN POETS

Introduction by Robert Penn Warren

Preface by Richard Wilbur

Back in 1984, The Academy of American Poets celebrated its first half-century of existence by publishing *Fifty Years of American Poetry*. The present volume brings that anthology up to date by the addition of some 75 poems, representing the Academy's recently elected Chancellors as well as its recent award-winners and honorees. For the earlier book, Robert Penn Warren wrote an introduction which still serves admirably as an account of the Academy, and of its place in American poetry and the history of patronage. The function of these words of mine is to do a little updating and then to make way for Mr. Warren.

I first met that exceptional woman Marie Bullock in 1960 or so, when, on the lawn of her house in Edgartown, she gave me an after-dinner lecture on the stars. One of the things she pointed out in the heavens was the star in Draco which was used as North Star in the days of the Pharaohs. Her lesson stuck in my mind, and I later put it into a poem, but that was assuredly the least of Marie Bullock's contributions to poetry. The Academy that she founded has for sixty and more years given concrete encouragement to poets in every phase of development—to college undergraduates just learning the trade, to first-book poets, to poets faced with the hurdle of the second book, to established poets in need of cash or commendation. Among the Academy's many other initiatives have been the popularizing of poetry through public readings and audiotapes, the fostering of verse translation, the establishment of poetry workshops for high school students, the administering of a fund that gives aid to poets in personal emergencies. It is a long list of excellent undertakings.

Marie Bullock would be glad to know how the goals of her Academy have been elaborated of late, under the leadership of Lyn Chase, so that it now sponsors readings and festivals on a truly national basis, has increased the number and richness of its prizes, and significantly furthers the publishing of poetry in book form. Under the Presidency of Jonathan Galassi, more new programs—the creation of a poetry book club, for example—are contemplated and will doubtless be realized. In the past, the word "academy" may sometimes have implied stodginess and a somnolent self-admiration, but the Academy of American Poets, which has accomplished so much in a venturesome, generous, and catholic spirit, gives the word a lively present ring. Speaking as one who just retired from the Academy's Board of Chancellors, I am proud to have been involved, for 35 years, with an organization that has made so real a difference to poetry and to American culture.

Richard Wilbur

INTRODUCTION

This is the semi-centennial of The Academy of American Poets, and this anthology, created at the suggestion of Harry N. Abrams, Inc., the distinguished publishing house, and the Book-of-the-Month Club, is one of the various celebrations of that event. In it are represented, with óne poem each, the Chancellors, Fellows, and Award Winners since 1934—a hundred and twenty-six poets in all—a sort of cross-section of American poetry in the last half-century. A glance at the table of contents will show that no one school, bailiwick, method, or category of poetry has dominated the interest of the Academy. The Academy has been interested in poetry, not in cults or schools, in helping, as best it could, though no doubt with some human failing, serious poets of whatsoever persuasion.

What does the Academy do? According to its certificate of incorporation, its purpose is "To encourage, stimulate, and foster the production of American poetry. . . ." The responsibility for its activities lies with the Board of Directors (with Mrs. Hugh Bullock as president and many board members of distinguished reputation) and the Board of twelve Chancellors, which has included, over the years, such figures as Louise Bogan, W.H. Auden, Witter Bynner, Randall Jarrell, Robert Lowell, Robinson Jeffers, Marianne Moore, James Merrill, Robert Fitzgerald, F.O. Matthiessen, and Archibald MacLeish—certainly not members of the same poetic church. The primary duty of the Chancellors is to determine the winners of the various Fellowship Awards and, upon request, to advise the Board of Directors. As for the Fellowships, from 1937 to 1969, the value of each was $5,000, and since then $10,000. The first

Fellowship was awarded in 1947 to Edgar Lee Masters, a prefatory award having been made in 1937 to Edwin Markham. To date there are forty-seven Fellows.

Very significantly, the Academy has tried to reach beyond the professional level to the young, from whom the new poets must spring, or the new readers of poetry. For instance, the program of Poetry-in-the-Schools, fostered by the Academy, is now national. Furthermore, the Academy has assumed that its mission is not "Eastern provincial," as the awards and the books vouched for by the Academy and its various other activities clearly show. Behind all of these lies the assumption that poetry is not for poets only, but for readers, and that the cultivation of readers—the explanation of what poetry really is, what and how it "means," what it is about, how it may affect the reader— is essential for the health of poetry.

American education has become debased in this department since the old-fashioned days when, in almost all grades, there were usually required recitations of memorized poems, and often a discussion of them. We may compare the present perfunctory attention to poetry to the French system by which poems, even in early grades, simple for the very young, but by a master, must be memorized each week, recited, and then analyzed in a written theme based on specific questions. To have great poets there must be great audiences, Whitman said, to the more or less unheeding ears of American educators. Ambitiously, hopefully, the Academy has undertaken to remedy this plight.

Let us look back a half century to the moment in which

the Academy was founded. At that time the modern poetic revolution was already here. Robinson, the forerunner, had only a year or so to live. Frost was at the height of his fame, as was Eliot. Hart Crane was already dead. Ransom had written most of his poems. William Carlos Williams published his first *Collected Poems*, with an introduction by Wallace Stevens, almost simultaneously with the founding of the Academy. A new generation, offspring of that revolution, was about to appear.

The fact of such a background in no way diminishes the importance of the founding of the Academy, even though it may have given preparation for it. To those already sunk in poetry, it had been an exhilarating period, but many literates, or semi-such readers, and many established professors had not heard the news (except for Robinson and Frost, and more remotely the rumor of Eliot), or took it as bad news. There were not many F.O. Matthiessens and Cleanth Brookses around in those days. Furthermore, most graduate students, even in important universities, were above such trivialities, a fact I can vouch for from my own experience. In other words, most of the poetic ferment had been in the scum afloat at the top of the pot and not in the heart of the brew. This is not, however, to say that many writers or readers who felt the necessity of the achievements of modernism were not solidly, or adequately, grounded in the old literature and devoted to it. They simply felt, instinctively, that literature must be a constantly expanding growth in a world of inevitable change. The Academy recognized the inevitability of change, and that literature is an expanding growth, as the limited tenure of Chancellors most obviously testifies. The poetry of today is not that of the 1920s and 1930s, and certain contemporary poets of real achievement find little or no direct inspiration from that earlier revolution.

If we look for the genesis of the Academy, we see a young woman, Marie Graves, of French birth but American parentage, raised in France (except for the years of World War I), steeped in music from all the festivals of Europe, from study, and from the musicians, along with artists and writers, frequenting the house of her family, and those of their friends. And there was, too, the Sorbonne.

When, in 1933, she married an American, Mr. Hugh Bullock, and came to New York, she was in for a surprise. "I found no poets (or other artists) at social events I attended in New York City, as I had done constantly on the Continent; and when poets I had looked forward to hearing in class [she had registered at Columbia] were not given time off from such jobs as soda-fountain jerk, or salesman in a clothing store, to come and read, my sense of artistic appreciation, nurtured in Europe, was immensely outraged."

She knew, of course, that things much more important than social life were involved; that situation was merely a symptom. Life itself—bread—was involved. Poverty was a common lot of poets unless they had the stamina to carry a job, menial or not, or a profession, with poetry an occupation of stolen time. Yes, there had been hungry and shabby poets even in France—the Nervals and Verlaines, the poets *maudits*. (Though Verlaine, in old age, did receive some private help.) And the same was true of England, from Chatterton to Francis Thompson, for example. The Continent was a little short of Utopia. But on that Continent there was a much more widespread, even official, recognition of poetry, and the other arts, as a basic national asset. In the early 1930s, a friend of mine, a poet of high reputation, was living with his family in a small French village, where he was often seen publicly carrying garbage from the kitchen. A delegation of the ladies of the village called on my friend's wife, and finally worked up the courage to tell her that it was not seemly for a poet to be seen in that role; it gave the village a bad name. Comedy, yes. But something else, too.

Even though poetry was regarded in various European countries as a national asset, prime ministers and bureaucrats did not necessarily retain much more than the fading recollection of it from the lycée or university; however, they knew an asset when they saw it. And a number of high officials have been writers of stature, most recently and famously St. John Perse as a poet, and Winston Churchill as a historian and prose stylist.

The long tradition of patronage, as Mrs. Bullock well knew, runs from the Greeks to modern Europe, accounting, quite literally, for many world masterpieces. Though the private patron survived, the governments themselves were assuming more and more responsibility. In England, from the late Middle Ages, private bounty was not uncommon and eventually the Crown provided substantial subsidy, and in following centuries, along with much important private munificence, there was a drift toward a consistent governmental patronage, ending in the annual Civil List— where once a name is inscribed, an annuity follows for life.

It is true that in America, in the nineteenth century, the government occasionally appointed a literary man to a post at home, most famously the Custom House, or abroad as a consul, Hawthorne having served, not always happily or productively, in both capacities. But we remember that the great Melville, fallen on evil days, served in the Custom House in New York—though not as a political appointee—grubbing away for many years at $4.00 a day, working at his poetry at night.

It was not until Theodore Roosevelt that an American poet received government patronage with any degree of understanding. When Robinson was in middle life, the author of only two books, a son of Roosevelt called the president's attention to one of them, *Children of the Night*, which the youth admired. The father, that strange combination of a sprawling diversity of qualities, recognized the talent in the poems and arranged an interview with the poet in which he said, "I regret that no Civil List exists in this country as in England and elsewhere. In its absence, I am forced to offer you a post in the Custom House. If you accept it, I urge you to put poetry first and the United States Treasury second." Apparently Robinson followed that advice, and a score of volumes followed—and great fame.

Theodore Roosevelt has had no successor of the same kidney.

Our government has, however, lately shown a new awareness of the arts, and has a number of very definite achievements to its credit. We should, of course, be grateful for this fact, and should hope for permanence and development. But should we assume that a political solution, however high-minded, is adequate? Certainly such a program would be the most vulnerable when budget-cutters get to work. That, however, is not my real point. Private aid to the arts seems to be more in the American individualistic tradition. Even a great foundation represents an individual's sense of values. And the individual who writes a $10.00 check for The Academy of American Poets has, however slightly, a new relation to the art of poetry; it is in a sense, "his." This is not to say that poetry or the reading of it should be the primary concern of mankind: but it is an activity, for writer or reader, valuable and unique, and a fundamental measure of the quality of any civilization.

I may seem to have wandered far from the founding of the Academy, but much of what I have said presumably lies in the background of that event, and in the Founder's determination, in her first distress about the American scene, to try "to do something about it." First, for discussion and advice, she turned to the poets she had, in fact, met, among whom were Robinson, Ridgely Torrence (poetry editor of the *New Republic*), Joseph Auslander (a teacher of hers at Columbia). Then, on the practical side, there was her husband, with his knowledge of the world of finance and law (and whose commitment was to grow to the point where he served as Secretary of the Academy). Those early days of struggle and hope come now to the Founder's mind: "We used many odd means to try to secure interest and funds. . . . It was hard work. I well remember the first early contributions, and how exciting it was to receive the first $50.00 or $100.00 check. And how much it meant when a bricklayer sent a $1.00 bill, because he 'loved poetry.'" It is easy to understand the symbolic weight of that $1.00, a meaning deeper, and more justifying, than that of munificent impersonal gifts from great corporations or foundations or governmental agencies.

The Academy has long since become a significant American institution. The originally vague, but dauntless, impulse "to do something about it" took form, bit by bit, with the aid of many other dauntless hearts and able workers. And here should be mentioned Elizabeth Kray, who, for many years, ingeniously and devotedly, committed herself and her great skills to the office of Executive Director.

It is hard to think back to the time, which some of us can still remember, when a public poetry reading was a rarity and, when one did occur, was often the subject of a jest. But now they are numberless, good and bad, in all sorts of places, and usually to well populated or packed houses. And not uncommonly Universities, great and famous or small, welcome poets to their faculties. But these items are merely symptoms of a change in American society —society in the broadest sense—to which the Academy has so vitally contributed. We should remember, however, that the Academy is engaged in a mission that is endless. That mission is as endless as we hope our civilization to be.

Robert Penn Warren
Vermont, Spring 1984

The Poems

E. A. ROBINSON

For a Dead Lady

No more with overflowing light
Shall fill the eyes that now are faded,
Nor shall another's fringe with night
Their woman-hidden world as they did.

No more shall quiver down the days
The flowing wonder of her ways,
Whereof no language may requite
The shifting and the many-shaded.

The grace, divine, definitive,
Clings only as a faint forestalling;
The laugh that love could not forgive
Is hushed, and answers to no calling;
The forehead and the little ears
Have gone where Saturn keeps the years;
The breast where roses could not live
Has done with rising and with falling.

The beauty, shattered by the laws
That have creation in their keeping,
No longer trembles at applause,
Or over children that are sleeping;
And we who delve in beauty's lore
Know all that we have known before
Of what inexorable cause
Makes Time so vicious in his reaping.

The Hill

Where are Elmer, Herman, Bert, Tom and Charley,
The weak of will, the strong of arm, the clown, the boozer,
    the fighter?
All, all, are sleeping on the hill.

One passed in a fever,
One was burned in a mine,
One was killed in a brawl,
One died in a jail,
One fell from a bridge toiling for children and wife—
All, all are sleeping, sleeping, sleeping on the hill.

Where are Ella, Kate, Mag, Lizzie and Edith,
The tender heart, the simple soul, the loud, the proud,
    the happy one?—
All, all, are sleeping on the hill.

One died in shameful child-birth
One of a thwarted love,
One at the hands of a brute in a brothel,
One of a broken pride, in the search for her heart's desire,
One after life in far-away London and Paris
Was brought to her little space by Ella and Kate and Mag—
All, all are sleeping, sleeping, sleeping on the hill.

Where are Uncle Isaac and Aunt Emily,
And old Towny Kincaid and Sevigne Houghton,
And Major Walker who had talked
With venerable men of the revolution—
All, all, are sleeping on the hill.

They brought them dead sons from the war,
And daughters whom life had crushed,
And their children fatherless, crying—
All, all are sleeping, sleeping, sleeping on the hill.

Where is Old Fiddler Jones
Who played with life all his ninety years,
Braving the sleet with bared breast,
Drinking, rioting, thinking neither of wife nor kin,
Nor gold, nor love, nor heaven?
Lo! he babbles of the fish-frys of long ago,
Of the horse-races of long ago at Clary's Grove,
Of what Abe Lincoln said
One time at Springfield.

EZRA POUND

The River-Merchant's Wife: A Letter

While my hair was still cut straight across my forehead
Played I about the front gate, pulling flowers.
You came by on bamboo stilts, playing horse,
You walked about my seat, playing with blue plums.
And we went on living in the village of Chokan:
Two small people, without dislike or suspicion.

At fourteen I married My Lord you.
I never laughed, being bashful.
Lowering my head, I looked at the wall.
Called to, a thousand times, I never looked back.

At fifteen I stopped scowling,
I desired my dust to be mingled with yours
Forever and forever and forever.
Why should I climb the look out?

At sixteen you departed,
You went into far Ku-to-yen, by the river of swirling eddies,
And you have been gone five months.
The monkeys make sorrowful noise overhead.

You dragged your feet when you went out.
By the gate now, the moss is grown, the different mosses,
Too deep to clear them away!
The leaves fall early this autumn, in wind.
The paired butterflies are already yellow with August
Over the grass in the West garden;
They hurt me. I grow older.
If you are coming down through the narrows of the river Kiang,
Please let me know beforehand,
And I will come out to meet you
                    As far as Cho-fu-Sa.

PADRAIC COLUM

An Old Woman of the Roads

Oh, to have a little house!
To own the hearth and stool and all!
The heaped-up sods upon the fire,
The pile of turf against the wall!

To have a clock with weights and chains
And pendulum swinging up and down,
A dresser filled with shining delph,
Speckled and white and blue and brown!

I could be busy all the day
Clearing and sweeping hearth and floor,
And fixing on their shelf again
My white and blue and speckled store!

I could be quiet there at night
Beside the fire and by myself,
Sure of a bed and loth to leave
The ticking clock and the shining delph!

Och! but I'm weary of mist and dark,
And roads where there's never a house nor bush,
And tired I am of bog and road,
And the crying wind and the lonesome hush!

And I am praying to God on high,
And I am praying him night and day,
For a little house, a house of my own—
Out of the wind's and the rain's way.

Driftwood

Come, warm your hands
From the cold wind of time.
I have built here under the moon,
A many-coloured fire
With fragments of wood
That have been part of a tree
And part of a ship.

Were leaves more real,
Or driven nails,
Or fingers of builders,
Than these burning violets?
Come, warm your hands
From the cold wind of time.
There's a fire under the moon.

CONRAD AIKEN

Two coffees in the Español, the last
Bright drops of golden Barsac in a goblet,
Fig paste and candied nuts . . . Hardy is dead,
And James and Conrad dead, and Shakspere dead,
And old Moore ripens for an obscene grave,
And Yeats for an arid one; and I, and you—
What winding sheet for us, what boards and bricks,
What mummeries, candles, prayers, and pious frauds?
You shall be lapped in Syrian scarlet, woman,
And wear your pearls, and your bright bracelets, too,
Your agate ring, and round your neck shall hang
Your dark blue lapis with its specks of gold.
And I, beside you—ah! but will that be?
For there are dark streams in this dark world, lady,
Gulf Streams and Arctic currents of the soul;
And I may be, before our consummation
Beds us together, cheek by jowl, in earth,
Swept to another shore, where my white bones
Will lie unhonored, or defiled by gulls.

What dignity can death bestow on us,
Who kiss beneath a streetlamp, or hold hands
Half hidden in a taxi, or replete
With coffee, figs and Barsac make our way
To a dark bedroom in a wormworn house?
The aspidistra guards the door; we enter,
Per aspidistra—then—*ad astra*—is it?—
And lock ourselves securely in our gloom
And loose ourselves from terror. . . . Here's my hand,
The white scar on my thumb, and here's my mouth
To stop your murmur; speechless let us lie,
And think of Hardy, Shakspere, Yeats and James;
Comfort our panic hearts with magic names;
Stare at the ceiling, where the taxi lamps
Make ghosts of light; and see, beyond this bed,
That other bed in which we will not move;
And, whether joined or separated, will not love.

Interval

Water pulls nervously whispering satin across
        cool roots, cold stones;
  And a bird balances his soul on a song flash, a
        desperate outcry:
These are the minor chords, the monotones;
  This the undefeated gesture against an armored sky.

The moment is metal; the sun crawling over it is a fly
  Head down on a bronze ceiling; the hot stillness
        drones:
And you go sliding through green sea shafts and I
  Am an old mountain warming his tired bones.

JOHN CROWE RANSOM

Judith of Bethulia

Beautiful as the flying legend of some leopard
She had not yet chosen her great captain or prince
Depositary to her flesh, and our defense;
And a wandering beauty is a blade out of its scabbard.
You know how dangerous, gentlemen of threescore?
May you know it yet ten more.

Nor by process of veiling she grew the less fabulous.
Grey or blue veils, we were desperate to study
The invincible emanations of her white body,
And the winds at her ordered raiment were ominous.
Might she walk in the market, sit in the council of soldiers?
Only of the extreme elders.

But a rare chance was the girl's then, when the Invader
Trumpeted from the south, and rumbled from the north,
Beleaguered the city from four quarters of the earth,
Our soldiery too craven and sick to aid her—
Where were the arms could countervail this horde?
Her beauty was the sword.

She sat with the elders, and proved on their blear visage
How bright was the weapon unrusted in her keeping,
While he lay surfeiting on their harvest heaping,
Wasting the husbandry of their rarest vintage—
And dreaming of the broad-breasted dames for concubine?
These floated on his wine.

He was lapped with bay-leaves, and grass and fumiter weed,
And from under the wine-film encountered his mortal vision,
For even within his tent she accomplished his derision;
She loosed one veil and another, standing unafraid;
And he perished. Nor brushed her with even so much as a daisy?
She found his destruction easy.

The heathen are all perished. The victory was furnished,
We smote them hiding in our vineyards, barns, annexes,
And now their white bones clutter the holes of foxes,
And the chieftain's head, with grinning sockets, and varnished—
Is it hung on the sky with a hideous epitaphy?
No, the woman keeps the trophy.

May God send unto our virtuous lady her prince.
It is stated she went reluctant to that orgy,
Yet a madness fevers our young men, and not the clergy
Nor the elders have turned them unto modesty since.
Inflamed by the thought of her naked beauty with desire?
Yes, and chilled with fear and despair.

WILLIAM ROSE BENÉT

Jesse James
(A Design in Red and Yellow for a Nickel Library)

JESSE JAMES was a two-gun man,
    (Roll on, Missouri!)
Strong-arm chief of an outlaw clan.
    (From Kansas to Illinois!)
He twirled an old Colt forty-five;
    (Roll on, Missouri!)
They never took Jesse James alive.
    (Roll, Missouri, roll!)

Jesse James 'was King of the Wes';
    (Cataracks in the Missouri!)
He'd a di'mon' heart in his lef' breas';
    (Brown Missouri rolls!)
He'd a fire in his heart no hurt could stifle;
    (Thunder, Missouri!)
Lion eyes an' a Winchester rifle.
    (Missouri, roll down!)

Jesse James rode a pinto hawse;
Come at night to a water-cawse;
Tetched with the rowel that pinto's flank;
She sprung the torrent from bank to bank.

Jesse rode through a sleepin' town;
Looked the moonlit street both up an' down;
Crack-crack-crack, the street ran flames
An' a great voice cried, "I'm Jesse James!"

Hawse an' afoot they're after Jess!
    (Roll on, Missouri!)
Spurrin' an' spurrin'—but he's gone Wes'.
    (Brown Missouri rolls!)
He was ten foot tall when he stood in his boots;
    (Lightnin' light the Missouri!)
More'n a match fer sich galoots.
    (Roll, Missouri, roll!)

Jesse James rode outa the sage;
Roun' the rocks come the swayin' stage;
Straddlin' the road a giant stan's
An' a great voice bellers, "Throw up yer han's!"

Jesse raked in the di'mon' rings,
The big gold watches an' the yuther things;
Jesse divvied 'em then an' thar
With a cryin' child had lost her mar.

The U.S. troopers is after Jess;
    (Roll on, Missouri!)
Their hawses sweat foam, but he's gone Wes';
    (Hear Missouri roar!)
He was broad as a b'ar, he'd a ches' like a drum,
    (Wind an' rain through Missouri!)
An' his red hair flamed like Kingdom Come.
    (Missouri down to the sea!)

Jesse James all alone in the rain
Stopped an' stuck up the Eas'-boun' train;
Swayed through the coaches with horns an' a tail,
Lit out with the bullion an' the registered mail.

Jess made 'em all turn green with fright
Quakin' in the aisles in the pitch-black night;
An' he give all the bullion to a pore ole tramp
Campin' nigh the cuttin' in the dirt an' damp.

The whole U. S. is after Jess;
    (Roll on, Missouri!)
The son-of-a-gun, if he ain't gone Wes';
    (Missouri to the sea!)
He could chaw cold iron an' spit blue flame;
    (Cataracks down the Missouri!)
He rode on a catamount he'd larned to tame.
    (Hear that Missouri roll!)

Jesse James rode into a bank;
Give his pinto a tetch on the flank;
Jumped the teller's window with an awful crash;
Heaved up the safe an' twirled his mustache;

He said, "So long, boys!" He yelped, "So long!
Feelin' porely today—I ain't feelin' strong!"
Rode right through the wall a-goin' crack-crack-crack—
Took the safe home to mother in a gunny-sack.

They're creepin', they're crawlin', they're stalkin' Jess;
    (Roll on, Missouri!)
They's a rumor he's gone much further Wes';
    (Roll, Missouri, roll!)
They's word of a cayuse hitched to the bars
    (Ruddy clouds on Missouri!)
Of a golden sunset that busts into stars.
    (Missouri, roll down!)

Jesse James rode hell fer leather;
He was a hawse an' a man together;
In a cave in a mountain high up in air
He lived with a rattlesnake, a wolf, an' a bear.

Jesse's heart was as sof' as a woman;
Fer guts an' stren'th he was sooper-human;
He could put six shots through a woodpecker's eye
And take in one swaller a gallon o' rye.

They sought him here an' they sought him there,
    (Roll on, Missouri!)
But he strides by night through the ways of the air;
    (Brown Missouri rolls!)
They say he was took an' they say he is dead,
    (Thunder, Missouri!)
But he ain't—he's a sunset overhead!
    (Missouri down to the sea!)

Jesse James was a Hercules.
When he went through the woods he tore up the trees.
When he went on the plains he smoked the groun'
An' the hull lan' shuddered fer miles aroun'.

Jesse James wore a red bandanner
That waved on the breeze like the Star Spangled Banner;
In seven states he cut up dadoes.
He's gone with the buffler an' the desperadoes.

Yes, Jesse James was a two-gun man
    (Roll on, Missouri!)
The same as when this song began;
    (From Kansas to Illinois!)
An' when you see a sunset bust into flames
    (Lightnin' light the Missouri!)
Or a thunderstorm blaze—that's Jesse James!
    (Hear that Missouri roll!)

ROBINSON JEFFERS

Hurt Hawks

I

The broken pillar of the wing jags from the clotted shoulder,
The wing trails like a banner in defeat,
No more to use the sky forever but live with famine
And pain a few days: cat nor coyote
Will shorten the week of waiting for death, there is game
      without talons.
He stands under the oak-bush and waits
The lame feet of salvation; at night he remembers freedom
And flies in a dream, the dawns ruin it.
He is strong and pain is worse to the strong, incapacity is worse.
The curs of the day come and torment him
At distance, no one but death the redeemer will humble
      that head,
The intrepid readiness, the terrible eyes.
The wild God of the world is sometimes merciful to those
That ask mercy, not often to the arrogant.
You do not know him, you communal people, or you
      have forgotten him;
Intemperate and savage, the hawk remembers him;
Beautiful and wild, the hawks, and men that are dying,
      remember him.

II

I'd sooner, except the penalties, kill a man than a hawk;
      but the great redtail
Had nothing left but unable misery
From the bone too shattered for mending, the wing that
      trailed under his talons when he moved.
We had fed him six weeks, I gave him freedom,
He wandered over the foreland hill and returned in the evening,
      asking for death,
Not like a beggar, still eyed with the old
Implacable arrogance. I gave him the lead gift in the
      twilight. What fell was relaxed,
Owl-downy, soft feminine feathers; but what
Soared: the fierce rush: the night-herons by the flooded river
      cried fear at its rising
Before it was quite unsheathed from reality.

EDNA ST. VINCENT MILLAY

The Cameo

Forever over now, forever, forever gone
That day. Clear and diminished like a scene
Carven in cameo, the lighthouse, and the cove between
The sandy cliffs, and the boat drawn up on the beach;
And the long skirt of a lady innocent and young,
Her hand resting on her bosom, her head hung;
And the figure of a man in earnest speech.

Clear and diminished like a scene cut in cameo
The lighthouse, and the boat on the beach, and the two shapes
Of the woman and the man; lost like the lost day
Are the words that passed, and the pain,—discarded, cut away
From the stone, as from the memory the heat of the tears escapes.

O troubled forms, O early love unfortunate and hard,
Time has estranged you into a jewel cold and pure;
From the action of the waves and from the action of sorrow
        forever secure,
White against a ruddy cliff you stand, chalcedony on sard.

OLIVER ST. JOHN GOGARTY

Anachronism

Tall and great-bearded: black and white,
The deep-eyed beggar gazed about,
For all his weight of years, upright;
He woke the morning with a shout,
One shout, one note, one rolling word;
But in my dreaming ears I heard
The sea-filled rhythm roll again,
And saw long-vanished boys and men
With eager faces ranged around
A dark man in a market place,
Singing to men of his own race,
With long blithe ripples in the sound,
Of isles enchanted, love and wrath,
And of Achilles' deadly path;
The great ash spear he used to fling;
The bow one man alone could string;
Odysseus in the sea immersed
Who never heard of "Safety First,"
Nor went to a Peace Conference:
For Homer was a man of sense,
And knew right well the only themes
Of Song, when men have time for dreams.
And then, indignant, down the lane
The great dark beggar roared again.

ARCHIBALD MacLEISH

You, Andrew Marvell

And here face down beneath the sun
And here upon earth's noonward height
To feel the always coming on
The always rising of the night:

To feel creep up the curving east
The earthy chill of dusk and slow
Upon those under lands the vast
And ever climbing shadow grow

And strange at Ecbatan the trees
Take leaf by leaf the evening strange
The flooding dark about their knees
The mountains over Persia change

And now at Kermanshah the gate
Dark empty and the withered grass
And through the twilight now the late
Few travelers in the westward pass

And Baghdad darken and the bridge
Across the silent river gone
And through Arabia the edge
Of evening widen and steal on

And deepen on Palmyra's street
The wheel rut in the ruined stone
And Lebanon fade out and Crete
High through the clouds and overblown

And over Sicily the air
Still flashing with the landward gulls
And loom and slowly disappear
The sails above the shadowy hulls

And Spain go under and the shore
Of Africa the gilded sand
And evening vanish and no more
The low pale light across that land

Nor now the long light on the sea:

And here face downward in the sun
To feel how swift how secretly
The shadow of the night comes on . . .

ALLEN TATE

Aeneas at Washington

I myself saw furious with blood
Neoptolemus, at his side the black Atridae,
Hecuba and the hundred daughters, Priam
Cut down, his filth drenching the holy fires.
In that extremity I bore me well
A true gentleman, valorous in arms,
Disinterested and honorable. Then fled:
That was a time when civilization
Run by the few fell to the many, and
Crashed to the shout of men, the clang of arms:
Cold victualing I seized, I hoisted up
The old man my father upon my back,
In the smoke made by sea for a new world
Saving little—a mind imperishable
If time is, a love of past things tenuous
As the hesitation of receding love.

(To the reduction of uncitied littorals
We brought chiefly the vigor of prophecy
Our hunger breeding calculation
And fixed triumphs)

                  The thirsty dove I saw
In the glowing fields of Troy, hemp ripening
And tawny corn, the thickening Blue Grass
All lying rich forever in the green sun.
I see all things apart, the towers that men
Contrive I too contrived long, long ago.
Now I demand little. The singular passion
Abides its object and consumes desire
In the circling shadow of its appetite.
There was a time when the young eyes were slow,
Their flame steady beyond the firstling fire,
I stood in the rain, far from home at nightfall
By the Potomac, the great Dome lit the water,
The city my blood had built I knew no more
While the screech-owl whistled his new delight
Consecutively dark.
                    Stuck in the wet mire
Four thousand leagues from the ninth buried city
I thought of Troy, what we had built her for.

EDWIN MARKHAM

The Third Wonder

'Two things,' said Kant, 'fill me with breathless awe:
The starry heavens and the moral law.'
I know a thing more awful and obscure—
The long, long patience of the plundered poor.

AUDREY WURDEMANN

Behold this brief hexagonal,
The honey and the honey-cell,
A tower of wax;—a touch, and see
These walls that could sustain a bee
Clinging with clawed and furry feet
Now bend and break and spill their sweet.

Behold, my dear, the dream we saw,
The thing we built without a flaw,
The amber and the agate rime,
The interstitial beat of time,
The microcosmos of our wit,
The sweetness that we sucked from it,
The honeycomb, the holy land
Broken and bleeding in my hand.

The Jerboa

Too Much

A Roman had an
artist, a freedman,
    contrive a cone—pine-cone
    or fir-cone—with holes for a fountain. Placed on
        the Prison of St. Angelo, this cone
        of the Pompeys which is known

now as the Popes', passed
for art. A huge cast
    bronze, dwarfing the peacock
    statue in the garden of the Vatican,
        it looks like a work of art made to give
        to a Pompey, or native

of Thebes. Others could
build, and understood
    making colossi and
    how to use slaves, and kept crocodiles and put
        baboons on the necks of giraffes to pick
        fruit, and used serpent magic.

They had their men tie
hippopotami
    and bring out dapple dog-
    cats to course antelopes, dikdik, and ibex;
        or used small eagles. They looked on as theirs,
        impallas and onigers,

the wild ostrich herd
with hard feet and bird
    necks rearing back in the
    dust like a serpent preparing to strike, cranes,
        mongooses, storks, anoas, Nile geese;
        and there were gardens for these—

combining planes, dates,
limes, and pomegranates,
    in avenues—with square
      pools of pink flowers, tame fish, and small frogs. Besides
        yarns dyed with indigo, and red cotton,
        they had a flax which they spun

into fine linen
cordage for yachtsmen.
    These people liked small things;
      they gave to boys little paired playthings such as
        nests of eggs, ichneumon and snake, paddle
        and raft, badger and camel;

and made toys for them-
selves: the royal totem;
    and toilet-boxes marked
      with the contents. Lords and ladies put goose-grease
        paint in round bone boxes with pivoting
        lid incised with the duck-wing

or reverted duck-
head; kept in a buck
    or rhinoceros horn,
      the ground horn; and locust oil in stone locusts.
        It was a picture with a fine distance;
        of drought, and of assistance

in time, from the Nile
rising slowly, while
    the pig-tailed monkey on
      slab-hands, with arched-up slack-slung gait, and the brown
        dandy, looked at the jasmine two-leafed twig
        and bud, cactus-pads, and fig.

62

Dwarfs here and there, lent
to an evident
    poetry of frog greys,
      duck-egg greens, and egg-plant blues, a fantasy
        and a verisimilitude that were
        right to those with, everywhere,

power over the poor.
The bees' food is your
    food. Those who tended flower-
    beds and stables were like the king's cane in the
      form of a hand, or the folding bedroom
      made for his mother of whom

he was fond. Princes
clad in queens' dresses,
    calla or petunia
    white, that trembled at the edge, and queens in a
      king's underskirt of fine-twilled thread like silk-
      worm gut, as bee-man and milk-

maid, kept divine cows
and bees; limestone brows,
    and gold-foil wings. They made
    basalt serpents and portraits of beetles; the
      king gave his name to them and he was named
      for them. He feared snakes, and tamed

Pharaoh's rat, the rust-
backed mongoose. No bust
    of it was made, but there
    was pleasure for the rat. Its restlessness was
      its excellence; it was praised for its wit;
      and the jerboa, like it,

a small desert rat,
and not famous, that
    lives without water, has
    happiness. Abroad seeking food, or at home
      in its burrow, the Sahara field-mouse
      has a shining silver house

of sand. O rest and
joy, the boundless sand,
    the stupendous sand-spout,
      no water, no palm-trees, no ivory bed,
        tiny cactus; but one would not be he
        who has nothing but plenty.

    Abundance

Africanus meant
the conqueror sent
    from Rome. It should mean the
    untouched: the sand-brown jumping-rat—free-born; and
        the blacks, that choice race with an elegance
        ignored by one's ignorance.

Part terrestrial,
and part celestial,
    Jacob saw, cudgel staff
    in claw-hand—steps of air and air angels; his
        friends were the stones. The translucent mistake
        of the desert, does not make

hardship for one who
can rest and then do
    the opposite—launching
    as if on wings, from its match-thin hind legs, in
        daytime or at night; with the tail as a weight,
        undulated by speed, straight.

Looked at by daylight,
the underside's white,
    though the fur on the back
    is buff-brown like the breast of the fawn-breasted
        bower-bird. It hops like the fawn-breast, but has
        chipmunk contours—perceived as

it turns its bird head—
the nap directed
    neatly back and blending
      with the ear which reiterates the slimness
        of the body. The fine hairs on the tail,
        repeating the other pale

markings, lengthen till
at the tip they fill
    out in a tuft—black and
      white; strange detail of the simplified creature,
        fish-shaped and silvered to steel by the force
        of the large desert moon. Course

the jerboa, or
plunder its food store,
    and you will be cursed. It
      honours the sand by assuming its colour;
        closed upper paws seeming one with the fur
        in its flight from a danger.

By fifths and sevenths,
in leaps of two lengths,
    like the uneven notes
      of the Bedouin flute, it stops its gleaning
        on little wheel castors, and makes fern-seed
        foot-prints with kangaroo speed.

Its leaps should be set
to the flageolet;
    pillar body erect
      on a three-cornered smooth-working Chippendale
        claw—propped on hind legs, and tail as third toe,
        between leaps to its burrow.

MURIEL RUKEYSER

Effort at Speech Between Two People

: Speak to me.   Take my hand.   What are you now?
I will tell you all.   I will conceal nothing.
When I was three, a little child read a story about a rabbit
who died, in the story, and I crawled under a chair :
a pink rabbit : it was my birthday, and a candle
burnt a sore spot on my finger, and I was told to be happy.

: Oh, grow to know me.   I am not happy.   I will be open :
Now I am thinking of white sails against a sky like music,
like glad horns blowing, and birds tilting, and an arm about me.
There was one I loved, who wanted to live, sailing.

: Speak to me.   Take my hand.   What are you now?
When I was nine, I was fruitily sentimental,
fluid : and my widowed aunt played Chopin,
and I bent my head on the painted woodwork, and wept.
I want now to be close to you.   I would
link the minutes of my days close, somehow, to your days.

I am not happy.   I will be open.
I have liked lamps in evening corners, and quiet poems.
There has been fear in my life.   Sometimes I speculate
On what a tragedy his life was, really.

: Take my hand.   Fist my mind in your hand.   What are
    you now?
When I was fourteen, I had dreams of suicide,
and I stood at a steep window, at sunset, hoping toward death :
if the light had not melted clouds and plains to beauty,
if light had not transformed that day, I would have leapt.
I am unhappy.   I am lonely.   Speak to me.

: I will be open.   I think he never loved me :
he loved the bright beaches, the little lips of foam
that ride small waves, he loved the veer of gulls :
he said with a gay mouth : I love you.   Grow to know me.

: What are you now?   If we could touch one another,
if these our separate entities could come to grips,
clenched like a Chinese puzzle . . . yesterday
I stood in a crowded street that was live with people,
and no one spoke a word, and the morning shone.
Everyone silent, moving. . . . Take my hand.   Speak to me.

CARL SANDBURG

An Englishman in the old days
presented the Empress of Russia
with a life-sized flea made of gold
and it could hop.

She asked the court:
"What can we Russians do
to equal this marvel?"

A minister took it away
and brought it back soon after.
He had seen to it
and had the monogram of the Empress
engraved on each foot of the flea
though it would no longer hop.

This is a case in point
as told by Salzman
who came from the Caucasus
and had it from a man who was there.

In Tiflis, his home town,
Salzman knew a merchant
who stood in the front door
and spoke to passersby,
to possible customers:
  "Come inside.
  We've got everything—
  even bird's milk."

And this merchant weighed his hand
along with what he sold his patrons
and each evening after business hours
he threw holy water on his hand
saying, "Cleanse thyself, cleanse thyself."

Among the peasants Salzman heard:
"He should be the owner of the land
who rubs it between his hands every spring."

Wood rangers in the forest of the czar
came in and talked all night.
They spoke of forest sounds:
"The cry of a virgin tree at its first cut of the ax stays in the air.
"The sound of the blow that kills a snake is in the
    air till sundown.
"The cry of the child wrongfully punished stays in the air."

And this was in the old days
and they are a fine smoke
a thin smoke.

The people move
in a fine thin smoke,
the people, yes.

DUDLEY FITTS

Ya Se Van Los Pastores

Lady, the shepherds have all gone
To Extremadura, taking their sheep with them,

Their musical instruments also, their singing:
We shall not see them again.

Therefore bring lute, flute, or other melodious machine,
And we shall sit under this plane-tree and perform upon it.

There is no help for it: use your eyes:

The shepherds, Lady, have gone into Extremadura,
Eastward, into sunrise.

PERCY MacKAYE

After Tempest

Shell-less, on your slimey trail,
In mornless dawn, I meet you, snail:
Sans house, sans home, sans bivouac,
No arc of wonder spans your back.

Here, on time's storm-shattered shelf,
Slug, you meet your crawling self,
Reaching towards eternity
All-unavailing antennae!

LEONORA SPEYER

Swans

With wings held close and slim neck bent,
Along dark water scarcely stirred,
Floats, glimmering and indolent,
The alabaster bird;

Floats near its mate—the lovely one!
They lie like snow, cool flake on flake,
Mild breast on breast of dimmer swan
Dim-mirrored in the lake.

They glide—and glides that white embrace,
Shy bird to bird with never a sound;
Thus leaned Narcissus toward his face,
Leaned lower till he drowned.

Leda leaned thus, subdued and spent
Beneath those vivid wings of love;
Along the lake, proud, indolent,
The vast birds scarcely move.

Silence is wisdom. Then how wise
Are these whose song is but their knell!
A god did well to choose this guise.
Truly, a god did well.

e.e. cummings

my father moved through dooms of love

my father moved through dooms of love
through sames of am through haves of give,
singing each morning out of each night
my father moved through depths of height

this motionless forgetful where
turned at his glance to shining here;
that if (so timid air is firm)
under his eyes would stir and squirm

newly as from unburied which
floats the first who,his april touch
drove sleeping selves to swarm their fates
woke dreamers to their ghostly roots

and should some why completely weep
my father's fingers brought her sleep:
vainly no smallest voice might cry
for he could feel the mountains grow.

Lifting the valleys of the sea
my father moved through griefs of joy;
praising a forehead called the moon
singing desire into begin

joy was his song and joy so pure
a heart of star by him could steer
and pure so now and now so yes
the wrists of twilight would rejoice

keen as midsummer's keen beyond
conceiving mind of sun will stand,
so strictly (over utmost him
so hugely) stood my father's dream

his flesh was flesh his blood was blood:
no hungry man but wished him food;
no cripple wouldn't creep one mile
uphill to only see him smile.

Scorning the pomp of must and shall
my father moved through dooms of feel;
his anger was as right as rain
his pity was as green as grain

septembering arms of year extend
less humbly wealth to foe and friend
than he to foolish and to wise
offered immeasurable is

proudly and (by octobering flame
beckoned) as earth will downward climb,
so naked for immortal work
his shoulders marched against the dark

his sorrow was as true as bread:
no liar looked him in the head;
if every friend became his foe
he'd laugh and build a world with snow.

My father moved through theys of we,
singing each new leaf out of each tree
(and every child was sure that spring
danced when she heard my father sing)

then let men kill which cannot share,
let blood and flesh be mud and mire,
scheming imagine,passion willed,
freedom a drug that's bought and sold

giving to steal and cruel kind,
a heart to fear,to doubt a mind,
to differ a disease of same,
conform the pinnacle of am

though dull were all we taste as bright,
bitter all utterly things sweet,
maggoty minus and dumb death
all we inherit,all bequeath

and nothing quite so least as truth
—i say though hate were why men breathe—
because my father lived his soul
love is the whole and more than all

MAX EASTMAN

Animal

Could you, so arrantly of earth, so cool,
With coarse harsh hair and rapid agile pace,
So built to beat boys in a swimming race
Or dive with sheer terns to a salty pool,
So lean, so animally beautiful—
Your breasts look sideways like a heifer's face,
And you stand sometimes with a surly grace
And mutinous blue eye-fires like a bull—
Could you from this most envied poise descend,
Moved by some force in me I know not of,
To mix with me and be to me a woman,
Diana down from heaven could not lend
More ecstasy, or fill my faltering human
Heart's hunger with a more celestial love.

JOHN NEIHARDT

From *The Song of Jed Smith*

> One more rendezvous—
> And only silence waiting after all!
>
> The nights were nippy with a tang of Fall
> Along the lone road leading to the States—
> The season when the dying Summer waits
> To listen for the whisper of the snow
> A long way off. Three horseback days below
> The Arkansaw, and twelve from Santa Fé
> I crossed the Cimarrone; another day
> Beyond the waterholes, and that was where
> He left the wagons.
>
> All around me there
> Was empty desert, level as a sea,
> And like a picture of eternity
> Completed for the holding of regret.
> But I could almost see the oxen yet
> Droop, panting, in the circled wagon train;
> The anxious eyes that followed on the plain
> A solitary horseman growing dim;
> And, riding south, I almost sighted him
> Along the last horizon—many moons
> Ahead of me.
>
> Beyond a strip of dunes
> I came upon the Cimarrone once more,
> A winding flat no wetter than the shore,
> Excepting when you clawed a hole, it filled.
> But hunting for the spot where he was killed
> Was weary work. There had to be a ledge
> Of sandstone jutting from the river's edge
> Southwestwardly; and, balanced at the tip,
> A bowlder, waiting for a flood, to slip
> And tumble in the stream; and just below,
> Not any farther than a good knife-throw,
> A hiding place behind a point of clay.
>
> But there was sand—and sand.

                                        The second day,
When I was sure the Mexicans had sold
The buyer's wish, with twilight getting cold
And blue along a northward bend, I came
Upon it with a start—the very same,
Except the bowlder bedded in the stream!
And like one helpless in an evil dream,
I seemed to see it all. The burning glare,
The pawing horse, and 'Diah clawing there
Beneath the ledge, beyond the reach of sound
To warn him of the faces peering round
The point of clay behind; a sheath-knife thrown,
Bows twanging; 'Diah fighting all alone,
A-bristle with the arrows and the knife—
Alone, alone, and fighting for his life
With twenty yelling devils; left for dead,
The bloody, feathered huddle that was Jed,
Half buried in Comanches, coming to;
The slow red trail, the hard, last trail that grew
Behind him, crawling up the bank to seek
The frightened horse; too dizzy sick and weak
To make it past the sepulcher of shade
The sandstone ledge and balanced bowlder made
Against the swimming dazzle of the sun;
The band returning for the horse and gun
To find him there, still moaning, in his tomb
And roll the bowlder on him.
                                        —Only gloom
And silence left!''

                    The voice of sorrow rose
And ceased. Assenting in a semi-doze,
The elder nodded sagely; and the Squire
Breathed deeper. Feeling by the fallen fire
The mystery of sorrow in the cry,
The dog sat up and, muzzle to the sky,
Mourned for the dear one mourning.

Adam's Dying

He dreamed first
   Of what seem
The things worst
   In the dream:

The lost bower,
   The grave's drouth,
The sword's power,
   The worm's mouth.

He dreamed last
   Of good things:
The pain past,
   The air's wings.

The seed furled,
   The stirred dust,
Sight's world,
   The hand's thrust.

Thought's birth,
   The mind's blade,
Work's worth,
   The thing made.

The wind's haste,
   The cloud's dove,
The fruit's taste,
   The heart's love.

The sky's dome,
   The sun's west,
A man's home,
   Eve's breast.

The wave's beach,
   The bird's wood,
Dreams, each,
   But all good.

Life finds rest
   Where life rose.
Which was best?
   The heart knows.

Never Again Would Birds' Song Be the Same

He would declare and could himself believe
That the birds there in all the garden round
From having heard the daylong voice of Eve
Had added to their own an oversound,
Her tone of meaning but without the words.
Admittedly an eloquence so soft
Could only have had an influence on birds
When call or laughter carried it aloft.
Be that as may be, she was in their song.
Moreover her voice upon their voices crossed
Had now persisted in the woods so long
That probably it never would be lost.
Never again would birds' song be the same.
And to do that to birds was why she came.

RANDALL JARRELL

At home, in my flannel gown, like a bear to its floe,
I clambered to bed; up the globe's impossible sides
I sailed all night—till at last, with my black beard,
My furs and my dogs, I stood at the northern pole.

There in the childish night my companions lay frozen,
The stiff furs knocked at my starveling throat,
And I gave my great sigh: the flakes came huddling,
Were they really my end? In the darkness I turned to my rest.

—Here, the flag snaps in the glare and silence
Of the unbroken ice. I stand here,
The dogs bark, my beard is black, and I stare
At the North Pole . . .
                              And now what? Why, go back.

Turn as I please, my step is to the south.
The world—my world spins on this final point
Of cold and wretchedness: all lines, all winds
End in this whirlpool I at last discover.

And it is meaningless. In the child's bed
After the night's voyage, in that warm world
Where people work and suffer for the end
That crowns the pain—in that Cloud-Cuckoo-Land

I reached my North and it had meaning.
Here at the actual pole of my existence,
Where all that I have done is meaningless,
Where I die or live by accident alone—

Where, living or dying, I am still alone;
Here where North, the night, the berg of death
Crowd me out of the ignorant darkness,
I see at last that all the knowledge

I wrung from the darkness—that the darkness flung me—
Is worthless as ignorance: nothing comes from nothing,
The darkness from the darkness. Pain comes from the darkness
And we call it wisdom. It is pain.

Strength Through Joy

Coming back over the col between
Isosceles Mountain and North Palisade,
I stop at the summit and look back
At the storm gathering over the white peaks
Of the Whitney group and the colored
Kaweahs. September, nineteen-thirty-nine.
This is the last trip in the mountains
This autumn, possibly the last trip ever.
The storm clouds rise up the mountainside,
Lightning batters the pinnacles above me,
The clouds beneath the pass are purple
And I see rising through them from the valleys
And cities a cold, murderous flood,
Spreading over the world, lapping at the last
Inviolate heights; mud streaked yellow
With gas, slimy and blotched with crimson,
Filled with broken bits of steel and flesh,
Moving slowly with the blind motion
Of lice, spreading inexorably
As bacteria spread in tissues,
Swirling with the precise rapacity of starved rats.
I loiter here like a condemned man

Lingers over his last breakfast, his last smoke;
Thinking of those heroes of the war
Of human skill, foresight, endurance and will;
The disinterested bravery,
The ideal combat of peace: Bauer
Crawling all night around his icecave
On snowbound Kanchenjunga, Tilman
And Shipton skylarking on Nanda Devi,
Smythe seeing visions on Everest,
The mad children of the Eigerwand—
What holidays will they keep this year?
Gun emplacements blasted in the rock;
No place for graves, the dead covered with quicklime
Or left in the snow till the spring thaw;
Machine gun duels between white robed ski troops,
The last screaming schusses marked with blood.
Was it for this we spent the years perfecting
The craft of courage? Better the corpse
Of the foolhardy, frozen on the Eiger
Accessible only to the storm,
Standing sentry for the avalanche.

Speaks the Whispering Grass

See young John Sutton with his Kathaleen
In love with life, alive to kiss and dreams;
A fairer couple I have never seen
Through April eyes of my green liquid stems!
Now let them love while spring is in their blood,
Know joy of living, ecstasy, and pain;
And let them know each coming season's mood,
Let them know life that will not come again.

Snakes, lizards, scorpions, boast eternal spring
But I shall drink their cold blood through my tendrils;
Fair Kathaleen and John who laugh and sing
Will give to me their portion for my petals!
Even, slow shell-protected terrapin
Shall give my fibers strength, bone for my stems;
I nurture everything but blowing wind,
The lamps of Heaven and earth's buried dreams.

MARK VAN DOREN

The Seven Sleepers

The liberal arts lie eastward of this shore.
Choppy the waves at first. Then the long swells
And the being lost. Oh, centuries of salt
Till the surf booms again, and comes more land.

Not even there, except that old men point
At passes up the mountains. Over which,
Oh, centuries of soil, with olive trees
For twisted shade, and helicons for sound.

Then eastward seas, boned with peninsulas.
Then, orient, the islands; and at last,
The cave, the seven sleepers. Who will rise
And sing to you in numbers till you know

White magic. Which remember. Do you hear?
Oh, universe of sand that you must cross,
And animal the night. But do not rest.
The centuries are stars, and stud the way.

In Praise of Limestone

If it form the one landscape that we the inconstant ones
    Are consistently homesick for, this is chiefly
Because it dissolves in water. Mark these rounded slopes
    With their surface fragrance of thyme and beneath
A secret system of caves and conduits; hear these springs
    That spurt out everywhere with a chuckle
Each filling a private pool for its fish and carving
    Its own little ravine whose cliffs entertain
The butterfly and the lizard; examine this region
    Of short distances and definite places:
What could be more like Mother or a fitter background
    For her son, for the nude young male who lounges
Against a rock displaying his dildo, never doubting
    That for all his faults he is loved, whose works are but
Extensions of his power to charm? From weathered outcrop
    To hill-top temple, from appearing waters to
Conspicuous fountains, from a wild to a formal vineyard,
    Are ingenious but short steps that a child's wish
To receive more attention than his brothers, whether
    By pleasing or teasing, can easily take.

Watch, then, the band of rivals as they climb up and down
    Their steep stone gennels in twos and threes, sometimes
Arm in arm, but never, thank God, in step; or engaged
    On the shady side of a square at midday in
Voluble discourse, knowing each other too well to think
    There are any important secrets, unable
To conceive a god whose temper-tantrums are moral
    And not to be pacified by a clever line
Or a good lay: for, accustomed to a stone that responds,
    They have never had to veil their faces in awe
Of a crater whose blazing fury could not be fixed;
    Adjusted to the local needs of valleys

Where everything can be touched or reached by walking,
    Their eyes have never looked into infinite space
Through the lattice-work of a nomad's comb; born lucky,
    Their legs have never encountered the fungi
And insects of the jungle, the monstrous forms and lives
    With which we have nothing, we like to hope, in common.
So, when one of them goes to the bad, the way his mind works
    Remains comprehensible: to become a pimp
Or deal in fake jewelry or ruin a fine tenor voice
    For effects that bring down the house could happen to all
But the best and the worst of us . . .
                    That is why, I suppose,
    The best and worst never stayed here long but sought
Immoderate soils where the beauty was not so external,
    The light less public and the meaning of life
Something more than a mad camp. "Come!" cried
      the granite wastes,
    "How evasive is your humor, how accidental
Your kindest kiss, how permanent is death." (Saints-to-be
    Slipped away sighing.) "Come!" purred the
        clays and gravels,
"On our plains there is room for armies to drill; rivers
    Wait to be tamed and slaves to construct you a tomb
In the grand manner: soft as the earth is mankind and both
    Need to be altered." (Intendant Caesars rose and
Left, slamming the door.) But the really reckless were fetched
    By an older colder voice, the oceanic whisper:
"I am the solitude that asks and promises nothing;
    That is how I shall set you free. There is no love;
There are only the various envies, all of them sad."
    They were right, my dear, all those voices were right
And still are; this land is not the sweet home that it looks,
    Nor its peace the historical calm of a site

Where something was settled once and for all: A backward
  And dilapidated province, connected
To the big busy world by a tunnel, with a certain
  Seedy appeal, is that all it is now? Not quite:
It has a worldly duty which in spite of itself
  It does not neglect, but calls into question
All the Great Powers assume; it disturbs our rights. The poet,
  Admired for his earnest habit of calling
The sun the sun, his mind Puzzle, is made uneasy
  By these solid statues which so obviously doubt
His antimythological myth; and these gamins,
  Pursuing the scientist down the tiled colonnade
With such lively offers, rebuke his concern for Nature's
  Remotest aspects: I, too, am reproached, for what
And how much you know. Not to lose time, not to get caught,
  Not to be left behind, not, please! to resemble

The beasts who repeat themselves, or a thing like water
  Or stone whose conduct can be predicted, these
Are our Common Prayer, whose greatest comfort is music
  Which can be made anywhere, is invisible,
And does not smell. In so far as we have to look forward
  To death as a fact, no doubt we are right: But if
Sins can be forgiven, if bodies rise from the dead,
  These modifications of matter into
Innocent athletes and gesticulating fountains,
  Made solely for pleasure, make a further point:
The blessed will not care what angle they are regarded from,
  Having nothing to hide. Dear, I know nothing of
Either, but when I try to imagine a faultless love
  Or the life to come, what I hear is the murmur
Of underground streams, what I see is a limestone landscape.

ROLFE HUMPHRIES

The Offering of the Heart
Tapestry from Arras, XV Century

Against a somber background, blue as midnight,
More blank and dark than cloud, as black as storm,
The almost moving leaves are almost golden,
The light is almost warm.

Seated, a lady, wearing a cloak with ermine
Holds on her hand, correctly gloved and bent,
A falcon, without feathered hood or jesses;
Her gaze appears intent

On what her hound, good little dog, is doing
Around her ankles, left front paw in air,
Regardless of the three white careless rabbits—
He does not see them there,

Or turn, as does the falcon, toward the gallant,
The gentleman, more elegant than smart,
Who comes, in crimson cloak with ermine lining,
And offers her a heart,

Holding it, chastely, between thumb and finger
Whose U it does not fill, a plum in size,
A somewhat faded strawberry in color—
She does not raise her eyes.

How can a heart be beating in the bosom,
And yet held up, so tiny, in the hand?
Innocence; mystery: an Age of Science
Would hardly understand.

ROBERT FRANCIS

Squash in Blossom

How lush, how loose, the uninhibited squash is.
If ever hearts (and these immoderate leaves
Are vegetable hearts) were worn on sleeves,
The squash's are. In green the squash vine gushes.

The flowers are cornucopias of summer,
Briefly exuberant and cheaply golden.
And if they make a show of being hidden,
Are open promiscuously to every comer.

Let the squash be what it was doomed to be
By the old Gardener with the shrewd green thumb.
Let it expand and sprawl, defenceless, dumb.
But let me be the fiber-disciplined tree

Whose leaf (with something to say in wind) is small,
Reduced to the ingenuity of a green splinter
Sharp to defy or fraternize with winter,
Or if not that, prepared in fall to fall.

ROBERT NATHAN

Now Blue October

ROBERT NATHAN

Now Blue October

93

Now blue October, smoky in the sun,
Must end the long, sweet summer of the heart.
The last brief visit of the birds is done;
They sing the autumn songs before they part.
Listen, how lovely—there's the thrush we heard
When June was small with roses, and the bending
Blossom of branches covered nest and bird,
Singing the summer in, summer unending—
Give me your hand once more before the night;
See how the meadows darken with the frost,
How fades the green that was the summer's light.
Beauty is only altered, never lost,
And love, before the cold November rain,
Will make its summer in the heart again.

Evening in the Sanitarium

The free evening fades, outside the windows fastened with
    decorative iron grilles.
The lamps are lighted; the shades drawn; the nurses are
    watching a little.
It is the hour of the complicated knitting on the safe bone
    needles; of the games of anagrams and bridge;
The deadly game of chess; the book held up like a mask.

The period of the wildest weeping, the fiercest delusion, is over.
The women rest their tired half-healed hearts;
    they are almost well.
Some of them will stay almost well always:
    the blunt-faced woman whose thinking dissolved
Under academic discipline; the manic depressive girl
Now leveling off; one paranoiac afflicted with jealousy.
Another with persecution. Some alleviation has been possible.

O fortunate bride, who never again will become
    elated after childbirth!
O lucky older wife, who has been cured of feeling unwanted!
To the suburban railway station you will return, return,
To meet forever Jim home on the 5:35.
You will be again as normal and selfish and heartless
    as anybody else.

There is life left: the piano says it with its octave smile.
The soft carpets pad the thump and splinter of the suicide to be.
Everything will be splendid: the grandmother
    will not drink habitually.
The fruit salad will bloom on the plate like a bouquet
And the garden produce the blue-ribbon aquilegia.

The cats will be glad; the fathers feel justified;
    the mothers relieved.
The sons and husbands will no longer need to pay the bills.
Childhoods will be put away, the obscene nightmare abated.

At the ends of the corridors the baths are running.
Mrs. C. again feels the shadow of the obsessive idea.
Miss R. looks at the mantel-piece, which must mean something.

LOUISE TOWNSEND NICHOLL

Smell of cigar smoke, Sunday, after dinner,
Our eyes upon the visitor, leaning back
From robust lengthy elegance of dining,
White fingers catching up the golden slack
Of watch chain slung across expansive chest,
Rippling the links into a silken banner. . . .
All else was solid, black and white and shining,
The polished shirt-front and the black mustache,
Even the smooth fine broadcloth of the vest
Shone with a dark and unaccustomed luster.

Save that the damask throws a burnished flash,
The room, the coffee and the talk, are lost;
Only lives on the one compelling cluster,
The composition masterfully glossed,
Portrait of manhood and its ease of manner,
Rich as cigar smoke after Sunday dinner,
And how the white hand flicked away the ash.

LÉONIE ADAMS

Grapes Making

Noon sun beats down the leaf; the noon
Of summer burns along the vine
And thins the leaf with burning air,
Till from the underleaf is fanned,
And down the woven vine, the light.
Still the pleached leaves drop layer on layer
To wind the sun on either hand,
And echoes of the light are bound,
And hushed the blazing cheek of light,
The hurry of the breathless noon,
And from the thicket of the vine
The grape has pressed into its round.

The grape has pressed into its round,
And swings, aloof chill green, clean won
Of light, between the sky and ground;
Those hid, soft-flashing lamps yet blind,
Which yield an apprehended sun.
Fresh triumph in a courteous kind,
Having more ways to be, and years,
And easy, countless treasuries,
You whose all-told is still no sum,
Like a rich heart, well-said in sighs,
The careless autumn mornings come,
The grapes drop glimmering to the shears.

Now shady sod at heel piles deep,
An overarching shade, the vine
Across the fall of noon is flung;
And here beneath the leaves is cast
A light to colour noonday sleep,
While cool, bemused the grape is swung
Beneath the eyelids of the vine;
And deepening like a tender thought
Green moves along the leaf, and bright
The leaf above, and leaf has caught,
And emerald pierces day, and last
The faint leaf vanishes to light.

WILLIAM CARLOS WILLIAMS

The Mental Hospital Garden

It is far to Assisi,
    but not too far:
        Over this garden,
brooding over this garden,
    there is a kindly spirit,
        brother to the poor
and who is poorer than he
    who is in love
        when birds are nesting
in the spring of the year?
    They came
        to eat from his hand
who had nothing,
    and yet
        from his plenty
he fed them all.
    All mankind
        grew to be his debtors,
a simple story.
    Love is in season.
At such a time,
    hyacinth time
        in
the hospital garden,
    the time
        of the coral-flowered
and early salmon-pink
    clusters, it is
        the time also of
abandoned birds' nests
    before
        the sparrows start
        to tear them apart
against the advent of that bounty
    from which
        they will build anew.

All about them
            on the lawns
                        the young couples
embrace
            as in a tale
                        by Boccaccio.
They are careless
            under license of the disease
                        which has restricted them
to these grounds.
            St. Francis forgive them
                        and all lovers
whoever they may be.
            They have seen
                        a great light, it
springs from their own bawdy foreheads.
            The light
                        is sequestered there
by these enclosing walls.
            They are divided
                        from their fellows.
It is a bounty
            from a last year's bird's nest.
                        St. Francis,
who befriended the wild birds,
            by their aid,
                        those who
have nothing
            and live
                        by the Holy light of love
that rules,
            blocking despair,
                        over this garden.

Time passes.
        The pace has slackened
                But with the falling off
of the pace
        the scene has altered.
                The lovers raise their heads,
at that which has come over them.
        It is summer now.
            The broad sun
shines!
        Blinded by the light
            they walk bewildered,
seeking
        between the leaves
            for a vantage
from which to view
        the advancing season.
            They are incredulous
of their own cure
        and half minded
            to escape
into the dark again.
        The scene
            indeed has changed.
By St. Francis
        the whole scene
            has changed.
They glimpse
        a surrounding sky
            and the whole countryside.
Filled with terror
        they seek
            a familiar flower
at which to warm themselves,
        but the whole field
            accosts them.

They hide their eyes
        ashamed
                before that bounty,
peering through their fingers
        timidly.
                The saint is watching,
his eyes filled with pity.
The year is still young
        but not so young
                as they
who face the fears
        with which
                they are confronted.
Reawakened
        after love's first folly
                they resemble children
roused from a long sleep.
        Summer is here,
                right enough.
The saint
        has tactfully withdrawn.
                One
emboldened,
        parting the leaves before her,
                stands in the full sunlight,
alone
        shading her eyes
                as her heart
beats wildly
        and her mind
                drinks up
the full meaning
        of it
                all!

History

It is Leviathan, mountain and world,
Yet in its grandeur we perceive
This flutter of the impalpable arriving
Like moths and heartbeats, flakes of snow
Falling on wool, or clouds of thought
Trailing rain in the mind: some old one's dream
Of hauling canvas, or the joy of swording
Hard rascals with a smack—for lordly blood
Circulates tenderly and will seep away;
And the winds blowing across the day
From quarters numberless, going where words go
And songs go, even the holy songs, or where
Leaves, showering, go with the spindling grasses.
Into this mountain shade everything passes.
The slave lays down his bones here and the hero,
Thrown, goes reeling with blinded face;
The long desired opens her scorched armpits.
A mountain; so a gloom and air of ghosts,
But charged with utter light if this is light,
A feathery mass, where this beholding
Shines among lustrous fiddles and codices,
Or dusky angels painted against gold
With lutes across their knees. Magical grain
Bound up in splay sheaves on an evening field,
And a bawling calf butchered—these feed
The curious coil of man. A man, this man,
Bred among lakes and railway cars and smoke,
The salt of childhood on his wintry lips,
His full heart ebbing toward the new tide
Arriving, arriving, in laughter and cries,
Down the chaotic dawn and eastern drift,

Would hail the unforeseen, and celebrate
On the great mountainside those sprites,
Tongues of delight, that may remember him—
The yet unborn, trembling in the same rooms,
Breakfasting before the same grey windows,
Lying, grieving again; yet all beyond him,
Who knew he lived in rough Jehovah's breath,
And burned, a quiet wick in a wild night,
Loving what he beheld and will behold.

DANIEL BERRIGAN

The Beautiful Ruined Orchard

                      What had November done?
It wore its trees at breast like English swans
on the green swell triumphant and immortal
through spring and summer: so seeing them
from the edge, caught one's breath, to have discovered

perfection in a long single line, dawn to dusk.

But was it threats and mutters of the envious dead
infected, frightened them, that they arose
an immense fleet sailing the autumn storm
fleeing before dawn?
                     Shadow of those wings
fell in blight on the acres, turned their choral surf
to a hoarse whisper through a common sedge.

And where each swan rode like a king to throne: only
a bony ghost the contemptuous wind makes light of.

Earliness at the Cape

The color of silence is the oyster's color
Between the lustres of deep night and dawn.
Earth turns to absence; the sole shape's the sleeping
Light—a mollusk of mist. Remote,
A sandspit hinges the valves of that soft monster
Yawning at Portugal. Alone wakeful, lanterns
Over a dark hull to eastward mark
The tough long pull, hidden, the killing
Work, hidden, to feed a hidden world.
Muteness is all. Even the greed of the gulls
Annulled, the hush of color everywhere
The hush of motion. This is the neap of the blood,
Of memory, thought, desire; if pain visits
Such placelessness, it has phantom feet.
What's physical is lost here in ignorance
Of its own being. That solitary boat,
Out fishing, is a black stroke on vacancy.
Night, deaf and dumb as something from the deeps,
Having swallowed whole bright yesterday, replete
With radiance, is gray as abstinence now.
But in this nothingness, a knife point: pleasure
Comes pricking; the hour's pallor, too, is bladed
Like a shell, and as it opens, cuts.

ROBERT HILLYER

Nocturne

If the deep wood is haunted, it is I
Who am the ghost; not the tall trees
Nor the white moonlight slanting down like rain,
Filling the hollows with bright pools of silver.

A long train whistle serpentines around the hill
Now shrill, now far away.
Tell me, from what dark smoky terminal
What train sets out for yesterday?

Or, since our spirits take off and resume
Their flesh as travellers their cloaks, O tell me where,
In what age and what country you will come,
That I may meet you there.

NED O'GORMAN

The Kiss

Talk of passion is a winter thing,
a huddle of girls, descending wind.
There is no vehicle in a kiss
to carry fury and originality.
In that wherewithal of mouth
the body greets with cannon
the profundis and halt clamavi
of the virgin. Dying is a kiss,
it has broken me. It rimes with tiger
and the gallow tree.

Advice to a Prophet

When you come, as you soon must, to the streets of our city,
Mad-eyed from stating the obvious,
Not proclaiming our fall but begging us
In God's name to have self-pity,

Spare us all word of the weapons, their force and range,
The long numbers that rocket the mind;
Our slow, unreckoning hearts will be left behind,
Unable to fear what is too strange.

Nor shall you scare us with talk of the death of the race.
How should we dream of this place without us?—
The sun mere fire, the leaves untroubled about us,
A stone look on the stone's face?

Speak of the world's own change. Though we cannot conceive
Of an undreamt thing, we know to our cost
How the dreamt cloud crumbles, the vines are blackened
      by frost,
How the view alters. We could believe,

If you told us so, that the white-tailed deer will slip
Into perfect shade, grown perfectly shy,
The lark avoid the reaches of our eye,
The jack-pine lose its knuckled grip

On the cold ledge, and every torrent burn
As Xanthus once, its gliding trout
Stunned in a twinkling. What should we be without
The dolphin's arc, the dove's return,

These things in which we have seen ourselves and spoken?
Ask us, prophet, how we shall call
Our natures forth when that live tongue is all
Dispelled, that glass obscured or broken

In which we have said the rose of our love and the clean
Horse of our courage, in which beheld
The singing locust of the soul unshelled,
And all we mean or wish to mean.

Ask us, ask us whether with the worldless rose
Our hearts shall fail us; come demanding
Whether there shall be lofty or long standing
When the bronze annals of the oak-tree close.

X. J. KENNEDY

In a Prominent Bar in Secaucus One Day

To the tune of "The Old Orange Flute"
or the tune of "Sweet Betsy from Pike"

In a prominent bar in Secaucus one day
Rose a lady in skunk with a topheavy sway,
Raised a knobby red finger—all turned from their beer—
While with eyes bright as snowcrust she sang high and clear:

'Now who of you'd think from an eyeload of me
That I once was a lady as proud as could be?
Oh I'd never sit down by a tumbledown drunk
If it wasn't, my dears, for the high cost of junk.

'All the gents used to swear that the white of my calf
Beat the down of the swan by a length and a half.
In the kerchief of linen I caught to my nose
Ah, there never fell snot, but a little gold rose.

'I had seven gold teeth and a toothpick of gold,
My Virginia cheroot was a leaf of it rolled
And I'd light it each time with a thousand in cash—
Why the bums used to fight if I flicked them an ash.

'Once the toast of the Biltmore, the belle of the Taft,
I would drink bottle beer at the Drake, never draft,
And dine at the Astor on Salisbury steak
With a clean tablecloth for each bite I did take.

'In a car like the Roxy I'd roll to the track,
A steel-guitar trio, a bar in the back,
And the wheels made no noise, they turned over so fast,
Still it took you ten minutes to see me go past.

'When the horses bowed down to me that I might choose,
I bet on them all, for I hated to lose.
Now I'm saddled each night for my butter and eggs
And the broken threads race down the backs of my legs.

'Let you hold in mind, girls, that your beauty must pass
Like a lovely white clover that rusts with its grass.
Keep your bottoms off barstools and marry you young
Or be left—an old barrel with many a bung.

'For when time takes you out for a spin in his car
You'll be hard-pressed to stop him from going too far
And be left by the roadside, for all your good deeds,
Two toadstools for tits and a face full of weeds.'

All the house raised a cheer, but the man at the bar
Made a phonecall and up pulled a red patrol car
And she blew us a kiss as they copped her away
From that prominent bar in Secaucus, N.J.

JOHN HALL WHEELOCK

Hippopotamothalamium 111

A hippopotamus had a bride
    Of rather singular beauty,
When he lay down at her side
    'Twas out of love, not duty—
    Hers was an exceptional beauty.
Take, oh take those lips away, etc.

He met her in Central Nigeria,
    While she was resident there,
Where life is distinctly superior
    And a hippo can take down her hair—
    And, Gód, but she was fair!
Take, oh take those lips away, etc.

She was coming up from her morning swim
    When first they chanced to meet:
He looked at her, she looked at him,
    And stood with reluctant feet
    Where mud and river meet.
Take, oh take those lips away, etc.

Their eye-beams, twisted on one thread,
    Instantaneously did twine,
And he made up poetry out of his head,
    Such as: "Dear heart, be mine"—
    And he quoted, line for line,
"Hail to thee, blithe spirit", etc.

Now, hippopotamoid courtesy
    Is strangely meticulous—
A beautiful thing, you will agree,
    In a hippopotamus—
    And she answered, briefly, thus:
"Hail to thee, blithe spirit", etc.

Perhaps she was practising the arts
    That grace old Hippo's daughter,
The coquetries that win all hearts,
    For, even as he besought her,
    She slid into the water.
Out, out, brief candle, etc.

Now, on the borders of the wood,
    Whence love had drawn him hither,
He paces in an anguished mood,
    Darting hither and thither
    In a terrific dither.
Out, out, brief candle, etc.

The course of true love never yet
    Ran smooth, so we are told,
With thorns its pathway is beset
    And perils manifold,
    So was it from of old.
Out, out, brief candle, etc.

Yet soon a happier morning smiles,
    The marriage feast is spread—
The flower girls were crocodiles,
    When hippopotamus led
    Hippopotamus, with firm tread,
    A bride to the bridal bed.
Milton, thou should'st be living at this hour.

JOHN UPDIKE

They have been with us a long time.
They will outlast the elms.
Our eyes, like the eyes of a savage sieving the trees
In his search for game,
Run through them. They blend along small-town streets
Like a race of giants that have faded into mere mythology.
Our eyes, washed clean of belief,
Lift incredulous to their fearsome crowns of bolts, trusses, struts,
    nuts, insulators, and such
Barnacles as compose
These weathered encrustations of electrical debris—
Each a Gorgon's head, which, seized right,
Could stun us to stone.

Yet they are ours. We made them.
See here, where the cleats of linemen
Have roughened a second bark
Onto the bald trunk. And these spikes
Have been driven sideways at intervals handy for human legs.
The Nature of our construction is in every way
A better fit than the Nature it displaces.
What other tree can you climb where the birds' twitter,
Unscrambled, is English? True, their thin shade is negligible,
But then again there is not that tragic autumnal
Casting-off of leaves to outface annually.
These giants are more constant than evergreens
By being never green.

JOHN BERRYMAN

114

Dream Song #48

He yelled at me in Greek,
my God!—It's not his language
and I'm no good at—his is Aramaic,
was—I am a monoglot of English
(American version) and, say pieces from
a baker's dozen others: where's the bread?

but rising in the Second Gospel, pal:
The seed goes down, god dies.
a rising happens,
some crust, and then occurs   an eating. He said so,
a Greek idea,
troublesome to imaginary Jews,

like bitter Henry, full of the death of love,
Cawdor-uneasy, disambitious, mourning
the whole implausible necessary thing.
He dropped his voice & sybilled of
the death of the death of love.
I óught to get going.

ROBERT LOWELL

For the Union Dead
  "Relinquunt omnia servare rem publicam."

The old South Boston Aquarium stands
in a Sahara of snow now. Its broken windows are boarded.
The bronze weathervane cod has lost half its scales.
The airy tanks are dry.

Once my nose crawled like a snail on the glass;
my hand tingled
to burst the bubbles
drifting from the noses of the cowed, compliant fish.

My hand draws back. I often sigh still
for the dark downward and vegetating kingdom
of the fish and reptile. One morning last March,
I pressed against the new barbed and galvanized

fence on the Boston Common. Behind their cage,
yellow dinosaur steamshovels were grunting
as they cropped up tons of mush and grass
to gouge their underworld garage.

Parking spaces luxuriate like civic
sandpiles in the heart of Boston.
A girdle of orange, Puritan-pumpkin colored girders
braces the tingling Statehouse,

shaking over the excavations, as it faces Colonel Shaw
and his bell-cheeked Negro infantry
on St. Gaudens' shaking Civil War relief,
propped by a plank splint against the garage's earthquake.

Two months after marching through Boston,
half the regiment was dead;
at the dedication,
William James could almost hear the bronze Negroes breathe.

Their monument sticks like a fishbone
in the city's throat.
Its Colonel is as lean
as a compass-needle.

He has an angry wrenlike vigilance,
a greyhound's gentle tautness;
he seems to wince at pleasure,
and suffocate for privacy.

He is out of bounds now. He rejoices in man's lovely,
peculiar power to choose life and death—
when he leads his black soldiers to death,
he cannot bend his back.

On a thousand small town New England greens,
the old white churches hold their air
of sparse, sincere rebellion; frayed flags
quilt the graveyards of the Grand Army of the Republic.

The stone statues of the abstract Union Soldier
grow slimmer and younger each year—
wasp-wasted, they doze over muskets
and muse through their sideburns . . .

Shaw's father wanted no monument
except the ditch,
where his son's body was thrown
and lost with his "niggers."

The ditch is nearer.
There are no statues for the last war here;
on Boyleston Street, a commercial photograph
shows Hiroshima boiling

over a Mosler Safe, the "Rock of Ages"
that survived the blast. Space is nearer.
When I crouch to my television set,
the drained faces of Negro school-children rise like balloons.

Colonel Shaw
is riding on his bubble,
he waits
for the blesséd break.

The Aquarium is gone. Everywhere,
giant finned cars nose forward like fish;
a savage servility
slides by on grease.

ADRIEN STOUTENBERG

Ants and Others

Their spare, fanatic sentry comes
across the miles of afternoon
and finds us out, our single crumb
left dozing in a yellowed spoon;
sets up his wireless, reports
to Brown Shirts, comrades, pantry thieves.
(Their army goes like coffee grounds
down doorknobs, drains, up balconies
we meant to guard from minor lusts,
but lacked the key or missed the time.)
Defenseless now the last crust leans
beside a cup. The brown knots climb,
as neat as clocks. I feel the heat
of other lives, and hungers bent
on honeycombs that are not there,
and do not ask what sweet is meant
for which of us, there being such need
of loaves and fishes everywhere.

DAVID WAGONER

The Shooting of John Dillinger Outside the Biograph Theater,

  July 22, 1934

Chicago ran a fever of a hundred and one that groggy Sunday.
A reporter fried an egg on a sidewalk; the air looked shaky.
And a hundred thousand people were in the lake like shirts in
    a laundry.
Why was Johnny lonely?
Not because two dozen solid citizens, heat-struck, had keeled
    over backward.
Not because those lawful souls had fallen out of their sockets
    and melted.
But because the sun went down like a lump in a furnace or a
    bull in the Stockyards.
Where was Johnny headed?
Under the Biograph Theater sign that said, "Our Air is
    Refrigerated."
Past seventeen FBI men and four policemen who stood in
    doorways and sweated.
Johnny sat down in a cold seat to watch Clark Gable get
    electrocuted.
Had Johnny been mistreated?
Yes, but Gable told the D.A. he'd rather fry than be shut up
    forever.
Two women sat by Johnny. One looked sweet, one looked like
    J. Edgar Hoover.
Polly Hamilton made him feel hot, but Anna Sage made him
    shiver.
Was Johnny a good lover?
Yes, but he passed out his share of squeezes and pokes like a
    jittery masher
While Agent Purvis sneaked up and down the aisle like an
    extra usher,
Trying to make sure they wouldn't slip out till the show was
    over.
Was Johnny a fourflusher?
No, not if he knew the game. He got it up or got it back.

But he liked to take snapshots of policemen with his own Kodak,
And once in a while he liked to take them with an automatic.
Why was Johnny frantic?
Because he couldn't take a walk or sit down in a movie
Without being afraid he'd run smack into somebody
Who'd point at his rearranged face and holler, "Johnny!"
Was Johnny ugly?
Yes, because Dr. Wilhelm Loeser had given him a new profile
With a baggy jawline and squint eyes and an erased dimple,
With kangaroo-tendon cheekbones and a gigolo's mustache
        that should've been illegal.
Did Johnny love a girl?
Yes, a good-looking, hard-headed Indian named Billie Frechette.
He wanted to marry her and lie down and try to get over it,
But she was locked in jail for giving him first-aid and comfort.
Did Johnny feel hurt?
He felt like breaking a bank or jumping over a railing
Into some panicky teller's cage to shout, "Reach for the ceiling!"
Or like kicking some vice president in the bum checks and
        smiling.
What was he really doing?
Going up the aisle with the crowd and into the lobby
With Polly saying, "Would you do what Clark done?" And
        Johnny saying, "Maybe."
And Anna saying, "If he'd been smart, he'd of acted like
        Bing Crosby."
Did Johnny look flashy?
Yes, his white-on-white shirt and tie were luminous.
His trousers were creased like knives to the tops of his shoes,
And his yellow straw hat came down to his dark glasses.
Was Johnny suspicious?
Yes, and when Agent Purvis signalled with a trembling cigar,
Johnny ducked left and ran out of the theater,
And innocent Polly and squealing Anna were left nowhere.

Was Johnny a fast runner?
No, but he crouched and scurried past a friendly liquor store
Under the coupled arms of double-daters, under awnings,
    under stars,
To the curb at the mouth of an alley. He hunched there.
Was Johnny a thinker?
No, but he was thinking more or less of Billie Frechette
Who was lost in prison for longer than he could possibly wait,
And then it was suddenly too hard to think around a bullet.
Did anyone shoot straight?
Yes, but Mrs. Etta Natalsky fell out from under her picture hat.
Theresa Paulus sprawled on the sidewalk, clutching her left foot.
And both of them groaned loud and long under the streetlight.
Did Johnny like that?
No, but he lay down with those strange women, his face
    in the alley,
One shoe off, cinders in his mouth, his eyelids heavy.
When they shouted questions at him, he talked back to nobody.
Did Johnny lie easy?
Yes, holding his gun and holding his breath as a last trick,
He waited, but when the Agents came close, his breath
    wouldn't work.
Clark Gable walked his last mile; Johnny ran half a block.
Did he run out of luck?
Yes, before he was cool, they had him spread out on dished-in
    marble
In the Cook County Morgue, surrounded by babbling people
With a crime reporter presiding over the head of the table.
Did Johnny have a soul?
Yes, and it was climbing his slippery wind-pipe like a trapped
    burglar.
It was beating the inside of his ribcage, hollering, "Let me
    out of here!"
Maybe it got out, and maybe it just stayed there.

Was Johnny a money-maker?

Yes, and thousands paid 25¢ to see him, mostly women,

And one said, "I wouldn't have come, except he's a moral
lesson,"

And another, "I'm disappointed. He feels like a dead man."

Did Johnny have a brain?

Yes, and it always worked best through the worst of dangers,

Through flat-footed hammerlocks, through guarded doors,
around corners,

But it got taken out in the morgue and sold to some doctors.

Could Johnny take orders?

No, but he stayed in the wicker basket carried by six men

Through the bulging crowd to the hearse and let himself be
locked in,

And he stayed put as it went driving south in a driving rain.

And he didn't get stolen?

No, not even after his old hard-nosed dad refused to sell

The quick-drawing corpse for $10,000 to somebody in a
carnival.

He figured he'd let *Johnny* decide how to get to Hell.

Did anyone wish him well?

Yes, half of Indiana camped in the family pasture,

And the minister said, "With luck, he could have been a
minister."

And up the sleeve of his oversized gray suit, Johnny twitched
a finger.

Does anyone remember?

Everyone still alive. And some dead ones. It was a new kind of
holiday

With hot and cold drinks and hot and cold tears. They planted
him in a cemetery

With three unknown vice presidents, Benjamin Harrison, and
James Whitcomb Riley,

Who never held up anybody.

DONALD JUSTICE

Bus Stop

Lights are burning
In quiet rooms
Where lives go on
Resembling ours.

The quiet lives
That follow us—
These lives we lead
But do not own—

Stand in the rain
So quietly
When we are gone,
So quietly . . .

And the last bus
Comes letting dark
Umbrellas out—
Black flowers, black flowers.

And lives go on.
And lives go on
Like sudden lights
At street corners

Or like the lights
In quiet rooms
Left on for hours,
Burning, burning.

Some Small Shells from the Windward Islands

Their scrape and clink together of musical coin.
Than the tinkling of crickets more eerie, more thin.
Their click as of crystal, wood, carapace and bone.

A tintinabular fusion. The friction spinal and chill
as of ivory embryo fragments of horn
honed to whistles and flutes.

Windy Eustachian coils cold as the sea,
until held, then warm as the palm.
And snuggled naturally there, smoother than skin.

The curve and continuous spiral, intrinsic. Their role
eternal inversion. Closed
the undulant scroll.

Even when corrugate, sharpness rubbed from their forms,
licked by the mouth of the sea
to tactile charms.

Some blanched by the eye of the sun, a pumice shine
buffing their calcareous nakedness
clean as a tooth.

Some colored like flesh, yet more subtle than corpuscle dyes.
Some sunsets, some buttermilk skies,
or penumbras of moons in eclipse.

Malachite greens, fish-eyed icy blues,
pigeon-foot pinks, brindled fulvous browns.
Some black, like tektites.

Gathered here in a bowl, their ineradicable inks
vivid, declarative under water,
peculiar fossil-fruits.

They suck through ribbed lips and gaping sutures
into secret clefts
the sweet wet with a tame taste.

Vulviform creatures,
or rather their rocklike backs,
with labial bellies.

Some earhole-shaped,
or funnels with an overlap. Some stony worms
curled up and glazed, the egress like a trumpet.

Some cones, tight twisted sphincters
rugose and spiculate, cactus humped, or warted.
Others slick and simple pods where tender jellies hid.

The rigid souls, the amorphous ones
emptied from out their skeletons
that were their furled caves.

Each an eccentric mummy-case,
one facet mute and ultimate,
the other baffling in its ruffles as a rose.

The largest a valve of bone streaked like a cloud.
its shadowy crease, ambiguous vestibule a puckered trap ajar.
The sly, inviting smile into the labyrinth.

JAMES WRIGHT

The Minneapolis Poem

to John Logan

1.
I wonder how many old men last winter
Hungry and frightened by namelessness prowled
The Mississippi shore
Lashed blind by the wind, dreaming
Of suicide in the river.
The police remove their cadavers by daybreak
And turn them in somewhere.
Where?
How does the city keep lists of its fathers
Who have no names?
By Nicollet Island I gaze down at the dark water
So beautifully slow.
And I wish my brothers good luck
And a warm grave.

2.
The Chippewa young men
Stab one another shrieking
Jesus Christ.
Split-lipped homosexuals limp in terror of assault.
High school backfields search under benches
Near the Post Office. Their faces are the rich
Raw bacon without eyes.
The Walker Art Center crowd stare
At the Guthrie Theater.

3.

Tall Negro girls from Chicago
Listen to light songs.
They know when the supposed patron
Is a plainclothesman.
A cop's palm
Is a roach dangling down the scorched fangs
Of a light bulb.
The soul of a cop's eyes
Is an eternity of Sunday daybreak in the suburbs
Of Juárez, Mexico.

4.

The legless beggars are gone, carried away
By white birds.
The Artificial Limbs Exchange is gutted
And sown with lime.
The whalebone crutches and hand-me-down trusses
Huddle together dreaming in a desolation
Of dry groins.
I think of poor men astonished to waken
Exposed in broad daylight by the blade
Of a strange plough.

5.

All over the walls of comb cells
Automobiles perfumed and blindered
Consent with a mutter of high good humor
To take their two naps a day.
Without sound windows glide back
Into dusk.
The sockets of a thousand blind bee graves tier upon tier
Tower not quite toppling.
There are men in this city who labor dawn after dawn
To sell me my death.

6.
But I could not bear
To allow my poor brother my body to die
In Minneapolis.
The old man Walt Whitman our countryman
Is now in America our country
Dead.
But he was not buried in Minneapolis
At least.
And no more may I be
Please God.

7.
I want to be lifted up
By some great white bird unknown to the police,
And soar for a thousand miles and be carefully hidden
Modest and golden as one last corn grain,
Stored with the secrets of the wheat and the mysterious lives
Of the unnamed poor.

JAMES SCHUYLER

Salute

Past is past, and if one
remembers what one meant
to do and never did, is
not to have thought to do
enough? Like that gather-
ing of one of each I
planned, to gather one
of each kind of clover,
daisy, paintbrush that
grew in that field
the cabin stood in and
study them one afternoon
before they wilted. Past
is past; I salute
that various field.

For John Clare

Kind of empty in the way it sees everything, the earth gets to its feet and salutes the sky. More of a success at it this time than most others it is. The feeling that the sky might be in the back of someone's mind. Then there is no telling how many there are. They grace everything—bush and tree—to take the roisterer's mind off his caroling—so it's like a smooth switch back. To what was aired in their previous conniption fit. There is so much to be seen everywhere that it's like not getting used to it, only there is so much it never feels new, never any different. You are standing looking at that building and you cannot take it all in, certain details are already hazy and the mind boggles. What will it all be like in five years' time when you try to remember? Will there have been boards in between the grass part and the edge of the street? As long as that couple is stopping to look in that window over there we cannot go. We feel like they have to tell us we can, but they never look our way and they are already gone, gone far into the future—the night of time. If we could look at a photograph of it and say there they are, they never really stopped but there they are. There is so much to be said, and on the surface of it very little gets said.

There ought to be room for more things, for a spreading out, like. Being immersed in the details of rock and field and slope—letting them come to you for once, and then meeting them half-way would be so much easier—if they took an ingenuous pride in being in one's blood. Alas, we perceive them if at all as those things that were meant to be put aside—costumes of the sup-porting actors or voice trilling at the end of a narrow enclosed street. You can do nothing with them. Not even offer to pay.

It is possible that finally, like coming to the end of a long, barely perceptible rise, there is mutual cohesion and interaction. The whole scene is fixed in your mind, the music all present, as though you could see each note as well as hear it. I say this because there is an uneasiness in things just now. Waiting for something to be over before you are forced to notice it. The pollarded trees scarcely bucking the wind—and yet it's keen, it makes you fall over. Clabbered sky. Seasons that pass with a rush. After all it's their time too—nothing says they aren't to make something of it. As for Jenny Wren, she cares, hopping about on her little twig like she was tryin' to tell us somethin', but that's just it, she couldn't even if she wanted to—dumb bird. But the others—and they in some way must know too—it would never occur to them to want to, even if they could take the first step of the terrible journey toward feeling somebody should act, that ends in utter confusion and hopelessness, east of the sun and west of the moon. So their comment is: "No com-ment." Meanwhile the whole history of probabilities is coming to life, starting in the upper left-hand corner, like a sail.

Locus
        (for Ralph)

Here redbuds like momentary trees
        of an illusionist;
here Cherokee rose, acacia, and mimosa;
here magnolias—totemic flowers
        wreathing legends of this place.
Here violent metamorphosis,
        with every blossom turning
deadly and memorial soldiers,
their sabres drawn, charging
        firewood shacks,
apartheid streets. Here wound-red earth
        and blinding cottonfields,
rock hills where sachems counseled,
where scouts gazed stealthily
        upon the glittering death march
of De Soto through Indian wilderness.
        Here mockingbird and
cottonmouth, fury of rivers.
Here swamp and trace and bayou
        where the runagate hid,
the devil with Spanish pistols rode.
        Here spareness, rankness, harsh
brilliances; beauty of what's hardbitten,
knotted, stinted, flourishing
        in despite, on thorny meagerness
thriving, twisting into grace.
        Here symbol houses
where the brutal dream lives out its lengthy
dying. Here the past, adored and
        unforgiven. Here the past—
soulscape, Old Testament battleground
of warring shades whose weapons kill.

SYLVIA PLATH

Last Words

I do not want a plain box, I want a sarcophagus
With tigery stripes, and a face on it
Round as the moon, to stare up.
I want to be looking at them when they come
Picking among the dumb minerals, the roots.
I see them already—the pale, star-distance faces.
Now they are nothing, they are not even babies.
I imagine them without fathers or mothers, like the first gods.
They will wonder if I was important.
I should sugar and preserve my days like fruit!
My mirror is clouding over—
A few more breaths, and it will reflect nothing at all.
The flowers and the faces whiten to a sheet.

I do not trust the spirit. It escapes like steam
In dreams, through mouth-hole or eye-hole. I can't stop it.
One day it won't come back. Things aren't like that.
They stay, their little particular lusters
Warmed by much handling. They almost purr.
When the soles of my feet grow cold,
The blue eye of my turquoise will comfort me.
Let me have my copper cooking pots, let my rouge pots
Bloom about me like night flowers, with a good smell.
They will roll me up in bandages, they will store my heart
Under my feet in a neat parcel.
I shall hardly know myself. It will be dark,
And the shine of these small things sweeter than the face
        of Ishtar.

The Testing-Tree

1
On my way home from school
    up tribal Providence Hill
        past the Academy ballpark
where I could never hope to play
    I scuffed in the drainage ditch
        among the sodden seethe of leaves
hunting for perfect stones
    rolled out of glacial time
        into my pitcher's hand;
then sprinted lickety-
    split on my magic Keds
        from a crouching start,
scarcely touching the ground
    with my flying skin
        as I poured it on
for the prize of the mastery
    over that stretch of road,
        with no one no where to deny
when I flung myself down
    that on the given course
        I was the world's fastest human.

2
Around the bend
    that tried to loop me home
        dawdling came natural
across a nettled field
    riddled with rabbit-life
        where the bees sank sugar-wells

in the trunks of the maples
    and a stringy old lilac
        more than two stories tall
blazing with mildew
    remembered a door in the
        long teeth of the woods.
All of it happened slow:
    brushing the stickseed off,
        wading through jewelweed
strangled by angel's hair,
    spotting the print of the deer
        and the red fox's scats.
Once I owned the key
    to an umbrageous trail
        thickened with mosses
where flickering presences
    gave me right of passage
        as I followed in the steps
of straight-backed Massassoit
    soundlessly heel-and-toe
        practicing my Indian walk.

3
Past the abandoned quarry
    where the pale sun bobbed
        in the sump of the granite,
past copperhead ledge,
    where the ferns gave foothold,
        I walked, deliberate,

on to the clearing,
　　　with the stones in my pocket
　　　　　changing to oracles
and my coiled ear tuned
　　　to the slightest leaf-stir.
　　　　　I had kept my appointment.
There I stood in the shadow,
　　　at fifty measured paces,
　　　　　of the inexhaustible oak,
tyrant and target,
　　　Jehovah of acorns,
　　　　　watchtower of the thunders,
that locked King Philip's War
　　　in its annulated core
　　　　　under the cut of my name.
Father wherever you are
　　　I have only three throws
　　　　　bless my good right arm.
In the haze of afternoon,
　　　while the air flowed saffron,
　　　　　I played my game for keeps—
for love, for poetry,
　　　and for eternal life—
　　　　　after the trials of summer.

4
In the recurring dream
　　　my mother stands
　　　　　in her bridal gown

under the burning lilac,
    with Bernard Shaw and Bertie
        Russell kissing her hands;
the house behind her is in ruins;
    she is wearing an owl's face
        and makes barking noises.
Her minatory finger points.
    I pass through the cardboard doorway
        askew in the field
and peer down a well
    where an albino walrus huffs.
        He has the gentlest eyes.
If the dirt keeps sifting in,
    staining the water yellow,
        why should I be blamed?
Never try to explain.
    That single Model A
        sputtering up the grade
unfurled a highway behind
    where the tanks maneuver,
        revolving their turrets.
In a murderous time
    the heart breaks and breaks
        and lives by breaking.
It is necessary to go
    through dark and deeper dark
        and not to turn.
I am looking for the trail.
    Where is my testing-tree?
        Give me back my stones!

The Brother

When morning came
I rose and made tea
and sent off my brother.
In the quiet house
I sat down to wait.

The day knocked on my door
with its sack of wares. The evening
looked in my window
with its inconsolable gray eyes.
On the table the lamp was lit.

My brother came home then,
white dust on his shoes
and a tiny blue flower in his cap,
weary
as if he'd danced a long time
or met a girl in the fields.

When I touched his sleeve
my fingers brought away
a fragrance of mint and grass.

Now my brother wants sleep
and moons foolishly at my bed.
What I want
is to wash his feet
and send him off again, tomorrow,
with a stone in each shoe
and one for each hand
and no bread in his pocket.

RICHMOND LATTIMORE

Those were countries simple to observe, difficult
to interpret. Young men are sage and bearded; grandmothers
are pretty; the married care little for marriage, but have

many babies; black and white were never so close and cordial,
and never hated so much; elder counsellors are brainless
but play good tennis. Their heroes, who are genuine

heroes, are also killers. These people can do anything
difficult, but nothing easy: catch and tame sight
and sound out of space; stroll in it; fly tons of steel

and come down on a handkerchief, yet can not realize a simple
covenant. Hundreds of wise men are united by subtle
communication, to form one mind and talk like a single idiot.

We have seen angels dropping fire on straw villages,
and fiends sentimentally entertained by pitiful
musicians imitating the entertainers of angels.

We have seen more good than ever we saw before
accomplishing unendurable evil.

We have seen a whole world ruled by a handful of men.
No two from one country.

Transformation Scene

> *"But there is the danger," he said, "of trying to keep*
> *the past alive at the expense of one's own reality . . ."*

Returned, a wraith from her defrauded tomb,
she haunts an empty house,
stares through a window at a scrawl of boughs,
wanders from room to legendary room.

Weightless, she roams; with printless fingertips
touches the polished table-tops, and looks
at the long rows of books;
turns then, and slips

through an unopened door and past the stair.
Nothing can be neglected; she must check
lest there be change, lest there be flaw or fleck
to dim the house whose keeping is her care . . .

till, in a sunlight grown lackluster, she
who cast no shadow even in full sun,
comes on a mirror where there should be none,
sees her reflection who had none to see—

watches it sharpen, grow opaque and clear,
while silence gathers and like summer thunder
splits the high cupola, swells downward under
a gray light, and explodes upon her ear

here in a house that will not fall but fade
as her own body takes on life once more.
Not she is unsubstantial, but the door
she passes through, its locks again betrayed.

She walks on ground grown firm; the house, receding,
dissolves behind her. From a bough she breaks
a branch of blossom, and the branch-end rakes
her arm, her flesh, warm in the sun, and bleeding.

JOHN BALABAN

How still he stands as mists begin to move,
as morning, curling, billows creep across
his cooplike, concrete sentry perched mid-bridge
over mid-muddy river. Stares at bush green banks
which bristle rifles, mortars, men—perhaps.
No convoys shake the timbers. No sound
but water slapping boat sides, bank sides, pilings.
He's slung his carbine barrel down to keep
the boring dry, and two banana-clips instead of one
are taped to make, now, forty rounds instead
of twenty. Droplets bead from stock to sight;
they bulb, then strike his boot. He scrapes his heel,
and sees no box bombs floating towards his bridge.
Anchored in red morning mist a narrow junk
rocks its weight. A woman kneels on deck
staring at lapping water. Wets her face.
Idly the thick Rach Binh Thuy slides by.
He aims. At her. Then drops his aim. Idly.

Family

When you swim in the surf off Seal Rocks, and your family
Sits in the sand
Eating potato salad, and the undertow
Comes which takes you out away down
To loss of breath loss of play and the power of play
Holler, say
Help, help, help. Hello, they will say,
Come back here for some potato salad.

It is then that a seventeen year old cub
Cruising in a helicopter from Antigua,
A jackstraw expert speaking only Swedish
And remote from this area as a camel, says
Look down there, there is somebody drowning.
And it is you. You say, yes, yes,
And he throws you a line.
This is what is called the brotherhood of man.

RICHARD HUGO

Those who favor our plan to alter the river
raise your hand. Thank you for your vote.
Last week, you'll recall, I spoke about how water
never complains. How it runs where you tell it,
seemingly at home, flooding grain or pinched
by geometric banks like those in this graphic
depiction of our plan. We ask for power:
a river boils or falls to turn our turbines.
The river approves our plans to alter the river.

Due to a shipwreck downstream, I'm sad to report
our project is not on schedule. The boat
was carrying cement for our concrete rip rap
balustrade that will force the river to run
east of the factory site through the state-owned
grove of cedar. Then, the uncooperative
carpenters union went on strike. When we get
that settled, and the concrete, given good weather
we can go ahead with our plan to alter the river.

We have the injunction. We silenced the opposition.
The workers are back. The materials arrived
and everything's humming. I thank you
for this award, this handsome plaque I'll keep
forever above my mantle, and I'll read
the inscription often aloud to remind me
how with your courageous backing I fought
our battle and won. I'll always remember
this banquet this day we started to alter the river.

Flowers on the bank? A park on Forgotten Island?
Return of cedar and salmon? Who are these men?
These Johnnys-come-lately with plans to alter the river?
What's this wild festival in May
celebrating the runoff, display floats on fire
at night and a forest dance under the stars?
Children sing through my locked door, 'Old stranger,
we're going to alter, to alter, alter the river.'
Just when the water was settled and at home.

Singing Death

Illustrious One, in whom death is the vagrom wound
& who wanders on the wet grasses singing, sing no more
to me. I have heard your voice plenty & I hunger for health.
Yes, though it is beautiful & seduces, Hush. Come no more
glaze-eyed to my arms asking for pity then push me aside
when the urge strikes to start singing. Transfixed
& then unhinged, crazed with the wish to die & then with the
    fear
the wish might be granted. I have heard your song
and it shall not drag me yet down with it on the wet grasses.

Illustrious One, in whom death goes on living season by season,
drawing its strength from your singing, lovely
& deadly, Listen: I will not make myself
dead to nourish the death
blooming within you, vagrom intensity. Rather than that I'd see
you wandering lost on the white watery lawns at midnight
singing for the police to come get you, yes, even rather
see you staring at a white wall trying to sing the shapes
out of the whiteness than continue this dying together.

Illustrious One, in whom death is no longer a solid block
but a network, sing no more to me of the waterglass & the
    stopped clock.
Against such songs we've crashed enough, enough.
That which was from the heart and was heart's song
has been transformed, a heartless net in which to sing
is to struggle and suffer humiliation at the hour of death.
You who sing out of the vagrom flower-mouth-wound, go back!
The white grasses will release you, bones & voice & dress
one entity, dignity regained, deathsong left where you leave
your shape on the lawn in the wet blades. Singing yet.

Poem

About the size of an old-style dollar bill,
American or Canadian,
mostly the same whites, gray greens, and steel grays
—this little painting (a sketch for a larger one?)
has never earned any money in its life.
Useless and free, it has spent seventy years
as a minor family relic
handed along collaterally to owners
who looked at it sometimes, or didn't bother to.

It must be Nova Scotia; only there
does one see gabled wooden houses
painted that awful shade of brown.
The other houses, the bits that show, are white.
Elm trees, low hills, a thin church steeple
—that gray-blue wisp—or is it? In the foreground
a water meadow with some tiny cows,
two brushstrokes each, but confidently cows;
two minuscule white geese in the blue water,
back-to-back, feeding, and a slanting stick.
Up closer, a wild iris, white and yellow,
fresh-squiggled from the tube.
The air is fresh and cold; cold early spring
clear as gray glass; a half inch of blue sky
below the steel-gray storm clouds.
(They were the artist's specialty.)
A specklike bird is flying to the left.
Or is it a flyspeck looking like a bird?

Heavens, I recognize the place, I know it!
It's behind—I can almost remember the farmer's name.
His barn backed on that meadow. There it is,
titanium white, one dab. The hint of steeple,
filaments of brush-hairs, barely there,
must be the Presbyterian church.
Would that be Miss Gillespie's house?
Those particular geese and cows
are naturally before my time.

A sketch done in an hour, "in one breath,"
once taken from a trunk and handed over.
Would you like this? I'll probably never
have room to hang these things again.
Your Uncle George, no, mine, my Uncle George,
he'd be your great-uncle, left them all with Mother
when he went back to England.
You know, he was quite famous, an R.A. . . .

I never knew him. We both knew this place,
apparently, this literal small backwater,
looked at it long enough to memorize it,
our years apart. How strange. And it's still loved,
or its memory is (it must have changed a lot).
Our visions coincided—"visions" is
too serious a word—our looks, two looks:
art "copying from life" and life itself,
life and the memory of it so compressed
they've turned into each other. Which is which?
Life and the memory of it cramped,
dim, on a piece of Bristol board,
dim, but how live, how touching in detail
—the little that we get for free,
the little of our earthly trust. Not much.
About the size of our abidance
along with theirs: the munching cows,
the iris, crisp and shivering, the water
still standing from spring freshets,
the yet-to-be-dismantled elms, the geese.

PHILIP BOOTH

Stove

I wake up in the bed my grandmother died in.
November rain. The whole house is cold.
Long stairs, two rooms through to the kitchen:
walls that haven't been painted
in sixty years. They must have shone then:
pale sun, new pumpkin, old pine.

Nothing shines now but the nickel trim
on the grandmother stove, an iron invention
the whole room leans to surround; even
when it is dead the dogs sleep close behind it.
Now they bark out, but let rain return them;
they can smell how the stove is going to be lit.

Small chips of pine from the woodshed. Then
hardwood kindling. I build it all into the firebox,
on top of loose wads of last June's *Bangor News*.
Under the grate, my first match
catches. Flames congregate, the dogs watch,
the stove begins to attend old wisdom.

After the first noisy moments, I listen for Lora;
she cooked all the mornings my grandmother died,
she ruled the whole kitchen the year I was seven:
I can see Boyd Varnum, a post outside the side door;
he's waiting for Lora, up in the front of the house,
to get right change for his winter squash. Lora says

Boyd's got the best winter squash in the village.
When Boyd gets paid, she ties her apron back on
and lets in the eggman. He has a green wagon.
Lora tells him how last night her husband hit her;
she shows him the marks. All her bruised arms
adjust dampers and vents; under the plates where turnips

are coming to boil, she shifts both pies in the oven.
The dogs feel warmer now. I bank on thick coal.
The panes steam up as sure as November: rain,
school, a talkative stove to come home to at noon;
and Lora sets my red mittens to dry on the nickel shelves
next to the stovepipe. Lora knitted my mittens.

I can still smell the litter of spaniels
whelped between the stove and the wall; there's
venison cooking, there's milktoast being warmed on
the furthest back plate, milktoast to send upstairs
to my dead mother's mother. Because, Lora says,
she is sick. Lora says she is awful sick. When Lora goes up

to my grandmother's bed, I play with the puppies
under the stove; after they suckle and go back to sleep,
because I am in second grade and am seven, I practice
reading the black iron letters raised on the black oven door;
even though I don't know who Queen Clarion was,
I'm proud I can read what the oven door says: it says
                    Queen Clarion
                    Wood & Bishop
                    Bangor, Maine
                    1911

Elegy and Flame

It stepped into my room:
A deep, yet luminous shadow clung to the wall,
Steadied itself, then came up taller,
And took on character.
                    It turned its head,
Smiled, bent over me:
Portly, red-cheeked, benign.
                    It was Dudley Fitts:
" 'From Carthage I have come—'
All in quotation marks," he said,
"By God, I am a pedant. I always 'pull
For Prime.'
            Do you hear bells ringing?
When I read aloud
                Death of Patrokles,
ILIAD, BOOK XVI,
                    I made a schoolboy football-captain
                    weep!
O Helios-Achilles, thy brightness over me!
And with Meleager of Gadara

                              I walked with Heliodora:
Petals in her hair: white violets, narcissi,
Myrtle, and chiming lilies,
Innocent crocus, dark, clever hyacinths,
Roses, heavy with dew—
                              Heliodora, Heliodora.''
Behind his voice, there were strains of music:
Vivaldi at Evensong.
                    And above the altar,
Dudley at the keys.
                    Beyond the transept,
Gold shafts of light,
                    then increasing darkness,
And his voice again,
                    ''Being a thimbleful of ashes
Among the shades,
                    I have enjoyed a loss of earth.
I have come a long way
                    after Death.''

JAMES MERRILL

Lost in Translation
   (For Richard Howard)

> Diese Tage, die leer dir scheinen
> und wertlos für das All,
> haben Wurzeln zwischen den Steinen
> und trinken dort überall.

A card table in the library stands ready
To receive the puzzle which keeps never coming.
Daylight shines in or lamplight down
Upon the tense oasis of green felt.
Full of unfulfillment, life goes on,
Mirage arisen from time's trickling sands
Or fallen piecemeal into place:
German lesson, picnic, see-saw, walk
With the collie who "did everything but talk"—
Sour windfalls of the orchard back of us.
A summer without parents is the puzzle,
Or should be. But the boy, day after day,
Writes in his Line-a-Day *No puzzle.*

He's in love, at least. His French Mademoiselle,
In real life a widow since Verdun,
Is stout, plain, carrot-haired, devout.
She prays for him, as does a curé in Alsace,
Sews costumes for his marionettes,
Helps him to keep behind the scene
Whose sidelit goosegirl, speaking with his voice,
Plays Guinevere as well as Gunmoll Jean.
Or else at bedtime in his tight embrace
Tells him her own French hopes, her German fears,
Her—but what more is there to tell?
Having known grief and hardship, Mademoiselle

Knows little more. Her languages. Her place.
Noon coffee. Mail. The watch that also waited
Pinned to her heart, poor gold, throws up its hands—
No puzzle! Steaming bitterness
Her sugars draw pops back into his mouth, translated:
"Patience, chéri. Geduld, mein Schatz."
(Thus, reading Valéry the other evening
And seeming to recall a Rilke version of "Palme,"
That sunlit paradigm whereby the tree
Taps a sweet wellspring of authority,
The hour came back. Patience dans l'azur.
Geduld im . . . Himmelblau? Mademoiselle.)

Out of the blue, as promised, of a New York
Puzzle-rental shop the puzzle comes—
A superior one, containing a thousand hand-sawn,
Sandal-scented pieces. Many take
Shapes known already—the craftsman's repertoire
Nice in its limitation—from other puzzles:
Witch on broomstick, ostrich, hourglass,
Even (surely not just in retrospect)
An inchling, innocently branching palm.
These can be put aside, made stories of
While Mademoiselle spreads out the rest face-up,
Herself excited as a child; or questioned
Like incoherent faces in a crowd,
Each with its scrap of highly colored
Evidence the Law must piece together.
Sky-blue ostrich? Likely story.
Mauve of the witch's cloak white, severed fingers
Pluck? Detain her. The plot thickens
As all at once two pieces interlock.

Mademoiselle does borders—(Not so fast.
A London dusk, December last.
Chatter silenced in the library
This grown man reenters, wearing gray.
A medium. All except him have seen
Panel slid back, recess explored,
An object at once unique and common
Displayed, planted in a plain tole
Casket the subject now considers
Through shut eyes, saying in effect:
"Even as voices reach me vaguely
A dry saw-shriek drowns them out,
Some loud machinery—a lumber mill?
Far uphill in the fir forest
Trees tower, tense with shock,
Groaning and cracking as they crash groundward.
But hidden here is a freak fragment
Of a pattern complex in appearance only.
What it seems to show is superficial
Next to that long-term lamination
Of hazard and craft, the karma that has
Made it matter in the first place.
Plywood. Piece of a puzzle." Applause
Acknowledged by an opening of lids
Upon the thing itself. A sudden dread—
But to go back. All this lay years ahead.)

Mademoiselle does borders. Straight-edge pieces
Align themselves with earth or sky
In twos and threes, naive cosmogonists
Whose views clash. Nomad inlanders meanwhile
Begin to cluster where the totem
Of a certain vibrant egg-yolk yellow

Or pelt of what emerging animal
Acts on the straggler like a trumpet call
To form a more sophisticated unit.
By suppertime two ragged wooden clouds
Have formed. In one, a Sheik with beard
And flashing sword hilt (he is all but finished)
Steps forward on a tiger skin. A piece
Snaps shut, and fangs gnash out at us!
In the second cloud—they gaze from cloud to cloud
With marked if undecipherable feeling—
Most of a dark-eyed woman veiled in mauve
Is being helped down from her camel (kneeling)
By a small backward-looking slave or page-boy
(Her son, thinks Mademoiselle mistakenly)
Whose feet have not been found. But lucky finds
In the last minutes before bed
Anchor both factions to the scene's limits
And, by so doing, orient
Them eye to eye across the green abyss.
The yellow promises, oh bliss,
To be in time a sumptuous tent.

Puzzle begun I write in the day's space
Then, while she bathes, peek at Mademoiselle's
Page to the curé: ". . . cette innocente mère,
Ce pauvre enfant, que deviendront-ils?"
Her azure script is curlicued like pieces
Of the puzzle she will be telling him about.
(Fearful incuriosity of childhood!
"Tu as l'accent allemand," said Dominique.
Indeed. Mademoiselle was only French by marriage.
Child of an English mother, a remote
Descendant of the great explorer Speke,
And Prussian father. No one knew. I heard it

Long afterwards from her nephew, a UN
Interpreter. His matter-of-fact account
Touched old strings. My poor Mademoiselle,
With 1939 about to shake
This world where "each was the enemy, each the friend"
To its foundations, kept, though signed in blood,
Her peace a shameful secret to the end.)
"Schlaf wohl, chéri." Her kiss. Her thumb
Crossing my brow against the dreams to come.

This World that shifts like sand, its unforeseen
Consolidations and elate routine,
Whose Potentate had lacked a retinue?
Lo! it assembles on the shrinking Green.

Gunmetal-skinned or pale, all plumes and scars,
Of Vassalage the noblest avatars—
The very coffee-bearer in his vair
Vest is a swart Highness, next to ours.

Kef easing Boredom, and iced syrups, thirst,
In guessed-at glooms old wives who know the worst
Outsweat that virile fiction of the New:
"Insh'Allah, he will tire—" "—or kill her first!"

(Hardly a proper subject for the Home,
Work of—dear Richard, I shall let *you* comb
Archives and learned journals for his name—
A minor lion attending on Gérôme.)

While, thick as Thebes whose presently complete
Gates close behind them, Houri and Afreet
Both claim the Page. He wonders whom to serve,
And what his duties are, and where his feet,

And if we'll find, as some before us did,
That piece of Distance deep in which lies hid
Your tiny apex sugary with sun,
Eternal Triangle, Great Pyramid!

Then sky alone is left, a hundred blue
Fragments in revolution, with no clue
To where a Niche will open. Quite a task,
Putting together Heaven, yet we do.

It's done. Here under the table all along
Were those missing feet. It's done.
The dog's tail thumping. Mademoiselle sketching
Costumes for a coming harem drama
To star the goosegirl. All too soon the swift
Dismantling. Lifted by two corners,
The puzzle hung together—and did not.
Irresistibly a populace,
Unstitched of its attachments, rattled down.
Power went to pieces as the witch
Slithered easily from Virtue's gown.
The blue held out for time, but crumbled, too.
The city had long fallen, and the tent,
A separating sauce mousseline,
Been swept away. Remained the green
On which the grown-ups gambled. A green dusk.
First lightning bugs. Last glow of west
Green in the false eyes of (coincidence)
Our mangy tiger safe on his bared hearth.

Before the puzzle was boxed and readdressed
To the puzzle shop in the mid-Sixties,
Something tells me that one piece contrived
To stay in the boy's pocket. How do I know?
I know because so many later puzzles

Had missing pieces—Maggie Teyte's high notes
Gone at the war's end, end of the vogue for collies,
A house torn down; and hadn't Mademoiselle
Kept back her pitiful bit of truth as well?
I've spent the last days, furthermore,
Ransacking Athens for that translation of "Palme."
Neither the Goethehaus nor the National Library
Seems able to unearth it. Yet I can't
Just be imagining. I've seen it. Know
How much of the sun-ripe original
Felicity Rilke made himself forego
(Who loved French words—verger, mûr, parfumer)
In order to render its underlying sense.
Know already in that tongue of his
What Pains, what monolithic Truths
Shadow stanza to stanza's symmetrical
Rhyme-rutted pavement. Know that ground plan left
Sublime and barren, where the warm Romance
Stone by stone faded, cooled; the fluted nouns
Made taller, lonelier than life
By leaf-carved capitals in the afterglow.
The owlet umlaut peeps and hoots
Above the open vowel. And after rain
A deep reverberation fills with stars.

Lost, is it, buried? One more missing piece?

But nothing's lost. Or else: all is translation
And every bit of us is lost in it
(Or found—I wander through the ruin of S
Now and then, wondering at the peacefulness)
And in that loss a self-effacing tree,
Color of context, imperceptibly
Rustling with its angel, turns the waste
To shade and fiber, milk and memory.

JANE COOPER

Rent

If you want my apartment, sleep in it
but let's have a clear understanding:
the books are still free agents.

If the rocking chair's arms surround you
they can also let you go,
they can shape the air like a body.

I don't want your rent, I want
a radiance of attention
like the candle's flame when we eat,

I mean a kind of awe
attending the spaces between us—
Not a roof but a field of stars.

LAURA GILPIN

The Two-Headed Calf

Tomorrow when the farm boys find this
freak of nature, they will wrap his body
in newspaper and carry him to the museum.

But tonight he is alive and in the north
field with his mother. It is a perfect
summer evening: the moon rising over
the orchard, the wind in the grass. And
as he stares into the sky, there are
twice as many stars as usual.

Couplets, XX

Don't be afraid of dying. The glass of water
Is quickly poured into the waiting goblet.

Your face that will be of no further use to mirrors
Grows more and more transparent, nothing is hidden.

It's night in the remotest provinces of the brain,
Seeing falls back into the great sea of light.

How strange to see that glittering green fly
Walk onto the eyeball, rubbing its hands and praying.

Don't be afraid, you're going to where you were
Before birth pushed you into this cold light.

Lie down here, next to Empedocles;
Be joined to the small grains of the brotherhood.

Mae West

She comes on drenched in a perfume called Self Satisfaction
from feather boa to silver pumps.

She does not need to be loved by you
though she'll give you credit for good taste.
Just because you say you love her
she's not throwing herself at your feet in gratitude.

Every other star reveals how worthless she feels
by crying when the hero says he loves her,
or how unhoped-for the approval is
when the audience applauds her big number—
but Mae West takes it as her due.
She knows she's good.

She expects the best for herself
and knows she's worth what she costs,
and she costs plenty.
She's not giving anything away.

She enjoys her admirers, fat daddy or muscleman,
and doesn't confuse vanity and sex,
though she never turns down pleasure,
lapping it up.

Above all she enjoys her Self,
swinging her body that says, Me me me me.
Why not have a good time?
As long as you amuse me, go on,
I like you slobbering over my hand, big boy.
I have a right to.

Most convincing, we know all this
not by her preaching it
but by her presence—it's no act.
Every word and look and movement
spells independence:
She likes being herself.

And we who don't
can only look on, astonished.

DONALD HALL

Ox Cart Man

In October of the year,
he counts potatoes dug from the brown field,
counting the seed, counting
the cellar's portion out,
and bags the rest on the cart's floor.

He packs wool sheared in April, honey
in combs, linen, leather
tanned from deerhide,
and vinegar in a barrel
hooped by hand at the forge's fire.

He walks by his ox's head, ten days
to Portsmouth Market, and sells potatoes,
and the bag that carried potatoes,
flaxseed, birch brooms, maple sugar, goose
feathers, yarn.

When the cart is empty he sells the cart.
When the cart is sold he sells the ox,
harness and yoke, and walks
home, his pockets heavy
with the year's coin for salt and taxes,

and at home by fire's light in November cold
stitches new harness
for next year's ox in the barn,
and carves the yoke, and saws planks
building the cart again.

I.

Beyond the last house, where home was,

Past the marsh we found the old skull in, all nameless

And cracked in a star-shape from stone-smack,

Up the hill where the grass was tangled waist-high and
    wind-tousled,

To the single great oak that, in leaf-season, hung like

A thunderhead black against whatever blue the sky had,

And here, at the widest circumference of shade, when shade was,

Ran the trench, six feet long,

And wide enough for a man to lie down in,

In comfort, if comfort was still any object. No sign there

Of any ruined cabin, foundation, or well,

So Pap must have died of camp-fever,

And the others pushed on, God knows where.

II.

The Dark and Bloody Ground, so the teacher
    romantically said,

But one look out the window, and woods and ruined
    cornfields we saw:

A careless flung corner of country, no hope and no history here.

No hope but the Pullman lights that swept

Night-fields—glass-glint from some farmhouse and
    flicker of ditches—

Or the night freight's moan on the rise where

You might catch a ride on the rods,

Just for hell, or if need had arisen.

No history either—no Harrod, or Finley, or Boone.

No tale how the Bluebellies broke at the Rebel yell
    and cold steel.

So we had to invent it all, our Bloody Ground, K and I,

And him the best shot in ten counties and could call any
    bird-note back,

But school out, not big enough for the ballgame,
And in the full tide of summer, not ready
For the twelve-gauge yet, or even a job, so what
Can you do but pick up your BBs and Benjamin,
Stick corn pone in pocket, and head out
"To Rally in the Cane-Brake and Shoot the Buffalo"—
As my grandfather's cracked old voice would sing it
From days of his own grandfather—and often enough
It was only a Plymouth Rock, or maybe a fat Dominecker,
That fell to the crack of the unerring Decherd.

    III.
Yes, imagination is strong. But not strong enough in the face of
The sticky feathers and BBs a mother's hand held out.
But no liberal concern was evinced for the Redskin,
As we trailed and out-tricked the sly Shawnees
In a thicket of ironweed, and I wrestled one naked
And slick with his bear-grease, till my hunting knife
Bit home, and the tomahawk
Slipped from his hand. And what mother cared about Bluebellies,
Who came charging our trench? But we held
To pour the last volley at face-gape before
The tangle and clangor of bayonet.

Yes, a day is merely forever
In memory's shiningness,
And a year but a gust or a gasp
In the summer's heat of Time, and in that last summer
I was almost ready to learn
What imagination is—it is only
The lie we must learn to live by, if ever
We mean to live at all. Times change.
Things change. And K up and gone, and the summer
Gone, and I yearned to know the world's name.

IV.
Well, what I remember most
In a world, long Time-paled and powdered
Like a vision still clinging to plaster
Set by Piero della Francesca,
Is how K, through lane-dust or meadow,
Seemed never to walk, but float
With a singular joy and silence,
In his cloud of bird dogs, like angels
With their eyes on his eyes like God,
And the sun on his uncut hair bright
As he passed through the ramshackle town and odd folks there
With pants on and vests and always soft gabble of money—
Polite in his smiling, but never much to say.

V.
To pass through to what? No, not
To some wild white peak dreamed westward,
And each sunrise a promise to keep. No, only
The Big Leagues, not even a bird dog,
And girls that popped gum while they screwed.

Yes, that was his path, and no batter
Could do what booze finally did:
Just blow him off the mound—but anyway,
He had always called it a fool game, just something
For children who hadn't yet dreamed what
A man is, or barked a squirrel, or raised
A single dog from a pup.

VI.

And I, too, went on my way, the winning or losing, or what
Is sometimes of all things the worst, the not knowing
One thing from the other, nor knowing
How the teeth in Time's jaws all snag backward,
And whatever enters therein
Has less hope of remission than shark-meat,

And one Sunday afternoon, in the idleness of summer,
I found his farm and him home there,
With the bird dogs crouched round in the grass,
And their eyes on his eyes as he whispered
Whatever to bird dogs it was.
Then yelled: "Well, for Christ's sake, it's you!"

Yes, me, for Christ's sake, and some sixty
Years blown like a hurricane past! But what can you say—
Can you say—when *all-to-be-said* is the *done?*
So our talk ran to buffalo hunting, and the look on his
        mother's face,

And the sun sank low as he stood there,
All Indian-brown from waist up, who never liked tops
        to his pants,
And standing nigh straight, but the arms and the pitcher's
Great shoulders, they were thinning to old-man thin.
Sun low, all silence, then sudden:
"But Jesus," he cried, "what makes a man do what he does—
Him living until he dies!"

Sure all of us live till we die, but bingo!
Like young David at brookside, he swooped down,
Snatched a stone, wound up, and let fly,
And high on a pole over yonder the big brown insulator
Simply exploded. "See, I still got control!" he said.

VII.
Late, late, toward sunset, I wandered
Where old dreams had once been Life's truth, and where
Sank the trench of our valor, now nothing
But a ditch full of late-season weed-growth,
Beyond the rim of shade.

There was nobody there, hence no shame to be saved from, so I
Just lie in the trench on my back and see high,
Beyond tall ironweed stalks, or oak leaves
If I happened to look that way,
How the late summer's thinned-out sky moves,
Drifting on, drifting on, like forever,
From *where* on to *where*, and I wonder
What it would be like to die,
Like the nameless old skull in the swamp, lost,
And know yourself dead lying under
The infinite motion of sky.

VIII.
But why should I lie here longer?
I am not yet dead though in years,
And the world's way is yet long to go,
And I love the world even in my anger,
And love is a hard thing to outgrow.

Ice

breaks up in obelisks on the river,
as I stand beside your grave.
I tip my head back.
Above me, the same sky you loved,
that shawl of cotton wool,
frozen around the shoulders of Minnesota.
I'm cold and so far from Texas
and my father, who gave me to you.
I was twelve, a Choctaw, a burden.
A *woman*, my father said, raising my skirt.
Then he showed you the roll of green gingham,
stained red, that I'd tried to crush to powder
with my small hands. I close my eyes,

and it is March 1866 again.
I'm fourteen, wearing a white smock.
I straddle the rocking horse you made for me
and stroke the black mane cut from my own hair.
Sunrise hugs you from behind,
as you walk through the open door
and lay the velvet beside me.

I give you the ebony box
with the baby's skull inside
and you set it on your work table,
comb your pale blond hair with one hand,
then nail it shut.
When the new baby starts crying, I cover my ears,

watching as you lift him from the cradle
and lay him on the pony-skin rug.
I untie the red scarf, knotted at my throat,
climb off the horse and bend over you.
I slip the scarf around your neck,
and pull it tight, remembering:
I strangled the other baby,
laid her on your stomach while you were asleep.
You break my hold and pull me to the floor.
I scratch you, bite your lips, your face,
then you cry out,
and I open and close my hands
around a row of bear teeth.

I open my eyes.
I wanted you then and now,
and I never let you know.
I kiss the headstone.
Tonight, wake me like always.
Talk and I'll listen,
while you lie on the pallet
resting your arms behind your head,
telling me about the wild rice in the marshes
and the empty .45 you call *Grace of God* that keeps you alive,
as we slide forward, without bitterness, decade by decade,
becoming transparent. Everlasting.

Old Apple Trees

Like battered old millhands, they stand in the orchard—
Like drunk legionnaires, heaving themselves up,
Lurching to attention. Not one of them wobbles
The same way as another. Uniforms won't fit them—
All those cramps, humps, bulges. Here, a limb's gone;
There, rain and corruption have eaten the whole core.
They've all grown too tall, too thick, or too something.
Like men bent too long over desks, engines, benches,
Or bent under mailsacks, under loss.
They've seen too much history and bad weather, grown
Around rocks, into high winds, diseases, grown
Too long to be wilful, too long to be changed.

Oh, I could replant, bulldoze the lot,
Get nursery stock, all the latest ornamentals,
Make the whole place look like a suburb,
Each limb sleek as a teenybopper's—pink
To the very crotch— each trunk smoothed, ideal
As the fantasy life of an adman.
We might just own the Arboreal Muscle Beach:
Each tree disguised as its neighbor. Or each disguised
As if not its neighbor— each doing its own thing
Like executives' children.

                              At least I could prune.
At least I should trim the dead wood; fill holes
Where rain collects and decay starts. Well, I should;
I should. There's a red squirrel nests here someplace.
I live in the hope of hearing one saw-whet owl.
Then, too, they're right about Spring. Bees hum
Through these branches like lascivious intentions. The white
Petals drift down, sift across the ground; this air's so rich
No man should come here except on a working pass;
No man should leave here without going to confession.
All Fall, apples nearly crack the boughs;
They hang here red as candles in the
White oncoming snow.

Tonight we'll drive down to the bad part of town
To the New Hungarian Bar or the Klub Polski,
To the Old Hellas where we'll eat the new spring lamb;
Drink good *mavrodaphne*, say, at the Laikon Bar,
Send drinks to the dancers, those meatcutters and laborers
Who move in their native dances, the archaic forms.
Maybe we'll still find our old crone selling chestnuts,
Whose toothless gums can spit out fifteen languages,
Who turns, there, late at night, in the center of the floor,
Her ancient dry hips wheeling their slow, slow *tsamikos*;
We'll stomp under the tables, whistle, we'll all hiss
Till even the belly dancer leaves, disgraced.

We'll drive back, lushed and vacant, in the first dawn;
Out of the light gray mists may rise our flowering
Orchard, the rough trunks holding their formations
Like elders of Colonus, the old men of Thebes
Tossing their white hair, almost whispering,

> Soon, each one of us will be taken
> By dark powers under this ground
> That drove us here, that warped us.
> Not one of us got it his own way.
> Nothing like any one of us
> Will be seen again, forever.
> Each of us held some noble shape in mind.
> It seemed better that we kept alive.

GALWAY KINNELL

Saint Francis and the Sow

The bud
stands for all things,
even for those things that don't flower,
for everything flowers, from within, of self-blessing;
though sometimes it is necessary
to reteach a thing its loveliness,
to put a hand on its brow
of the flower
and retell it in words and in touch
it is lovely
until it flowers again from within, of self-blessing;
as Saint Francis
put his hand on the creased forehead
of the sow, and told her in words and in touch
blessings of earth on the sow, and the sow
began remembering all down her thick length,
from the earthen snout all the way
through the fodder and slops to the spiritual curl of the tail,
from the hard spininess spiked out from the spine
down through the great broken heart
to the sheer blue milken dreaminess spurting and shuddering
from the fourteen teats into the fourteen mouths sucking and
    blowing beneath them:
the long, perfect loveliness of sow.

JARED CARTER

At the Sign-Painter's

Of them all—those laboring men who knew my first name
And called out to me as I watched them coming up the walk;
The ones with birthmarks and missing fingers and red hair,
Who had worked for my grandfather, and now my father;
Who had gone home to wash up and put on a clean shirt;
Who came to the back door Friday evenings for their checks;
Who drove a Ford coupe and had a second wife and three kids
And were headed for town to have a drink and buy groceries—

Of the ones too old to work—in their black shoes laced up
With hooks, and their string ties, who stood on the sidewalk
When we were building something, and asked my father
If he remembered the house-moving business back during
The Depression: how you squirmed through all that dust
And broken glass in the crawl space, nudging ten-by-twelves
Twenty feet long, and lugged the house-jacks behind you
One at a time, setting them up just right. How you moved
On your back like a crab through darkness, cobwebs
Brushing your face, an iron bar in your hands, a voice
Calling somewhere from outside, asking for a quarter-turn—

Of them all—plumbers, tinners, roofers, well-diggers,
Carpenters, cement finishers with their padded knees—
I liked the sign-painters best: liked being taken there
By my father, following after him, running my fingers
Along the pipe railing, taking his hand as we climbed up
The concrete embankment to their back-street shop looking
Out across the Nickel Plate yard—
                                                    liked being left to wander
Among piles of fresh pine planks, tables caked and smeared
And stacked with hundreds of bottles and jars leaking color
And fragrance, coffee cans jammed with dried brushes, skylight
Peppered with dead flies, narrow paths that wound among
Signs shrouded with tape and newspaper—all the way back
To the airshaft, the blackened sink, the two-burner hotplate,
Spoons sticking from china mugs, behind the curtain the bed
With its torn army blanket—liked feeling beneath my toes
The wood floors patterned with forgotten colors, soft
To the step, darkened with grime and soot from the trains—

Liked them most of all—those solemn old men with skin
Bleached and faded as their hair, white muslin caps
Speckled with paint, knuckles and fingers faintly dotted—
Liked them for their listening to him about the sign
He wanted painted, for pretending not to notice me watching—
For the wooden rod with its black knob resting lightly
Against the primed surface, for the slow sweep and whisper
Of the brush—liked seeing the ghost letters in pencil
Gradually filling out, fresh and wet and gleaming, words
Forming out of all that darkness, that huge disorder.

STEPHEN DOBYNS

A great cry went up from the stockyards and
slaughterhouses, and Death, tired of complaint
and constant abuse, withdrew to his underground garage.
He was still young and his work was a torment.
All over, their power cut, people stalled like street cars.
Their gravity taken away, they began to float.
Without buoyancy, they began to sink. Each person
became a single darkened room. The small hand
pressed firmly against the small of their backs
was suddenly gone and people swirled to a halt
like petals fallen from a flower. Why hurry?
Why get out of bed? People got off subways,
on subways, off subways all at the same stop.
Everywhere clocks languished in antique shops
as their hands composed themselves in sleep.
Without time and decay, people grew less beautiful.
They stopped eating and began to study their feet.
They stopped sleeping and spent weeks following stray dogs.
The first to react were remnants of the church.
They falsified miracles: displayed priests posing
as corpses until finally they sneezed or grew lonely.
Then governments called special elections to choose those
to join the ranks of the volunteer dead: unhappy people
forced to sit in straight chairs for weeks at a time.
Interest soon dwindled. Then the army seized power
and soldiers ran through the street dabbling the living
with red paint. You're dead, they said. Maybe

tomorrow, people answered, today we're just breathing:
look at the sky, look at the color of the grass.
For without Death each color had grown brighter.
At last a committee of businessmen met together,
because with Death gone money had no value.
They went to where Death was waiting in a white room,
and he sat on the floor and looked like a small boy
with pale blond hair and eyes the color of clear water.
In his lap was a red ball heavy with the absence of life.
The businessmen flattered him. We will make you king,
they said. I am king already, Death answered. We will
print your likeness on all the money of the world.
It is there already, Death answered. We adore you
and will not live without you, the businessmen said.
Death said, I will consider your offer.

How Death was restored to his people:

At first the smallest creatures began to die—
bacteria and certain insects. No one noticed. Then fish
began to float to the surface; lizards and tree toads
toppled from sun-warmed rocks. Still no one saw them.
Then birds began tumbling out of the air,
and as sunlight flickered on the blue feathers
of the jay, brown of the hawk, white of the dove,
then people lifted their heads and pointed to the sky
and from the thirsty streets cries of welcome rose up
like a net to catch the delicate and plummeting bodies.

ANTHONY HECHT

The Transparent Man

I'm mighty glad to see you, Mrs. Curtis,
And thank you very kindly for this visit—
Especially now when all the others here
Are having holiday visitors, and I feel
A little conspicuous and in the way.
It's mainly because of Thanksgiving. All these mothers
And wives and husbands gaze at me soulfully
And feel they should break up their box of chocolates
For a donation, or hand me a chunk of fruitcake.
What they don't understand and never guess
Is that it's better for me without a family;
It's a great blessing. Though I mean no harm.
And as for visitors, why, I have you,
All cheerful, brisk and punctual every Sunday,
Like church, even if the aisles smell of phenol.
And you always bring even better gifts than any
On your book-trolley. Though they mean only good,
Families can become a sort of burden.
I've only got my father, and he won't come,
Poor man, because it would be too much for him.
And for me, too, so it's best the way it is.
He knows, you see, that I will predecease him,
Which is hard enough. It would take a callous man
To come and stand around and watch me failing.
(Now don't you fuss; we both know the plain facts.)
But for him it's even harder. He loved my mother.
They say she looked like me; I suppose she may have.
Or rather, as I grew older I came to look
More and more like she must one time have looked,
And so the prospect for my father now

178

Of losing me is like having to lose her twice.
I know he frets about me. Dr. Frazer
Tells me he phones in every single day,
Hoping that things will take a turn for the better.
But with leukemia things don't improve.
It's like a sort of blizzard in the bloodstream,
A deep, severe, unseasonable winter,
Burying everything. The white blood cells
Multiply crazily and storm around,
Out of control. The chemotherapy
Hasn't helped much, and it makes my hair fall out.
I know I look a sight, but I don't care.
I care about fewer things; I'm more selective.
It's got so I can't even bring myself
To read through any of your books these days.
It's partly weariness, and partly the fact
That I seem not to care much about the endings,
How things work out, or whether they even do.
What I do instead is sit here by this window
And look out at the trees across the way.
You wouldn't think that was much, but let me tell you,
It keeps me quite intent and occupied.
Now all the leaves are down, you can see the spare,
Delicate structures of the sycamores,
The fine articulation of the beeches.
I have sat here for days studying them,
And I have only just begun to see
What it is that they resemble. One by one,
They stand there like magnificent enlargements
Of the vascular system of the human brain.

I see them there like huge discarnate minds,
Lost in their meditative silences.
The trunks, branches and twigs compose the vessels
That feed and nourish vast immortal thoughts.
So I've assigned them names. There, near the path,
Is the great brain of Beethoven, and Kepler
Haunts the wide spaces of that mountain ash.
This view, you see, has become my Hall of Fame.
It came to me one day when I remembered
Mary Beth Finley who used to play with me
When we were girls. One year her parents gave her
A birthday toy called "The Transparent Man."
It was made of plastic, with different colored organs,
And the circulatory system all mapped out
In rivers of red and blue. She'd ask me over
And the two of us would sit and study him
Together, and do a powerful lot of giggling.
I figure he's most likely the only man
Either of us would ever get to know
Intimately, because Mary Beth became
A Sister of Mercy when she was old enough.
She must be thirty-one; she was a year
Older than I, and about four inches taller.
I used to envy both those advantages
Back in those days. Anyway, I was struck
Right from the start by the sea-weed intricacy,
The fine-haired, silken-threaded filiations
That wove, like Belgian lace, throughout the head.
But this last week it seems I have found myself
Looking beyond, or through, individual trees

At the dense, clustered woodland just behind them,
Where those great, nameless crowds patiently stand.
It's become a sort of complex, ultimate puzzle
And keeps me fascinated. My eyes are twenty-twenty,
Or used to be, but of course I can't unravel
The tousled snarl of intersecting limbs,
That mackled, cinder grayness. It's a riddle
Beyond the eye's solution. Impenetrable.
If there is order in all that anarchy
Of granite mezzotint, that wilderness,
It takes a better eye than mine to see it.
It set me on to wondering how to deal
With such a thickness of particulars,
Deal with it faithfully, you understand,
Without blurring the issue. Of course I know
That within a month the sleeving snows will come
With cold, selective emphases, with massings
And arbitrary contrasts, rendering things
Deceptively simple, thickening the twigs
To frosty veins, bestowing epaulets
And decorations on every birch and aspen.
And the eye, self-satisfied, will be misled,
Thinking the puzzle solved, supposing at last
It can look forth and comprehend the world.
That's when you have to really watch yourself.
So I hope that you won't think me plain ungrateful
For not selecting one of your fine books,
And I take it very kindly that you came
And sat here and let me rattle on this way.

HOWARD NEMEROV

The Makers

Who can remember back to the first poets,
The greatest ones, greater even than Orpheus?
No one has remembered that far back
Or now considers, among the artifacts
And bones and cantilevered inference
The past is made of, those first and greatest poets,
So lofty and disdainful of renown
They left us not a name to know them by.

They were the ones that in whatever tongue
Worded the world, that were the first to say
Star, water, stone, that said the visible
And made it bring invisibles to view
In wind and time and change, and in the mind
Itself that minded the hitherto idiot world
And spoke the speechless world and sang the towers
Of the city into the astonished sky.

They were the first great listeners, attuned
To interval, relationship, and scale,
The first to say above, beneath, beyond,
Conjurors with love, death, sleep, with bread and wine,
Who having uttered vanished from the world
Leaving no memory but the marvelous
Magical elements, the breathing shapes
And stops of breath we build our Babels of.

MARILYN HACKER

La Fontaine de Vaucluse

for Marie Ponsot

"Why write unless you praise the sacred places . . . ?"
  Richard Howard: "Audiences"

1
Azure striation swirls beyond the stones
flung in by French papas and German boys.
The radio-guide emits trilingual noise.
"Always 'two ladies alone'; we were not alone."
Source, cunt, umbilicus, resilient blue
springs where the sheer gorge spreads wooded, mossed thighs:
unsounded female depth in a child-sized
pool boys throw rocks at. Hobbled in platform shoes,
girls stare from the edge. We came for the day
on a hot bus from Avignon. A Swed-
ish child hurls a chalk boulder; a tall girl,
his sister, twelve, tanned, crouches to finger shell-
whorls bedded in rock-moss. We find our way
here when we can; we take away what we need.

2
Here, when we can, we take away what we need:
stones, jars of herb-leaves, scrap-patch workbags stored
in the haphazard rooms we can afford.
Marie and I are lucky: we can feed
our children and ourselves on what we earn.
One left the man who beat her, left hostages
two daughters; one weighs her life to her wages,
finds both wanting and, bought out, stays put, scorn-
ful of herself for not deserving more.
The concierge at Le Régent is forty-six;
there fifteen years, widowed for one, behind
counters a dun perpetual presence, fixed
in sallow non-age till Marie talked to her.
I learn she is coeval with my friends.

3
I learn she is coeval with my friends:
the novelist of seventy who gives

us tea and cakes; the sister with whom she lives
a dialogue; the old Hungarian
countess' potter daughter, British, dyke,
bravely espoused in a medieval hill
town in Provence; Jane whom I probably will
never know and would probably never like;
Liliane the weaver; Liliane's daughter
the weaver; Liliane's housewifely other
daughter, mothering; the great-grandmother
who drove us through gnarled lanes at Avignon;
the virgin at the source with wedgies on;
Iva, who will want to know what I brought her.

4
Iva, who will want to know what I brought her
(from Selfridge's, a double-decker bus,
a taxi, Lego; a dark blue flowered dress
from Uniprix; a wickerwork doll's chair
from the Vence market; books; a wrapped-yarn deer;
a batik: girl guitarist who composes
sea creatures, one of three I chose,
two by the pupil, one by the woman who taught her),
might plunge her arms to the elbows, might shy stones,
might stay shy. I'll see her in ten days.
Sometimes she still swims at my center; sometimes
she is a four-year-old an ocean away
and I am on vertiginous terrain
where I am nobody's mother and nobody's daughter.

5
"Where I am, nobody's mother and nobody's daughter
can find me," words of a woman in pain
or self-blame, obsessed with an absent or present man,
blindfolded, crossing two swords, her back to the water.
The truth is, I wake up with lust and loss
and only half believe in something better;
the truth is that I still write twelve-page letters
and blame my acne and my flabby ass

that I am thirty-five and celibate.
Women are lustful and fickle and all alike,
say the hand-laid flower-pressed sheets at the papermill.
I pay attention to what lies they tell
us here, but at the flowered lip, hesitate,
one of the tamed girls stopped at the edge to look.

6
One of the tamed girls stopped at the edge to look
at her self in the water, genital self that stains
and stinks, that is synonymous with drains,
wounds, pettiness, stupidity, rebuke.
The pool creates itself, cleansed, puissant, deep
as magma, maker, genetrix. Marie
and I, each with a notebook on her knee,
begin to write, homage the source calls up
or force we find here. There is another source
consecrate in the pool we perch above:
our own intelligent accord that brings
us to the lucid power of the spring
to work at re-inventing work and love.
We may be learning how to tell the truth.

7
We may be learning how to tell the truth.
Distracted by a cinematic sky,
Paris below two dozen shades of grey,
in borrowed rooms we couldn't afford, we both
work over words till we can tell ourselves
what we saw. I get up at eight, go down
to buy fresh croissants, put a saucepan on
and brew first shared coffee. The water solves
itself, salves us. Sideways, hugging the bank,
two stocky women helped each other, drank
from leathery cupped palms. We make our own
descent downstream, getting our shoes wet, care-
fully hoist cold handsful from a crevice where
azure striation swirls beyond the stones.

WILLIAM MEREDITH

Parents 185

What it must be like to be an angel
or a squirrel, we can imagine sooner.

The last time we go to bed good,
they are there, lying about darkness.

They dandle us once too often,
these friends who become our enemies.

Suddenly one day, their juniors
are as old as we yearn to be.

They get wrinkles where it is better
smooth, odd coughs, and smells.

It is grotesque how they go on
loving us, we go on loving them.

The effrontery, barely imaginable,
of having caused us. And of how.

Their lives: surely
we can do better than that.

This goes on for a long time. Everything
they do is wrong, and the worst thing,

they all do it, is to die,
taking with them the last explanation,

how we came out of the wet sea
or wherever they got us from,

taking the last link
of that chain with them.

Father, mother, we cry, wrinkling,
to our uncomprehending children and grandchildren.

My Mother on an Evening in Late Summer

1

When the moon appears
and a few wind-stricken barns stand out
in the low-domed hills
and shine with a light
that is veiled and dust-filled
and that floats upon the fields,
my mother, with her hair in a bun,
her face in shadow, and the smoke
from her cigarette coiling close
to the faint yellow sheen of her dress,
stands near the house
and watches the seepage of late light
down through the sedges,
the last gray islands of cloud
taken from view, and the wind
ruffling the moon's ash-colored coat
on the black bay.

2

Soon the house, with its shades drawn closed, will send
small carpets of lampglow
into the haze and the bay
will begin its loud heaving
and the pines, frayed finials
climbing the hill, will seem to graze
the dim cinders of heaven.
And my mother will stare into the starlanes,
the endless tunnels of nothing,
and as she gazes,
under the hour's spell,
she will think how we yield each night
to the soundless storms of decay
that tear at the folding flesh,
and she will not know
why she is here
or what she is prisoner of
if not the conditions of love that brought her to this.

3
My mother will go indoors
and the fields, the bare stones
will drift in peace, small creatures—
the mouse and the swift—will sleep
at opposite ends of the house.
Only the cricket will be up,
repeating its one shrill note
to the rotten boards of the porch,
to the rusted screens, to the air, to the rimless dark,
to the sea that keeps to itself.
Why should my mother awake?
The earth is not yet a garden
about to be turned. The stars
are not yet bells that ring
at night for the lost.
It is much too late.

These Green-Going-to-Yellow

This year,
I'm raising the emotional ante,
putting my face
in the leaves to be stepped on,
seeing myself among them, that is;
that is, likening
leaf-vein to artery, leaf to flesh,
the passage of a leaf in autumn
to the passage of autumn,
branch-tip and winter spaces
to possibilities, and possibility
to God. Even on East 61st Street
in the blowzy city of New York,
someone has planted a gingko
because it has leaves like fans like hands,
hand-leaves, and sex. Those lovely
Chinese hands on the sidewalks
so far from delicacy
or even, perhaps, another gender of gingko—
do we see them?
No one ever treated us so gently
as these green-going-to-yellow hands
fanned out where we walk.
No one ever fell down so quietly
and lay where we would look
when we were tired or embarrassed,
or so bowed down by humanity
that we had to watch out lest our shoes stumble,
and looked down not to look up
until something looked like parts of people
where we were walking. We have no
experience to make us see the gingko
or any other tree,
and, in our admiration for whatever grows tall
and outlives us,
we look away, or look at the middles of things,
which would not be our way
if we truly thought we were gods.

III. Blue

Everyone is gone. Everyone.
At a gutted store building
in his old neighborhood
Willie idles, kicking the rubbish.
By chance the odd pieces gather
into a stick figure—a boy.
Willie adds bits of cloth
and an old mop head for hair,
but he finds no object to be
a word to coax his boy to talk.
The face is a cracked white plate.
Willie throws it in the road
hoping a tire explodes.
The image exists when it confirms
our sense of being. Willie feels blue
like the sky, so close so far away.
When he opens his mouth
there is no sound but a window
opened wide to show more air.

For the Sleepwalkers

Tonight I want to say something wonderful
for the sleepwalkers who have so much faith
in their legs, so much faith in the invisible

arrow carved into the carpet, the worn path
that leads to the stairs instead of the window,
the gaping doorway instead of the seamless mirror.

I love the way that sleepwalkers are willing
to step out of their bodies into the night,
to raise their arms and welcome the darkness,

palming the blank spaces, touching everything.
Always they return home safely, like blind men
who know it is morning by feeling shadows.

And always they wake up as themselves again.
That's why I want to say something astonishing
like: *Our hearts are leaving our bodies.*

Our hearts are thirsty black handkerchiefs
flying through the trees at night, soaking up
the darkest beams of moonlight, the music

of owls, the motion of wind-torn branches.
And now our hearts are thick black fists
flying back to the glove of our chests.

We have to learn to trust our hearts like that.
We have to learn the desperate faith of sleep-
walkers who rise out of their calm beds

and walk through the skin of another life.
We have to drink the stupefying cup of darkness
and wake up to ourselves, nourished and surprised.

Yes, I only got here on my own.
Nothing miraculous. An old woman
opened her door expecting the milk,
and there I was, seven years old, with
a bulging suitcase of wet cardboard
and my hair plastered down and stiff
in the cold. She didn't say, "Come in,"
she didn't say anything. Her luck
had always been bad, so she stood
to one side and let me pass, trailing
the unmistakable aroma of badger
which she mistook for my underwear,
and so she looked upward, not
to heaven but to the cracked ceiling
her husband had promised to mend,
and she sighed for the first time
in my life that sigh which would tell
me what was for dinner. I found my room
and spread my things on the sagging bed:
the bright ties and candy-striped shirts,
the knife to cut bread, the stuffed weasel
to guard the window, the silver spoon
to turn my tea, the pack of cigarettes
for the life ahead, and at last
the little collection of worn-out books
from which I would choose my only name—
Morgan the Pirate, Jack Dempsey, the Prince
of Wales. I chose Abraham Plain
and went off to school wearing a cap
that said "Ford" in the right script.
The teachers were soft-spoken women
smelling like washed babies and the students

fierce as lost dogs, but they all hushed
in wonder when I named the 400 angels
of death, the planets sighted and unsighted,
the moment at which creation would turn
to burned feathers and blow every which way
in the winds of shock. I sat down
and the room grew quiet and warm. My eyes
asked me to close them. I did, and so
I discovered the beauty of sleep and that
to get ahead I need only say I was there,
and everything would open as the darkness
in my silent head opened onto seascapes
at the other end of the world, waves
breaking into mountains of froth, the sand
running back to become the salt savor
of the infinite. Mrs. Tarbox woke me
for lunch—a tiny container of milk
and chocolate cookies in the shape of Michigan.
Of course I went home at 3:30, with
the bells ringing behind me and four stars
in my notebook and drinking companions
on each arm. If you had been there
in your yellow harness and bright hat
directing traffic you would never
have noticed me—my clothes shabby
and my eyes bright—; to you I'd have been
just an ordinary kid. Sure, now you
know, now it's obvious, what with the light
of the Lord streaming through the nine
windows of my soul and the music of rain
following in my wake and the ordinary air
on fire every blessed day I waken the world.

LARRY LEVIS

For Zbigniew Herbert, Summer, 1971, Los Angeles

No matter how hard I listen, the wind speaks
One syllable, which has no comfort in it—
Only a rasping of air through the dead elm.

Once a poet told me of his friend who was torn apart
By two pigs in a field in Poland. The man
Was a prisoner of the Nazis, and they watched,
He said, with interest and a drunken approval . . .
If terror is a state of complete understanding,

Then there was probably a point at which the man
Went mad, and felt nothing, though certainly
He understood everything that was there: after all,
He could see blood splash beneath him on the stubble,
He could hear singing float toward him from the barracks.

And though I don't know much about madness,
I know it lives in the thin body like a harp
Behind the rib cage. It makes it painful to move.
And when you kneel in madness your knees are glass,
And so you must stand up again with great care.

Maybe this wind was what he heard in 1941.
Maybe I have raised a dead man into this air,
And now I will have to bury him inside my body,
And breathe him in, and do nothing but listen—
Until I hear the black blood rushing over
The stone of my skull, and believe it is music.

But some things are not possible on the earth.
And that is why people make poems about the dead.
And the dead watch over them, until they are finished:
Until their hands feel like glass on the page,
And snow collects in the blind eyes of statues.

GERALD STERN

I Remember Galileo

I remember Galileo describing the mind
as a piece of paper blown around by the wind,
and I loved the sight of it sticking to a tree
or jumping into the back seat of a car,
and for years I watched paper leap through my cities;
but yesterday I saw the mind was a squirrel caught crossing
Route 80 between the wheels of a giant truck,
dancing back and forth like a thin leaf,
or a frightened string, for only two seconds living
on the white concrete before he got away,
his life shortened by all that terror, his head
jerking, his yellow teeth ground down to dust.

It was the speed of the squirrel and his lowness to the ground,
his great purpose and the alertness of his dancing,
that showed me the difference between him and paper.
Paper will do in theory, when there is time
to sit back in a metal chair and study shadows;
but for this life I need a squirrel,
his clawed feet spread, his whole soul quivering,
the hot wind rushing through his hair,
the loud noise shaking him from head to tail.
    O philosophical mind, O mind of paper, I need a squirrel
finishing his wild dash across the highway,
rushing up his green ungoverned hillside.

MICHAEL VAN WALLEGHEN

Driving into Enid
   —for Louis Jenkins

Hundreds of migrating hawks are roosting in the hedgerows around Enid, Oklahoma. If the sun were out you could see they were a reddish-brown and had creamy, speckled bellies. But today it's raining in Enid and the rain is mixed with snow. The hawks are merely silhouetted today, far off.

On sunny days, driving into Enid might easily remind you of a scene in a grade school geography book: behind the hawk on the fencepost, a train goes speeding toward some grain elevators on the outskirts of the city . . . then the horizon, and an airplane flying low over a few tall buildings. But today the winter grasses tremble on the hillsides and the scarce trees tremble.

I was just thinking I had come a long way . . . I was just thinking that next year, for sure, I'd buy a new car. I must have been thinking something like that on the outskirts, passing the first small factories, the ragged fields strewn with junk. . . .

Then, at the first stop light, some kid waves at me from the back seat of a police car . . . inscrutable, fierce. He looks like a kid I knew in grade school. His mother wore a fur coat in the middle of summer and believed the Russians were shooting tornadoes at us.

What did he do? Where are they taking him? They found him in a culvert trying to gut a chicken with a piece of glass . . . they found him trying to build a fire out of cow-shit and wet sticks. They found him alright and now he's going back.

Later on, I'll find his sister quite by accident selling cameras in the discount store. She has a crooked, shy face and reddish-brown hair. She's married now and her chewed fingers are tatooed SUE on one hand DAVE on the other.

PETER DAVISON

The Money Cry

My daughter cries when we have to talk about money.
"I can't help it," she wails. "I don't want to cry,
I just cry." How can a father blame her?
I set her straight by setting her allowance
or trying to mold the world to snug her budget
or preaching homilies about expense
and self-sufficiency. Foresight . *Foresight.*
All the while, quietly, helplessly, she cries.

Dollars of course can give a girl her head
with beads and shawls, or buy her sweet shampoos
and the acrid clangor of recorded music.
But dollars too could set her hands to work,
scrubbing pots and pans, mucking out stables.
No wonder money makes her cry! I can't
help wincing when I sit to pay the bills
from Progressive Oil or Dr. Leon Leach,
recalling the time it cost to raise the money,
and shiver when paychecks hiss across my blotter:
What will smear off? What is the handling charge?

I'd warn you to be wary of anyone
whose eyes light up at each percentage point
as though life were an electronic game
with nothing to describe it but the score.
The hunt's the game, not the computation,
yet all the while the world presents its bills,
and we sit paying them on Friday night
while everybody else is at the movies.
Listen! Don't cry. You get it and you spend it.
Take it and pass it on. That stuff won't kill you.

CAROLYN FORCHÉ

The Visitor
197

In Spanish he whispers there is no time left.
It is the sound of scythes arcing in wheat,
the ache of some field song in Salvador.
The wind along the prison, cautious
as Francisco's hands on the inside, touching
the walls as he walks, it is his wife's breath
slipping into his cell each night while he
imagines his hand to be hers. It is a small country.

There is nothing one man will not do to another.

Angel

There between the riverbank
and half-submerged tree trunk
it's a kind of alleyway
inviting loiterers—
    in this case, water striders.

Their legs, twice body-length, dent
the surface, but why they don't
sink is a transparent riddle:
the springs of their trampoline
    are nowhere to be seen.

Inches and yet far below, thin
as compass needles, almost, min-
nows flicker through the sun's
tattered netting, circling past
    each other as if lost.

Enter an angel, in
the form of a dragon-
fly, an apparition whose
coloring, were it not real,
    would scarcely be possible:

see him, like a sparkler,
tossing lights upon the water,
surplus greens, reds, milky
blues, and violets blended
    with ebony. Suspended

like a conductor's baton,
he hovers, then goes the one
way no minnow points: straight
up, into that vast solution
    of which he's a concentrate.

MARGARET GIBSON

October Elegy

Precisely down invisible threads these oak leaves
fall, leaf by leaf in low afternoon
light. They spindle and settle.
The woods open.

Birds no longer
slide by without my noticing loneliness in the bold
stare of the night sky—a sphere
tight as an onion.
At night I wake to a cry like the tearing of silk.
I listen and listen. There is only an owl.
Again, owl. A dog barks.
A clock persists,
its parody of singlemindedness
heroic.

Then mornings, they begin in mists that lift
towards noon, but first as if you've dreamed them in a deep
breath inward the trees come shyly forward
like ribs. Then the doves,
their breasts the color of hewn
cedar, call and vanish.
No one, you beautiful one just beyond grasp,
slide your fingers along my arms
as gently as you slide down
oak and beech and shagbark
loosening the leaves.

Who's attached to you, *no one* . . . who could be?
In ordinary commotions of grief and joy
you're elusive, a radiance
that flashes so strangely different each time
or so seldom
we say of you, *once in a lifetime*
remembering perhaps a phragmite on fire
in salt-marsh light where river crossed into the Sound
or the blow of light that glanced between mother
and father nakedly, once. Just once
laying the fire, remember how I whistled,
myself entirely and no one?

No one would say this:
you may as well laugh in delight,
cut loose. Interpret in a moment's
surrender your heart.

I watch the oak leaves fall.
Surely by the time I'm old I'll be ready . . .
surely by then I'll have gathered loose moments
and let them go, no longer dreaming on the stair
sun-hazy, surely not the old woman who thinks that by ninety
she'll wake once, if a split-second only,
and live.

No one, if I were able to forget you, or find you, I might learn
to enter the cup I am washing, door I am closing, word
I am opening with careful incision, lover or child
embracing—
             and fall towards that moment fire cracks
from common stones, a sunrise in evening.

WILLIAM HARMON

Again the time and blood consuming sun crosses its corner
With a web of new born light
And there the last stars literally starve.

Grey among a hundred or so other greys
The dawn horse stirs,

Wakes to the waking manifold of new circumstance
And—totally inhuman and remote
Among deep empty drums of sound unreeling hungrily
As though long drowned or long ago
Among unsteady equinoctial darknesses—
Stands.

On the welcoming west slope of the world's first mountain
Half dark in the tilted dominion of imperial light
    and common grasses
He is standing up
As dew will stand on the difficult pitched deck of grass
In the looking light,

An ordinary model of simplicity,
Spotted
(As when water spots a smooth leaf
With many magnifying lenses
That evaporate in place
Or else slip in the inflammatory turn and sloping),
Cold,
Solid enough for anybody.

Not one that waits at a fence for forked hay
Or feedbag of fodder hung on a headstall in a stable,
It is only he,
The ghostly dawn horse,

Not maiden white but stone colored,
Not a martingale gnawing nightmare
Or rainbow shouldered unicorn at allegorical attention
Or one of those things with wings

But a shaking shadow
Like the remote beating of the timed beast heart
Begotten and blessed by something blooded and blood loving;

Lowering his head for a moment
He starts to step.

LISEL MUELLER

Monet Refuses the Operation

Doctor, you say there are no haloes
around the streetlights in Paris
and what I see is an aberration
caused by old age, an affliction.
I tell you it has taken me all my life
to arrive at the vision of gas lamps as angels,
to soften and blur and finally banish
the edges you regret I don't see,
to learn that the line I called the horizon
does not exist and sky and water,
so long apart, are the same state of being.
Fifty-four years before I could see
Rouen cathedral is built
of parallel shafts of sun,
and now you want to restore
my youthful errors: fixed
notions of top and bottom,
the illusion of three-dimensional space,
wisteria separate
from the bridge it covers.
What can I say to convince you
the Houses of Parliament dissolve
night after night to become

the fluid dream of the Thames?
I will not return to a universe
of objects that don't know each other,
as if islands were not the lost children
of one great continent. The world
is flux, and light becomes what it touches,
becomes water, lilies on water,
above and below water,
becomes lilac and mauve and yellow
and white and cerulean lamps,
small fists passing sunlight
so quickly to one another
that it would take long, streaming hair
inside my brush to catch it.
To paint the speed of light!
Our weighted shapes, these verticals,
burn to mix with air
and change our bones, skin, clothes
to gases. Doctor,
if only you could see
how heaven pulls earth into its arms
and how infinitely the heart expands
to claim this world, blue vapor without end.

Tide Turning

Through salt marsh, grassy channel where the shark's
A rumor—lean, alongside—rides our boat;
Four of us off with picnic-things and wine.
Past tufty clutters of the mud called *pluff*,
Sun on the ocean tingles like a kiss.
About the fourth hour of the falling tide.

The six-hour-falling, six-hour-rising tide
Turns heron-haunts to alleys for the shark.
Tide-waters kiss and loosen; loosen, kiss.
Black-hooded terns blurt kazoo-talk—our boat
Now in midchannel and now rounding pluff.
Lolling, we eye the mud-tufts. Eye the wine.

The Atlantic, off there, dazzles. Who said wine-
Dark sea? Not this sea. Not at noon. The tide
Runs gold as chablis over sumps of pluff.
Too shallow here for lurkings of the shark,
His nose-cone, grin unsmiling. *Cr-ush!* the boat
Shocks, shudders—grounded. An abrupt tough kiss.

Our outboard's dug a mud-trough. Call that *kiss?*
Bronze knee bruised. A fair ankle gashed. With "wine-
Dark blood" a bard's on target here. The boat
Swivels, propeller in a pit, as tide
Withdraws in puddles round us—shows the shark-
Grey fin, grey flank, grey broadening humps of pluff.

Fingers that trailed in water, fume in pluff.
Wrist-deep, they learn how octopuses kiss.
Then—shark fins? No. Three dolphins there—*shhh!*—arc
Coquettish. As on TV. Cup of wine
To you, slaphappy sidekicks! with the tide's
Last hour a mudflat draining round the boat.

The hourglass turns. Look, tricklings toward the boat.
The first hour, poky, picks away at pluff.
The second, though, swirls currents. Then the tide's
Third, fourth—abundance! the great ocean's kiss.
The last two slacken. So? We're free, for wine
And gaudier mathematics. Toast the shark,

Good shark, a no-show. Glory floats our boat.
We, with the wine remaining—done with pluff—
Carouse on the affluent kisses of the tide.

LAUREN SHAKELY

Definition

After our damp skins slid apart
I nearly starved, pulling
on my mother's drained tit.
She used all her strength
to shove me out of her body,
the last link stretched, slashed,
tied in a knot I wear on the beach,
flaunting the twisted emblem
of first rejection, the eye of flesh
that saw love couldn't last.

ALBERTO RÍOS

Lost on September Trail, 1967

There was a roof over our heads
and that was at least something.
Then came dances.
The energy for them came from
childhood, or before, from the time
when only warmth was important.
We had come to the New World
and become part of it.
If the roof would shelter us,
we would keep it in repair.
Roof then could be roof,
solid, visible, recognizable,
and we could be whatever it was
that we were at this moment.
Having lost our previous names
somewhere in the rocks as we ran,
we could not yet describe ourselves.
For two days the rain had been
steady, and we left the trail
because one of us remembered
this place. Once when I was young
I had yielded to the temptation
of getting drunk, and parts of it
felt like this, wet and hot,
timeless, in the care of someone
else. After the dances we sat
like cubs, and cried for that
which in another world might be
milk, but none came.
We had only ourselves, side by side
and we began a wrestling

that comes, like dances, out of
nowhere and leaves into the night
like sophisticated daughters
painted and in plumes, but young,
a night darker than its name.
We gave ourselves over to adoration
of the moon, but we did not call it
moon, the words that came out
were instead noises as we tried
to coax it close enough
to where we might jump,
overpower it, and bring it to our
mouths, which is, after all,
the final test of all things.
But we could not, it only circled us,
calmly, and we wanted it more.
We called it Carlos, but it did not
come, we called it friend, comrade,
but nothing. We used every word
until we fell, exhausted, and slept
with our eyes open, not trusting
each other, dark pushing us even
farther into childhood, into liquid,
making us crave eyelessness,
craving so hard we understand
prayer without knowing its name.
At some point we failed
ourselves, and eyelids fell.
We dreamt dreams of even farther
worlds, so different they cannot

210

be remembered, cannot be remembered
because they cannot be described
or even imagined. We woke
and did not remember, and the night
before became part of those farther
worlds, and we did not remember
speaking to the moon.
We got up from the centuries
and centuries, and called
each other by name.
Honey, the one that was me said,
drying her tears that were
really the rain from the night
before, which had taken her
without me knowing, *honey,*
again, but she did not understand.
She wanted only the sun
because she was cold, she pulled out
hair to offer it, from her head
and her arms. She understood me
only when I held her, made her
warm. She reached to her head
and offered now me more
of herself. I took it.
I put it to my mouth,
put it to a cupped tongue
and took it in. She moved
and I put my hands on her knees
which looked up at opposite ends
of the sky.

The Living Room

We've hung David's *La Vierge et Les Saintes*
Near the piano. The companionable blessed
Surround the Virgin, her eyes are tolerant,
Dull with fulfillment. She is perfectly dressed,
Silk sleeves, green velvet gown, and jeweled cap;
Waves cascade down her back. Her Book of Hours,
Unlatched and lying open on her lap
Reveals white, distant, miniature towers
Against a sky of pure, medieval blue,
Rude peasants worshipping, broad fields of wheat
Beneath the sun, moon, stars. A courtly zoo
Feeds in the letters, magnified, ornate,
The lion, monkey, fox, and snakes twining
Around the words amuse her. She chooses not
To read just now, but touches her wedding ring,
And round her waist a gold rope in a knot.
From where she sits, her eyes rest on the keys,
Watching my hands at practice. She enjoys
Bach in Heaven, his sacred Fantasies
For her alone spin like fabulous toys.
Lines shift and break, she finds it rich and right,
Such music out of black dots on the page,
Symbols, the world a symbol from her height,
Great voices rising like smoke from time's wreckage.

Bach, like an epoch, at his clavichord,
Paused listening, and shaking the great head
He watched his mind begin, pressing a chord.
Tonight he would compose. Upstairs in bed
Anna Magdalyn worried, one o'clock
And him so tired, straining the clouded eyes to
Blindness; blindly for hours the master shook
The notes like legible blood-drops onto
The page, Europe a small book in his palm,
Giants in history's pages: 'Study Bach,
There you'll find everything.' And he worked on,
His wife awoke the first on earth to hear
These silver lines beginning, plucked, revolved,
Unearthly trills spiraling up the stair,
The night dispelled, Leipzig itself dissolved,
And Paradise a figuring of air.

CHARLES SIMIC

Old Mountain Road
    for Goody and Maida Smith

In the dusk of the evening
When the goats come,
The two pale ones nodding as they pass,
Unattended, taking their time
To graze by the curve,
Its sharpness indicated by a broken arrow,
In the last bit of daylight

I saw a blonde little girl step
Out of nowhere, and bow to them, stiffly,
As one does at the conclusion of a school play,
And disappear, pinafore and all,
In the bushes, so that I sat
On my porch, dumbfounded . . .

The goats' intermittent tinkle
Growing fainter and fainter,
And then hushing, as if on cue,
For the whippoorwill to take over
Briefly, in the giant maple.

Child! I thought of calling out,
Knowing myself a born doubter.

The Spell Against Spelling
    (a poem to be inscribed in dark places and
    never to be spoken aloud)

My favorite student lately is the one who wrote about
    feeling clumbsy.
I mean if he wanted to say how it feels to be all thumbs he
Certainly picked the write language to right in in the first place
I mean better to clutter a word up like the old Hearst place
Than to just walk off the job and not give a dam.

Another student gave me a diagragm.
"The Diagragm of the Plot in Henry the VIIIth."

Those, though, were instances of the sublime.
The wonder is in the wonders they can come up with every time.

Why do they all say heighth, but never weighth?
If chrystal can look like English to them,
    how come chryptic can't?
I guess cwm, chthonic, qanat, or quattrocento
Always gets looked up. But never momento.
Momento they know. Like wierd. Like differant.
It is a part of their deep deep-structure vocabulary:
Their stone axe, their dark bent-offering to the gods:
Their protoCro-Magnon pre-pre-sapient
    survival-against-cultural-odds.

You won't get *me* deputized in some Spelling Constabulary.
I'd sooner abandon the bag-toke-whiff system and go decimal.
I'm on their side. I better be, after my
    brush with "infinitessimal."

There it was, right where I put it, in my brand-new book.
And my friend Peter Davison read it, and he gave me this look,
And he held the look for a little while and said, "George . . ."

I needed my students at that moment. I, their Scourge.
I needed them. Needed their sympathy. Needed their care.
"Their their," I needed to hear them say, "their their."

You see, there are *Spellers* in this world, I mean mean ones too.
They shadow us around like a posse of Joe Btfsplks
Waiting for us to sit down at our study-desks and go shrdlu
So they can pop in at the windows saying "tsk tsk."

I know they're there. I know where the beggars are,
With their flash cards looking like prescriptions
        for the catarrh
And their mnemnmonics, blast 'em. They go too farrh.
I do not stoop to impugn, indict, or condemn;
But I know how to get back at the likes of thegm.

For a long time, I keep mumb.
I let 'em wait, while a preternatural calmn
Rises to me from the depths of my upwardly opened palmb.
Then I raise my eyes like some wizened-and-wisened gnolmbn,
Stranger to scissors, stranger to razor and coslmbn,
And I fix those birds with my gaze till my
        gaze strikes hoslgmbn,
And I say one word, and the word that I say is "Oslgmbnh."

"Om?" they inquire. "No, not exactly. *Oslgmbnh.*
Watch me carefully while I pronounce it because you've got
    only two more guesses
And you only get one more hint: there's an odd number of esses,
And you only get ten more seconds no nine more seconds no eight
And a right answer doesn't count if it comes in late
And a wrong answer bumps you out of the losers' bracket
And disqualifies you for the National Spellathon
    Contestant jacket
And that's all the time extension you're going to gebt
So go pick up your consolation prizes from the usherebt
And don't be surprised if it's the bowdlerized regularized
    paperback abridgment of Pepys
Because around here, gentlemen, we play for kepys."

Then I drive off in my chauffeured Cadillac Fleetwood Brougham
Like something out of the last days of Fellini's Rougham
And leave them smiting their brows and exclaiming to
    each other "Ougham!
O-U-G-H-A-M Ougham!" and tearing their hair.

Intricate are the compoundments of despair.

Well, brevity must be the soul of something-or-other.

Not, certainly, of spelling, in the good old mother
Tongue of Shakespeare, Raleigh, Marvell, and Vaughan.
But something. One finds out as one goes aughan.

MONA VAN DUYN

Letters from a Father   **217**

I

Ulcerated tooth keeps me awake, there is
such pain, would have to go to the hospital to have
it pulled or would bleed to death from the blood thinners,
but can't leave Mother, she falls and forgets her salve
and her tranquilizers, her ankles swell so and her bowels
are so bad, she almost had a stoppage and sometimes
what she passes is green as grass. There are big holes
in my thigh where my leg brace buckles the size of dimes.
My head pounds from the high pressure. It is awful
not to be able to get out, and I fell in the bathroom
and the girl could hardly get me up at all.
Sure thought my back was broken, it will be next time.
Prostate is bad and heart has given out,
feel bloated after supper. Have made my peace
because am just plain done for and have no doubt
that the Lord will come any day with my release.
You say you enjoy your feeder, I don't see why
you want to spend good money on grain for birds
and you say you have a hundred sparrows, I'd buy
poison and get rid of their diseases and turds.

II

We enjoyed your visit, it was nice of you to bring
the feeder but a terrible waste of your money
for that big bag of feed since we won't be living
more than a few weeks longer. We can see
them good from where we sit, big ones and little ones
but you know when I farmed I used to like to hunt
and we had many a good meal from pigeons
and quail and pheasant but these birds won't
be good for nothing and are dirty to have so near
the house. Mother likes the redbirds though.
My bad knee is so sore and I can't hardly hear
and Mother says she is hoarse from yelling but I know
it's too late for a hearing aid. I belch up all the time
and have a sour mouth and of course with my heart
it's no use to go to a doctor. Mother is the same.
Has a scab she thinks is going to turn to a wart.

III
The birds are eating and fighting, Ha! Ha! All shapes
and colors and sizes coming out of our woods
but we don't know what they are. Your Mother hopes
you can send us a kind of book that tells about birds.
There is one the folks called snowbirds, they eat on the ground,
we had the girl sprinkle extra there, but say,
they eat something awful. I sent the girl to town
to buy some more feed, she had to go anyway.

IV
Almost called you on the telephone
but it costs so much to call thought better write.
Say, the funniest thing is happening, one
day we had so many birds and they fight
and get excited at their feed you know
and it's really something to watch and two or three
flew right at us and crashed into our window
and bang, poor little things knocked themselves silly.
They come to after while on the ground and flew away.
And they been doing that. We felt awful
and didn't know what to do but the other day
a lady from our Church drove out to call
and a little bird knocked itself out while she sat
and she brought it in her hands right into the house,
it looked like dead. It had a kind of hat
of feathers sticking up on its head, kind of rose
or pinky color, don't know what it was,
and I petted it and it come to life right there
in her hands and she took it out and it flew. She says
they think the window is the sky on a fair
day, she feeds birds too but hasn't got
so many. She says to hang strips of aluminum foil
in the window so we'll do that. She raved about
our birds. P.S. The book just come in the mail.

V
Say, that book is sure good, I study
in it every day and enjoy our birds.
Some of them I can't identify
for sure, I guess they're females, the Latin words
I just skip over. Bet you'd never guess
the sparrows I've got here, House Sparrows you wrote,
but I have Fox Sparrows, Song Sparrows, Vesper Sparrows,
Pine Woods and Tree and Chipping and White Throat
and White Crowned Sparrows. I have six Cardinals,
three pairs, they come at early morning and night,
the males at the feeder and on the ground the females.
Juncos, maybe 25, they fight
for the ground, that's what they used to call snowbirds. I miss
the Bluebirds since the weather warmed. Their breast
is the color of a good ripe muskmelon. Tufted Titmouse
is sort of blue with a little tiny crest.
And I have Flicker and Red-Bellied and Red-
Headed Woodpeckers, you would die laughing
to see Red-Bellied, he hangs on with his head
flat on the board, his tail braced up under,
wing out. And Dickcissel and Ruby Crowned Kinglet
and Nuthatch stands on his head and Veery on top
the color of a bird dog and Hermit Thrush with spot
on breast, Blue Jay so funny, he will hop
right on the backs of the other birds to get the grain.
We bought some sunflower seeds just for him.
And Purple Finch I bet you never seen,
color of a watermelon, sits on the rim
of the feeder with his streaky wife, and the squirrels,
you know, they are cute too, they sit tall
and eat with their little hands, they eat bucketfuls.
I pulled my own tooth, it didn't bleed at all.

VI
It's sure a surprise how well Mother is doing,
she forgets her laxative but bowels move fine.
Now that windows are open she says our birds sing
all day. The girl took a Book of Knowledge on loan
from the library and I am reading up
on the habits of birds, did you know some males have three
wives, some migrate some don't. I am going to keep
feeding all spring, maybe summer, you can see
they expect it. Will need thistle seed for Goldfinch and Pine
Siskin next winter. Some folks are going to come see us
from Church, some bird watchers, pretty soon.
They have birds in town but nothing to equal this.

So the world woos its children back for an evening kiss.

DAVID BOTTOMS

In a U-Haul North of Damascus   221

1

Lord, what are the sins
I have tried to leave behind me? The bad checks,
the workless days, the scotch bottles thrown across the fence
and into the woods, the cruelty of silence,
the cruelty of lies, the jealousy,
the indifference?

What are these on the scale of sin
or failure
that they should follow me through the streets of Columbus,
the moon-streaked fields between Benevolence
and Cuthbert where dwarfed cotton sparkles like pearls
on the shoulders of the road. What are these
that they should find me half-lost,
sick and sleepless
behind the wheel of this U-Haul truck parked in a field
        on Georgia 45
a few miles north of Damascus,
some makeshift rest stop for eighteen wheelers
where the long white arms of oaks slap across trailers
and headlights glare all night through a wall of pines?

2

What was I thinking, Lord?
That for once I'd be in the driver's seat, a firm grip
        on direction?

So the jon boat muscled up the ramp,
the Johnson outboard, the bent frame of the wrecked Harley
chained for so long to the back fence,
the scarred desk, the bookcases and books,
the mattress and box springs,
a broken turntable, a Pioneer amp, a pair
of three-way speakers, everything mine
I intended to keep. Everything else abandon.

But on the road from one state
to another, what is left behind nags back through the distance,
a last word rising to a scream, a salad bowl
shattering against a kitchen cabinet, china barbs
spiking my heel, blood trailed across the cream linoleum
like the bedsheet that morning long ago
just before I watched the future miscarried.

Jesus, could the irony be
that suffering forms a stronger bond than love?

3
Now the sun
streaks the windshield with yellow and orange, heavy beads
of light drawing highways in the dew-cover.
I roll down the window and breathe the pine-air,
the after-scent of rain, and the far-off smell
of asphalt and diesel fumes.

But mostly pine and rain
as though the world really could be clean again.

Somewhere behind me,
miles behind me on a two-lane that streaks across
west Georgia, light is falling
through the windows of my half-empty house.
Lord, why am I thinking about this? And why should I care
so long after everything has fallen
to pain that the woman sleeping there should be sleeping alone?
Could I be just another sinner who needs to be blinded
before he can see? Lord, is it possible to fall
toward grace? Could I be moved
to believe in new beginnings? Could I be moved?

HENRI COULETTE

Night Thoughts
    in memory of David Kubal

Your kind of night, David, your kind of night.
The dog would eye you as you closed your book;
Such a long chapter, such a time it took.
The great leaps! The high cries! The leash like a line drive!
The two of you would rove the perfumed street,
Pillar to post, and terribly alive.

Your kind of night, nothing more, nothing less;
A single lighted window, the shade drawn,
Your shadow enormous on the silver lawn,
The busy mockingbird, his rapturous fit,
The cricket keeping time, the loneliness
Of the man in the moon—and the man under it.

The word *elsewhere* was always on your lips,
A password to some secret, inner place
Where Wisdome smiled in Beautie's looking-glass
And Pleasure was at home to dearest Honour.
(The dog-eared pages mourn your fingertips,
And vehicle whispers, Y*et once more*, to tenor.)

Now you are elsewhere, *elsewhere* comes to this,
The thoughtless body, like a windblown rose,
Is gathered up and ushered toward repose.
To have to know this is our true condition,
The Horn of Nothing, the classical abyss,
The only cry a cry of recognition.

The priest wore purple; now the night does, too.
A dog barks, and another, and another.
There are a hundred words for the word *brother*.
We use them when we love, when we are sick,
And in our dreams when we are somehow you.
What are we if not wholly catholic?

LOUIS COXE

Nightsong

Just as a year might end
the world tonight may die
around the darkside moon
with one wipe of the eye.
The world makes something to see
if we go out and look
at fields of snow and stars:
the ogle eye of Mars
throbbing toc and tic
burns red in the dark.
See how it all ends,
this time that was never ready,
this future that never worked
fallen into our hands
and our hands deadly
and the dead, friends.

J. V. CUNNINGHAM

After so many decades of . . . of what?
I have a permanent sabbatical.
I pass my time on actuarial time,
Listen to music, and, going to bed
Leave something in the bottom of the glass,
A little wastefulness to end the day.

Lighting the Night Sky

Under clouds, at the tag end of August
all the splendid atoms
fly off into darkness. This

is the nick of time, our
fine tooth comb, it's nothing
doing, never too late—

And they kicked him out of the city
and kept him from voting
for saying the sun was no god
but was rather a hot rock
and larger, even
than the Peloponnese
                        (Anaxagoras)
which is no doubt what got them

            —Paul Klee
his pale face like a peeled egg
behind that upstairs window in Switzerland
looking out on what?
            looking down on what?
                        (gathering dust)

Stendhal
in exile, even at home
frenetically changing his name
the way other people change shirts

THESE PEOPLE

said Lord Byron, "these people
have an endemic incapacity
for telling the truth"
   (before they bled him to death)

and his name now, in Athens
has been given to a sidestreet
where they sell shoes (him being
a clubfoot—though that, in the long run
was thought less important
than his money)

O I don't want to paint great pictures
he said. In Greece
they don't understand great pictures.
I want to be famous, that's all
and to have all the newspapers talk
(he was 25)

And the phoenix flower died
(*phoenix* whatever)
that had lasted three months—

"Maybe someone they look at it"
Niko suggested. "One of the Spanish.
Or maybe George."

           And "You don't believe?"
when I looked somewhat quizzical. "In Greece
(triumphant)
        is superstition."

—taxing my faith in the nation.

It's paint, said Picasso
counting his rubles.

—Stendhal with a face like a fried egg
Paul Klee changing names like hats
and Lord Byron, fleet as Nadia Comaneci

    —and the phoenix
    flower dies
    and will not rise.
    "Once you're dead.

said the grocer
not all the flowers or the greens
will make you up—
as they placed a wreath
on the grave of Venizelos.

In the night sky
the fixed stars
are like nails in the atmosphere.
They are not lanterns.

"The world is perishable"
said Anaximenes

"and shaped like the top of a table."

RIKA LESSER

Of us
not much is known.
Our lives were not
extraordinary.
Our silence seals
a deeper silence.

Sharing the single bed, how close
we lie; fingers curved over palms
whose fable reads: *conjugal bliss*
is possible.

How simple it was. It is.
But the secret's lost. That's why
you look to us, how we carry
ourselves, our smile. We live
in that space where all's yet
to become: embrace—a tenderness,
an expectation, myth, tentative
gesture preceding touch. Before
the shock of contact, when caution
counsels: Leave.

Not at all easy, this, to speak
of love. And to survive. Our skin
glows red with passion in reserve.
Unbridled, it would deaden every
nerve. Feeling—the reins, the check,
restraint, repose, out of whose thousand
fragments we are restored. Loving
each other even after death. As if
life were not, had not been, enough.

We touch, we hold, we keep
one another free.

Jurgis Petraskas, the Workers' Angel, Organizes the
First Miners' Strike in Exeter, Pennsylvania

Draped in khaki, Jurgis
who steals chickens
makes his way in the black dust
among the workers—so tired
and slow—trying to persuade them
that some abstraction is worth their jobs.
Jurgis with fireflies in his head.
      The old women sipping from a little bottle
of whiskey shake their heads and pray
to Matka Boża, virgin of virgins,
to deliver us from this affliction,
this crazy man who tells everyone
God is not good enough to them.
The girls don't sing on the steps anymore,
Matka Boża, and all we hear is the tune
Jurgis's troublesome bones play.
      When the sun reaches the highest place in the sky
everyone stops and eats while the good lord of the day
spreads his shadows over the dreams of his people—
the hot bodies in the mines, the streets
where nothing moves
until we stir like flies. Tomorrow
the angel of his own lord,
the weight of his passion, digs his own grave
inciting the miners to riot in Memorial Street
where the troopers kneel hunched over
their black Fords, tipped off, waiting.

J. D. McCLATCHY

A Winter Without Snow

Even the sky here in Connecticut has it,
That wry look of accomplished conspiracy,
The look of those who've gotten away

With a petty but regular white collar crime.
When I pick up my shirts at the laundry,
A black woman, putting down her *Daily News*,

Wonders why and how much longer our luck
Will hold. "Months now and no kiss of the witch."
The whole state overcast with such particulars.

For Emerson, a century ago and farther north,
Where the country has an ode's jagged edges,
It was "frolic architecture." Frozen blue-

Print of extravagance, shapes of a shared life
Left knee-deep in transcendental drifts:
The isolate forms of snow are its hardest fact.

Down here, the plain tercets of provision do,
Their picket snow-fence peeling, gritty,
Holding nothing back, nothing in, nothing at all.

Down here, we've come to prefer the raw material
Of everyday and this year have kept an eye
On it, shriveling but still recognizable—

A sight that disappoints even as it adds
A clearing second guess to winter. It's
As if, in the third year of a "relocation"

To a promising notch way out on the Sunbelt,
You've grown used to the prefab housing,
The quick turnover in neighbors, the constant

Smell of factory smoke—like Plato's cave,
You sometimes think—and the stumpy trees
That summer slighted and winter just ignores,

And all the snow that never falls is now
Back home and mixed up with other piercing
Memories of childhood days you were kept in

With a Negro schoolmate, of later storms
Through which you drove and drove for hours
Without ever seeing where you were going.

Or as if you've cheated on a cold sickly wife.
Not in some overheated turnpike motel room
With an old flame, herself the mother of two,

Who looks steamy in summer-weight slacks
And a parrot-green pullover. Not her.
Not anyone. But every day after lunch

You go off by yourself, deep in a brown study,
Not doing much of anything for an hour or two,
Just staring out the window, or at a patch

On the wall where a picture had hung for ages,
A woman with planets in her hair, the gravity
Of perfection in her features—oh! her hair

The lengthening shadow of the galaxy's sweep.
As a young man you used to stand outside
On warm nights and watch her through the trees.

You remember how she disappeared in winter,
Obscured by snow that fell blindly on the heart,
On the house, on a world of possibilities.

W. S. MERWIN

Yesterday

My friend says I was not a good son
you understand
I say yes I understand

he says I did not go
to see my parents very often you know
and I say yes I know

even when I was living in the same city he says
maybe I would go there once
a month or maybe even less
I say oh yes

he says the last time I went to see my father
I say the last time I saw my father

he says the last time I saw my father
he was asking me about my life
how I was making out and he
went into the next room
to get something to give me

oh I say
feeling again the cold
of my father's hand the last time

he says and my father turned
in the doorway and saw me
look at my wristwatch and he
said you know I would like you to stay
and talk with me

oh yes I say

but if you are busy he said
I don't want you to feel that you
have to
just because I'm here

I say nothing

he says my father
said maybe
you have important work you are doing
or maybe you should be seeing
somebody I don't want to keep you

I look out the window
my friend is older than I am
he says and I told my father it was so
and I got up and left him then
you know

though there was nowhere I had to go
and nothing I had to do

Up a ladder weightless as bird legs, thinner
than the indelible grass
where thistle leafs out, sizzling like bacon fat,
I'm re-ascending to heaven, getting back into management.

In no time I've persuaded underweight creeks to
        invest themselves
in the Green, the Yampa, the San Juan, the Gunnison
as they go bandsawing deeper into their canyons.

I feed a magpie on seeds wanting to fly.
I remind burrowing prairie dogs to exchange and dissolve
into offspring. I nudge cottonwood lint across the Divide
while its tree stays behind
riffling, lacing the San Luis Valley with plankton.
I stock the sky's night waters with dim barge-loads
        of turquoise
before lofting them southerly, just under the moon.

Off seasons? There are none.

I go round stuffing fresh meadows under old snow,
arrange high-country silences so comprehensive
that only in them can each smallest cony or pine finch
or pipit
take its place and be heard.

I make certain no note is lost. I traffic in light
the eye has not seen.

Out of stumps and trunks and fallen limbs moldered,
out of the white-bellied slugs, out of silver leaves
trilling sage stalks; out of bindweed
scribbling its inexhaustible phrases, the sulphur-flowers
yellowing wind, the daytime galaxies thicker than powder,
quicker than number; out of pollen scum
dusting pools in the rock,
I send a fifth season up in the sky, rising always.

Is my ladder still there? One rung at a time
I begin to step out of heaven, a cloud's possibilities
descending, as if some pure volunteer—or common starling
dead in mid-flight,
flashing dark color off preen oil
in wings barely stirring, whispering
ever so lightly as its slow turn falls
perfectly aimed
through air's open doors
toward the exuberant wreckage of August.

SHARON OLDS

First Love

for Averell

It was Sunday morning, I had the *New York*
Times spread out on my dormitory floor, its
black print coming off dark silver on the
heels of my palms, it was Spring and I had the
dormer window of my room open, to
let it in, I even had the radio
on, I was letting it all in, the
tiny silvery radio voices—I
even let myself feel that it was Easter, the
dark flower of his life opening
again, his life being given back
again, I was in love and I could take it, the ink
staining my hands, the news on the radio
coming in my ears, there had been a wreck
and they said your name, son of the well-known they
said your name. Then they said where they'd
taken the wounded and the dead, and I called the
hospital, I remember kneeling by the
phone on the third-floor landing of the dorm, the
dark steep stairs down
next to me, I spoke to a young
man a young doctor there in the
Emergency Room, my open ear
pressed to the dark receiver, my open
life pressed to the world, I said
Which one of them died, and he said your name,
he was standing there in the room with you
saying your name.
                    I remember I leaned my
forehead against the varnished bars of the
baluster rails and held on,
pulling at the rails as if I wanted to
pull them together, shut them like a dark
door, close myself like a door
as you had been shut, closed off, but I could not
do it, the pain kept coursing through me like
life, like the gift of life.

What is Poetry

We know it doesn't rhyme much anymore
but is it beautiful is it true
does it transcend the moment
which moment

or is it ironic, does it echo, echo what
does it have ears

at night whom does it adore
yet at dawn
what dream would it go to the wall for

or is it vituperative, why not
doesn't it express powerful feeling,
an overflow of feeling, is it sincere
is that enough

does it lay bare the soul
or explore the give-and-take of intense personal
    interrelationships
which persons, what kinds of interrelationships
work or play or
why one and not the others

is it witty, profound, wittily profound, profoundly witty,
is it avant-garde does it shock the bourgeoisie
who love it

or is it above the social arena does it circle the earth,
    a satellite with a proper sense of gravity high
    above the winds of fashion
who put it up there
does it transmit breathtaking pictures of a tiny earth
to a tiny earth
if not, is it a vision of eternity
tell us about it

does it make anything happen
or does it die to itself, till others notice the smell
is it shrill does its voice crack
or must it be a baritone of honey
does it give pleasure, does it teach, delight, uplift
whom does it persuade
whom doesn't it

is it a set of rules a code of forms
what is the principle behind the rules
was it handed down and by whom
or pieced together in a workshop too long ago to remember
can it be rearranged on the shelf
who really cares
may it be dismantled

is it moving, either way moving
is it the imitation of an action
which action
is it a bunch of willy-nilly impressions
who is impressed

if it were a crib
would you trust your baby to sleep in it
bounce up and down in it
learn to stand up in it then
don't answer that

is it a world created by the poet
for the poet of the poet
does it exist for its own sake,
but if it's a way of breathing, whose way
do they smoke are they
breathing making love or getting off work

is it the ideology of a class or the puff of genius
genius for what what class
what are you talking about
is it a man speaking to men
a woman speaking to women
or universal human speaking
to no one in particular
that is, no one at all

is it a mirror held up to nature,
to human nature,
or is it an escape, is it
a mirror held up to nature, to escape human nature, or
a mirror held up to human nature
to escape human history

are you afraid of it
do you understand it

does it embody human values,
values as they are
or as they say they are,
which humans, which values
is it for or against
or does it take no position,
where did it go then
does it levitate, is it in heaven

is it then beyond all this
what is it, where, if you know tell us

but if you don't know
shut up, we'll understand

KAREN SNOW

Gifts

Transient Americans,
here we are once more,
coaxing our burden of possessions
into yet another house . . .
ruthlessly junking the excess.
But two treasures we'll never relinquish:

This bright blue ceramic thing
spotted with orange. It could be
a stubby snake with a thimble-bonnet
in place of a head. Or maybe the
carbon-smeared cavity makes it a
chubby tobacco pipe?

. . . and this mother-of-pearl lined
wooden leaf dish the size of my palm.

The sooty snake-pipe ringed with oozed
glue is our much-mended candle-snuffer.
Aran, age ten, made it for me.

After Thanksgiving dinner, when I blew out
the candles, my husband, Malcolm, scolded,
"Now look what you've done to this teak table."
Contrite, I said, "I need a candle-snuffer."
Aran touched the wax tears. "Mom, what's a
candle-snuffer?"
With an inverted spoon over the smoking
black wick, I demonstrated.

A week later, Aran entered the kitchen,
grinning, his whole face singing,
his extended arm singing,
and I took from his palm the Kleenex-
swaddled packet   and unveiled this
clay candle-snuffer   and the whole
kitchen was caroling.

In that moment, Aran was my father,
and it was my seventh birthday.
Grinning like Will Rogers, he was extending
a newspaper bundle toward me,
and wonky from measles, I saw in the core
three pink flowers such as I'd never seen
before   blossoms like baby cheeks
among quivering damp ferns. "Lady's-slippers,"
Daddy said, "from the marsh alongside the track."

"That's railroad property!" Mamma flailed.
"That's stealing!"
Pushing up his hat—just like Will Rogers—
Daddy handed me the bundle. "You hold them,
Mina, and I'll get the spade." And I watched
the bouquet, all but breathing.
"You can't transplant those," Mamma sputtered.
"They'll die. The sun."
Cradling the flowers, I followed my dad to the
north side of the house, where nothing grew.
"Get in here, Mina!" Mamma fussed. "The light.
I *told* you. Your eyes."
But I stood beside my dad while
he transplanted the flowers.

And every day I watered them.

"They won't come up next year," Mamma would
nag. "Don't be surprised if the neighbors
notify the police."

But they were up for my eighth birthday,
(I hadn't gone blind, and the cops never came.)
larger than before   plus a satiny white star
"A trillium," Daddy told me, and a small yellow
lady's-slipper, "or orchid," he said.
"Well, don't count on it next year," Mamma lashed.

She had flogged a piñata.

May after May
under papermill soot and Mamma's hectoring
and freight train smoke   the beauties sprang
up   bountifully   and always the bonus twins.
Seven   nine   eleven   lush pink pouches
and trilliums and yellow orchids.

Now for the leaf-shaped dish.

Scowling at a windowfull of these in an
imports shop newly opened in our suburb,
Malcolm scoffed, "Trash. I'd like to see
a stiff tariff slapped on those peon products."

A week later: December snowstorm, twilight
growing into dark. Tad's baked potato is
wrinkling in the warm oven. I'm wringing
my hands. Where IS that boy?

A stomping. A thumping. It's Tad,
his fair fleece snow-soaked, a soggy
brown sack in his blue clutch.
"Come here, Mom," he whispers, and I
follow his drowned shoes up the stairs.
His eyes gleaming like a saint's, his
stiff suffering hand extracts from the sack
"It's for Dad." the leaf dish. "Hand-made
in India. Pearl!"

I was in the presence of Galahad and
the holy grail.

I perch the leaf dish, as always,
on the top shelf of Malcolm's desk
in company with the Noh mask and African
ivory and Chinese Jade.
The candle-snuffer presides here,
between Malcolm's heirloom Haviland
and silver candlesticks.

I think of our lineage, usually,
as a skein of protein so widging and
widdershins that it's sagging towards
extinction.
I had forgotten these filaments that
flame forth, seasonally, to plait us into
the broad braid of humanity.

Only yesterday, Aran's girl-wife,
glancing toward the ceiling where the
bald light bulb had recently glared,
announced, shyly, to us, her brittle guests,
"Aran stayed up half the night making this—"
And the woven willow lampshade floated over
our Thanksgiving feast   like an angel.

We surmount our spoilers, sometimes.

FREDERICK SEIDEL

A Dimpled Cloud

Cold drool on his chin, warm drool in his lap, a sigh,
The bitterness of too many cigarettes
On his breath: portrait of the autist
Asleep in the arms of his armchair, age thirteen,
Dizzily starting to wake just as the sun
Is setting. The room is already dark while outside
Rosewater streams from a broken yolk of blood.

All he has to do to sleep is open
A book; but the wet dream is new, as if
The pressure of *De Bello Gallico*
And Willa Cather face down on his fly,
Spread wide, one clasping the other from behind,
Had added confusion to confusion, like looking
For your glasses with your glasses on,

A mystically clear, unknowing trance of being . . .
And then you feel them—like that, his first wet dream
Seated in a chair, though not his first.
Mr. Hobbs, the Latin master with
A Roman nose he's always blowing, who keeps
His gooey handkerchief tucked in his jacket sleeve,
Pulls his hanky out, and fades away.

French, English, math, history: masters one
By one arrive, start to do what they do
In life, some oddity, some thing they do,
Then vanish. The darkness of the room grows brighter
The darker it gets outside, because of the moonlight.
O adolescence! darkness of a hole
The silver moonlight fills to overflowing!

If only he could be von Schrader or
Deloges, a beautiful athlete or a complete
Shit. God, von Schrader lazily shagging flies,
The beautiful flat trajectory of his throw.
Instead of seeking power, being it!
Tomorrow Deloges will lead the school in prayer,
Not that the autist would want to take his place.

Naked boys are yelling and snapping wet towels
At each other in the locker room,
Like a big swordfighting scene from *The Three Musketeers*,
Parry and thrust, roars of laughter and rage,
Lush Turkish steam billowing from the showers.
The showers hiss, the air is silver fox.
Hot breath, flashes of swords, the ravishing fur!—

Swashbuckling boys brandishing their towels!
Depression, aggression, elation—and acne cream—
The eco-system of a boy his age.
He combs his wet hair straight, he hates his curls,
He checks his pimples. Only the biggest ones show,
Or rather the ointment on them caked like mud,
Supposedly skin-color, invisible; dabs

Of peanut butter that have dried to fossils,
That even a shower won't wash away, like flaws
Of character expressed by their concealment—
Secrets holding up signs—O adolescence!
O silence not really hidden by the words,
Which are not true, the words, the words, the words—
Unless you scrub, will not wash away.

But how sweetly they strive to outreach these shortcomings,
These boys who call each other by their last names,
Copying older boys and masters—it's why
He isn't wearing his glasses, though he can't see.
That fiend Deloges notices but says nothing.
Butting rams, each looks at the other sincerely,
And doesn't look away, blue eyes that lie.

He follows his astigmatism toward
The schoolbuses lined up to take everyone home,
But which are empty still, which have that smiling,
Sweet-natured blur of the retarded, oafs
In clothes too small, too wrong, too red and white,
And *painfully* eager to please a sadist so cruel
He wouldn't even hurt a masochist.

The sadistic eye of the autist shapes the world
Into a sort of, call it innocence,
Ready to be wronged, ready to
Be tortured into power and beauty, into
Words his phonographic memory
Will store on silence like particles of oil
On water—the rainbow of polarity

Which made this poem. I put my glasses on,
And shut my eyes. O adolescence, sing!
All the bus windows are open because it's warm.
I blindly face a breeze almost too sweet
To bear. I hear a hazy drone and float—
A dimpled cloud—above the poor white and poorer
Black neighborhoods which surround the small airfield.

Two Stories

Tonight, on the deck, the lights
Semaphore up at me through the atmosphere,
Town lights, familiar lights
                              pulsing and slacking off
The way they used to back on the ridge outside of Kingsport
35 years ago,
The moonlight sitting inside my head
Like knives,
              the cold like a drug I knew I'd settle down with.
I used to imagine them shore lights, as these are, then,
As something inside me listened with all its weight
For the sea-surge and the sea-change.

There's a soft spot in everything
Our fingers touch,
                    the one place where everything breaks
When we press it just right.
The past is like that with its arduous edges and blind sides,
The whorls of our fingerprints
                              embedded along its walls
Like fossils the sea has left behind.

This is a story I swear is true.

I used to sleepwalk, But only
On camping trips,
                  or whenever I slept outside.
One August, when I was 11, on Mount LeConte in Tennessee,
Campfire over, and ghost story over,
Everyone still asleep, apparently I arose
From my sleeping bag,
              opened the tent flap, and started out on the trail
That led to the drop-off, where the mountainside

Went straight down for almost a thousand feet.
Half-moon and cloud cover, so some light
As I went on up the path through the rhododendron,
The small pebbles and split roots

                                  like nothing under my feet.
The cliff-side was half-a-mile from the campsite.
As I got closer,

                 moving blindly, unerringly,
Deeper in sleep than the shrubs,
I stepped out, it appears,
Onto the smooth lip of the rock cape of the cliff,
When my left hand, and then my right hand,
Stopped me as they were stopped
By the breathing side of a bear which woke me
And there we were,

                the child and the black bear and the cliff-drop,
And this is the way it went—

                I stepped back, and I turned around,
And I walked down through the rhododendron
And never looked back,

                  truly awake in the throbbing world,
And I ducked through the low flap
Of the tent, so quietly, and I went to sleep
And never told anyone
Till years later when I thought I knew what it meant,

                     which now I've forgot.

          ————————————

And this one is questionable,

Though sworn to me by an old friend
Who'd killed a six-foot diamondback about seven o'clock
   in the morning

250

(He'd found it coiled in a sunny place),
And threw it into a croker sack with its head chopped off,
    and threw the sack in the back of a jeep,
Then left for his day's work
On the farm.
                That evening he started to show the snake
To someone, and put his hand in the sack to pull it out.
As he reached in, the snake's stump struck him.
His wrist was bruised for a week.

It's not age,
            nor time with its gold eyelid and blink,
Nor dissolution in all its mimicry
That lifts us and sorts us out.
It's discontinuity
                and all its spangled coming between
That sends us apart and keeps us there in a dread.
It's what's in the rearview mirror,
                            smaller and out of sight.

What do you do when the words don't come to you any more,
And all the embolisms fade in the dirt?
And the ocean sings in its hammock,
                                rocking itself back and forth?
And you live at the end of the road where the sky starts
    its dark decline?
The barking goes on and on
                        from the far hill, constantly
Sticking its noise in my good ear.

Goodbye, Miss Sweeney, goodbye.
I'm starting to think about the psychotransference of all things.
It's small bones in the next life.
It's small bones,
                and heel and toe forever and ever.

Hansel and Gretel

To be baked as cookies by the mad witch?
Not so funny. See *The Rise and Fall*
Of the Third Reich. What starts out as kitsch
All too soon becomes a form of evil.

The witch was wise. What sweet tooth can resist
A candy cottage? They were wiser still,
Scattering their breadcrumbs not to get lost.
How could the witch know that they were trained to kill?

They got back home all right, the cunning children,
Only to end up in Munich, years later,
Stirring up the witchcraft of their own cauldron,
She a drunk and he a sadistic waiter.

"Maybe it would have been better," she said,
One day in her cups, "to have roasted in the oven
Than to hobble around this city, half dead—
Old movie stars in some dreary love-in."

At which he struck her. "Peasant . . . *peasant!*"
Then, lunging toward her, "You ungrateful bitch!
I wasted my life on our stupid legend
When my one and only love was the dead witch."

JOSEPHINE JACOBSEN

The Chinese Insomniacs

It is good to know
the Chinese insomniacs.
How, in 495 A.D.,
in 500 B.C.,
the moon shining, and the pine-
trees shining back
at it, a poet had to walk
to the window.

It is companionable
to remember my fellow
who was unable to sleep
because of a sorrow, or not;
who had to watch
for the wind
to stir night flowers in the garden
instead of making the deep journey.

They live nine hun-
dred years apart,
and turn, and turn, restless.
She says her sleeve is wet
with tears; he says something difficult
to forget, like
music counts the heartbeat.

A date is only a mark
on paper—it has little to do
with what is long.
It is good to have their company
tonight: a lady, awake
until birdsong;
a gentleman who made
poems later out of frag-
ments of the dark.

DAVID FERRY

We were driving down a road.
Where was it we were going?
Where were we going to?
Nobody knew.

Behind the blur of trees
Along the river road,
Somewhere behind the blur,
A dark river ran.

The car bore us along.
We didn't know who we were
Or where we were going to.
Somebody must know,

Somebody in the car
Must know where we were going,
Beside the dark river,
Where we were going to.

All silent in the car
We sat staring ahead.
Where were the lights of a bar,
A gas station, a house?

Out in the dark the river
Was telling itself a story.
There in the car nobody
Could tell where we were going.

Gauguin's White Horse

There he stood, quite suddenly,
Innocent nose to foreleg,
Bent against no betrayal,

As though all the gods had laps
And were not inflamed. Shadows
Bore fruit. Edible mosses

Exhaled an eternity
Of breath. Someone asks whether
Gauguin held his when this horse

Flowed out into the foreground
Like an ethics of texture.
Now, it matters. We, with our

Breath as heavy, as rapid
As paint, reach to pluck the horse,
Letting time back in, and take

Flesh for the trope of the horse,
The horse for a trope of grace,
Perception in place of the

Acts of the heart, for granted.
It was all actual. Here,
The emptied frame has become

What fills in for the prior
Question—not the one about
Wanting our innocence back,

Or how to send it forward,
A wisdom of matted manes,
Nor where the laps of the gods

Fall to when the sun rises.
The question is behind mouths
And won't come out of the frame

As long as we keep choking.
Ease in your throat is what lets
The head of the white horse swing

Downward through air, toward water.
Ours are the mouths Gauguin's brush
Bends to, compelled to answer.

STEPHEN MITCHELL   (Trans.)

Evening
by Rainer Maria Rilke

The sky puts on the darkening blue coat
held for it by a row of ancient trees;
you watch: and the lands grow distant in your sight,
one journeying to heaven, one that falls;

and leave you, not at home in either one,
not quite so still and dark as the darkened houses,
not calling to eternity with the passion
of what becomes a star each night, and rises;

and leave you (inexpressibly to unravel)
your life, with its immensity and fear,
so that, now bounded, now immeasurable,
it is alternately stone in you and star.

NORMAN WILLIAMS

For a Girl Walking the Fields
of Michigan in Mourning

The girl walks with one knee almost stiff,
The way her father taught her, the way his father walked.
For generations now the family has moved as if
It were not yet accustomed to this earth.
Behind the haze the late March sun
Spreads along a distant bank of trees;
Water lies between the broken rows
Of corn, like wreckage at a battleground.
She thinks of her grandfather's collapse,
Magnificent, a plowhorse in the sun,
Nostrils flaring and sweat pouring off his back,
And remembers, too, the morning condensation
Beading on her window, like his final breath . . .
Behind her, in the distance now, the farmhouse
Resembles a full-masted ship edging off the world.
Soon the windows would be nailed shut,
And, near the workshed, mice would nest
Beneath the harrow he never quite got fixed.
Ahead, two robins toss a worm in flight;
This spring the worms lay gorged and drunken on the fields
As if, again, winter had been too generous.

MARK ANDERSON (Trans.)

Shadow Roses Shadow
by Ingeborg Bachmann

Beneath a foreign sky
shadow roses
shadow
on a foreign earth
between roses and shadows
in a foreign water
my shadow

Hôtel de la Paix

The burden of roses falls silent from the walls,
and through the rug shine floor and earth.
The heart of light breaks inside the lamp.
Darkness. Steps.
The bolt has been pushed before death.

WILLIAM ARROWSMITH (Trans.)

The Storm

by Eugenio Montala

Les princes n'ont point d'yeux pour voir ces grand's merveilles,
Leurs mains ne servent plus qu'a nous persécuter . . .
                              Agrippa D'Aubigné: *À Dieu*

The storm splattering the tough magnolia
leaves, with the long rolling March thunder
and hail,

(tinklings of crystal in your nocturnal
nest startle you, out of gold gone
from the mahoganies, on the edging
of bound books, a grain of sugar
still burns in the shell
of your eyelids)

the lightning blanching
walls and trees, freezing them in that
forever of an instant—marble manna
and destruction—which you carry sculpted
inside you for your damnation, and that binds you
to me, strange sister, more than love—
then the hard crack, the castanets, the shaking
of tambourines over the thieving ditch,
the stamp of the fandango, and overhead,
some gesture, groping . . .
As when you turned around and, with your hand, the cloud of
        hair
clearing from your forehead,

you waved to me—and stepped into darkness.

CORNELIUS EADY

Crows in a Strong Wind

Off go the crows from the roof.
The crows can't hold on.
They might as well
Be perched on an oil slick.

Such an awkward dance,
These gentlemen
In their spottled-black coats.
Such a tipsy dance,

As if they didn't know where they were.
Such a humorous dance,
As they try to set things right.
As the wind reduces them.

Such a sorrowful dance.
How embarrassing is love
When it goes wrong

In front of everyone.

PETER HARGITAI

Mother's Visit No. 29

I think I will allow myself to get caught.

And not bother to vacuum the pool:
there are roaches on the bottom
I would like you to see.
Neither is the floor swept
nor the windows washed.
There are hairs on the couch,
I think a dog's.

Something smells in here

like raw fish.
Or black hair that is wet,
matted, and close to the skin.

But do come in. Do come in.

It is Easter of course.

I am waiting with the perfect gift:
a tiny spool of thread, a thimble, a needle
all in one egg.
Stuffed into an egg, a white plastic egg,
is a rosary, lilac in color.
O I could wring her—

In a sense,
Mother is a lover

of incense and usefulness,
Eastern European among other things.
Thick with the accent.
Her friend is in her seventies: peacock feathers, green hat,
lots of rouge, and a Masters in Library Science.
They are coming over to see what is wrong with me.

LI-YOUNG LEE

From Blossoms

From blossoms comes
this brown paper bag of peaches
we bought from the boy
at the bend in the road where we turned toward
signs painted *Peaches.*

From laden boughs, from hands,
from sweet fellowship in the bins,
comes nectar at the roadside, succulent
peaches we devour, dusty skin and all,
comes the familiar dust of summer, dust we eat.

O, to take what we love inside,
to carry within us an orchard, to eat
not only the skin, but the shade,
not only the sugar, but the days, to hold
the fruit in our hands, adore it, then bite into
the round jubilance of peach.

There are days we live
as if death were nowhere
in the background; from joy
to joy to joy, from wing to wing,
from blossom to blossom to
impossible blossom, to sweet impossible blossom.

JANE SHORE

A Luna Moth

For Elizabeth Bishop

For six days and nights
a luna moth, pale green,
pinned herself to the sliding screen—
a prize specimen in a lepidopterist's dream.

Tuesday's wind knocked her off the deck.
She tacked herself back up again.
During Wednesday's rain she disappeared
and reappeared on Thursday
to meditate and sun herself,
recharging her dreams from dawn to dusk,
and all night draining the current from
the deck's electric lantern.

A kimono just wider than my hand,
her two pairs of flattened wings were pale
gray-green panels of the sheerest crepe de Chine.
Embroidered on each sleeve, a drowsing eye
appeared to watch the pair of eyes
on the wings below quite wide awake.
But they're *all* fake.
Nature's trompe l'oeil gives the luna
eyes of a creature twice her size.

The head was covered with snow-white fur.
Once, I got so close
it rippled when I breathed on her.
She held herself so still,
she looked dead. I stroked
the hems of her long, sweeping tail;
her wings dosed my fingers with a green gold dust.
I touched her feathery antennae.
She twitched and calmly
reattached herself a quarter-inch west,
tuning into the valley miles away
a moment-by-moment weather report
broadcast by a compatriot,
catching the scent of a purely
sexual call; hearing sounds
I never hear, having
the more primitive ear.

Serene
in the middle of the screen,
she ruled the grid of her domain
oblivious to her collected kin—
the homely, brown varieties of moth
tranced-out and immobile.
or madly fanning their paper wings,
bashing their brains out on the bulb.
Surrounded by her dull-witted cousins,
she is, herself, a sort of bulb,
and Beauty is a kind of brilliance,
burning self-absorbed, giving little,
indifferent as a reflecting moon.

Clinging to the screen despite my comings
and goings, she never seemed to mind the ride.
At night, when I slid the glass door shut,
I liked to think I introduced her
to her perfect match
hatched from an illusion
—like something out of Grimm—
who, mirroring her dreamy stillness,
pining for a long-lost twin,
regarded her exactly as she regarded him.

This morning,
a weekend guest sunbathing on the deck,
sun-blind, thought the wind had blown
a five dollar bill against the screen.
He grabbed the luna, gasped,
and flung her to the ground.
She lay a long moment in the grass,
then fluttered slowly to the edge of the woods
where, sometimes at dawn,
deer nibble the wild raspberry bushes.

Garments

Now the sun's yellow smock is falling again
from the heavens. It is night. The nurse
is taking off her white uniform,
the policeman is tearing off his badge
and his blue hat, the doctor
is silently pulling the stethoscope
from around his neck. Slowly, button
by terrible button, people are undoing
the chrysalis of quotidian robes—
the dentist unfastening his plaque-ridden bib,
the chimney sweep flinging his soot-drenched shirt
into a corner, the bellhop emptying money
from his beleaguered pockets. The boards
of the world's floors grow heavy again
with a huge flotsam of bankers' suits,
the unleavened airiness of dancers' leotards.
Even the President we have all loved
for the sheer tedium of his sartorial sense,
yes, even he, is returning his body now
to the high ornament of its original suit,
even the talk-show host is unclipping
the microphone from his lapel, the seductress
peeling the frilled underwear from her body
by her own hand. We are becoming, like it
or not, a kind of democracy. We are all
growing equal beneath the naked moon.
We are all going to sleep, now, in the same bed.

MELISSA GREEN

For years a pair of cherubs dallied
there, the ink turned aubergine
above their curls, the faithful office
of their wings. A link of lace
was powder where their hands had joined,
the heart's original magenta dulled

to bloodless rose. The mystery,
desire, tucked away, redeemed
her notion of another time,
abandoned artifacts entombed
before her parents' love was damned
in rose-leaves' fragile potpourri.

From attic raids, her cedar bridebox
slowly filled with relics, eased
in secret from a musty clothespress,
not the kind of theft a priest
could censure—they were hers because
they'd been her mother's first: an onyx

brooch, the bolts of Devonia lace,
the wheat-colored cuffs in *broderie*
anglaise: and nearly lost behind
a chimney in a trunk, the hand-
done water color of a dairy
maid, dressed in a brown pelisse.

Some amateur who'd never trudged
manured cow paths painted it.
Imagination made her face
unearthly. Laden pails, her fists,
deceptive moonlight hinted at
a wending toward some tragedy.

The girl was bound to think sometimes
it was her mother on the road
by Colby Hill, hearing the wheels
of his democrat scrape the gravel, swirls
of love-in-the-mist at her hem. But would
he come this time with his strapping team

to take her home? Could she, the last
firelight flushing her cheek, not say
husband, come to bed: in the hurricane
lamp's obscuring glass become
the dairy maid, seeing the child who sees
herself there, and their palimpsest?

You told me, if something is not used it is meaning-less, and took my temperature which I had thought to save for a more difficult day. In the mirror, every night, the same face, a bit more threadbare, a dress worn too long. The moon was out in the cold, along with the restless, dissatisfied wind that seemed to change the location of the sycamores. I expected reproaches because I had mentioned the word love, but you only accused me of stealing your pencil, and sadness disappeared with sense. You made a ceremony out of holding your head in your hands because, you said, it could not be contained in itself.

If we could just go on walking through these woods and let the pine branches brush our faces, living would still make beads of sweat on your forehead, but you wouldn't have to worry about what you call my exhibitionism. All you liked about trees was the way the light came through the leaves in sheets of pre-cise, parallel rays, like slant rain. This may be an incomplete explanation of our relation, but we've always feared the dark inside the body. You agreed there could be no seduction if the structures of propositions did not stand in a physical relation, so that we could get from one to the other. Even so, not every moment of happiness is to hang one's clothes on.

I might have known you wouldn't talk to me. But to claim you just didn't want to disguise your thoughts! We've walked along this road before, I said, though perhaps in heavier coats, not designed to reveal the form of the body. Later the moon came out and threw the shadows of branches across the street where they remained, broken. Feverishly you examined the tacit conventions on which conversation depends. I sighed as one does at night, looking down into the river. I wondered if by throwing myself in I could penetrate to the essence of its character, or should I wait for you to stab me as you had practiced in your dreams? You said this question, like most philosophical problems, arose from failing to understand the tale of the two youths, two horses and two lilies. You could prove to me that the deepest rivers are, in fact, no rivers at all.

From this observation we turned to consider passion. Looking at the glints of light on the water, you tried to make me tell you not to risk the excitement—to recommend cold baths. The lack of certainty, of direction, of duration, was its own argument, unlike going into a bar to get drunk and getting drunk. Your face was alternately hot and cold, as if translating one language into another—gusts from the storm in your heart, the pink ribbon in your pocket. Its actual color turned out to be unimportant, but its presence disclosed something essential about membranes. You said there was still time, you could still break it off, go abroad, make a movie. I said (politely, I thought) this wouldn't help you. You'd have to kill yourself.

Toward morning, walking along the river, you tossed simple objects into the air which was indifferent around us, though it moved off a little, and again as you put your hand back in your pocket to test the degree of hardness. Everything else remained the same. This is why, you said, there was no fiction.

JUDITH BAUMEL

after Sakai Hōitsu

Some are drunk. Some are mumbling.
Many are solitary, each in his way fixed.
They are all happy over their very good number,
an easy square; its root six,
itself a lovely number, exponential chrysalis.
And if, in the array of patterns
taken from nature—clouds, spider webs, starfish—
we might yet find a true square
not one of these thirty-six, not the one
whose square is on his sleeve or heart, cares.

My old group, my buddies, the Math Team
would measure our drunks by booming
the quadratic formula, gleaming
with rum, slopped over some parents' living-room
rug, like these bards in their curtained cabal.
No one of us flubbed our password,
the drinking song, that poem of radicals
pressed in our brains, no gauge at all, absurd.
Minus b plus or minus the square root of
b squared minus four a c over two a.
Now even sober I lose those cancelled lines of youth
and drunk I am easily distracted, say,
by the discriminant, the bee-squared et al.
Concentrating on minutiae, I am lost in the well-
folded sleeve of the great poet's silk kimono,
lost on the silkworm's trail winding through Japan
and wonder, drunk, watching my steps split by Xeno,
drunk, wonder what led me to the simple numerical plan
and then away like dust in the path of a paper fan.

JOHN HOLLANDER

The Mad Potter

Now at the turn of the year this coil of clay
Bites its own tail: a New Year starts to choke
On the old one's ragged end. I bite my tongue
As the end of me—of my rope of stuff and nonsense
(The nonsense held, it was the stuff that broke),
Of bones and light, of levity and crime,
Of reddish clay and hope—still bides its time.

Each of my pots is quite unusable,
Even for contemplating as an object
Of gross unuse. In its own mode of being
Useless, though, each of them remains unique,
Subject to nothing, and themselves unseeing,
Stronger by virtue of what makes them weak.

I pound at all my clay. I pound the air.
This senseless lump, slapped into something like
Something, sits bound around by my despair.
For even as the great Creator's free
Hand shapes the forms of life, so—what? This pot,
Unhollowed solid, too full of itself,
Runneth over with incapacity.
I put it with the others on the shelf.

These tiny cups will each provide one sip
Of what's inside them, aphoristic prose
Unwilling, like full arguments, to make
Its points, then join them in extended lines
Like long draughts from the bowl of a deep lake.
The honey of knowledge, like my milky slip,
Firms slowly up against what merely flows.

Some of my older pieces bore inscriptions
That told a story only when you'd learned
How not to read them: LIVE reverted to EVIL,
EROS kept running backwards into SORE.
Their words, all fired up for truth, got burned.
I'll not write on weak vessels any more.

My juvenilia? I gave them names
In those days: Hans was all handles and no spout;
Bernie believed the whole world turned about
Himself alone; Sadie was close to James
(But Herman touched her bottom when he could);
Paul fell to pieces; Peter wore away
To nothing; Len was never any good;
Alf was a flat, random pancake, May
An opened blossom; Bud was an ash-tray.
Even their names break off, though: Whatsisface,
That death-mask of Desire, and—you know!—
The smaller version of that (Oh, what was it?—
You know . . .) All of my pots now have to go
By number only. Which is no disgrace.

Begin with being—in an anagram
Of unending—conclude in some dark den;
This is no matter. What I've been, I am:
What I will be is what I make of all
This clay, this moment. Now begin again . . .
Poured out of emptiness, drop by slow drop,
I start up at the quarreling sounds of water.
Pots cry out silently at me to stop.

What are we like? A barrelfull of this
Oozy wet substance, shadow-crammed, whose smudges
Of darkness lurk within but rise to kiss
The fingers that disturb the gentle edges
Of their bland world of shapelessness and bliss.

The half-formed cup cries out in agony,
The lump of clay suffers a silent pain.
I heard the cup, though, full of feeling, say
"O clay be true, O clay keep constant to
Your need to take, again and once again,
This pounding from your mad creator who
Only stops hurting when he's hurting you."

What will I then have left behind me? Over
The years I have originated some
Glazes that wear away at what they cover
And weep for what they never can become.
My Deadware, widely imitated; blue
Skyware of an amazing lightness; tired
Hopewear that I abandoned for my own
Good reasons; Hereware; Thereware; ware that grew
Weary of everything that earth desired;
Hellware that dances while it's being fired,
Noware that vanishes while being thrown.

Appearing to be silly, wisdom survives
Like tribes of superseded gods who go
Hiding in caves of triviality
From which they laughingly control our lives.
So with my useless pots: safe from the blow
Of carelessness, or outrage at their flaws,
They brave time's lion and his smashing paws.
—All of which tempts intelligence to call
Pure uselessness one more commodity.
The Good-for-Nothing once became our Hero,
But images of him, laid-back, carelessly
Laughing, were upright statues after all.
From straight above, each cup adds up to zero.

Clay to clay: Soon I shall indeed become
Dumb as these solid cups of hardened mud
(Dull *terra cruda* colored like our blood);
Meanwhile the slap and thump of palm and thumb
On wet mis-shapenness begins to hum
With meaning that was silent for so long.
The words of my wheel's turning come to ring
Truer than Truth itself does, my great *Ding
Dong-an-sich* that echoes everything
(Against it even lovely bells ring wrong):
Its whole voice gathers up the purest parts
Of all our speech, the vowels of the earth,
The aspirations of our hopeful hearts
Or the prophetic sibilance of song.

Volcano House

for Charles Wright

Mists in the lantern ferns,
  green wings furled against the cold,
and a mountain wind
  starts its low moan through *ohia* trees.
The lava land blazes in primrose and thimbleberry,
scented fires of pink and blue
  racing through jungled underbrush.
I'm out feeding chickens,
  slopping a garbage of melon seeds and rind
over the broken stones and woodrot of the forest path.
I'm humming a blues,
  some old song about China Nights
and boarding a junk,
  taking me from my village.
Miles in the distance,
  Kilauea steams and vents
    through its sulphurous roads,
and a yellow light spills through
  a faultline in the clouds,
glazing the slick beaks of the feeding chickens,
  shining in their eyes
like the phosphorous glow
  from a cave tunneled miles through the earth.
What was my face before I was born?
  the white mask and black teeth
at the bottom of the pond? What is the mind's insensible,
  the gateless gate?
Through overgrowth and the leaning drizzle,
through the pile and dump of tree fern
  and the indigoed snare of lasiandra
shedding its collars of sadness by the broken fence,
I make my way down a narrow path
  to the absolute and the house of my last days,
a dazzle of light scripting in the leaves and on the weeds,
  tremors in the shivering trees.

RICHARD LYONS

At the Window

1.

Each mind drifts in and out of the evening.
In Wertmüller's *Seven Beauties*
a man surrounded by a blue fog
lifts a German Luger to his friend's head.
Later, he wakes screaming about the gigantic hams
of the commandant who swats him with her riding crop.
He can't abbreviate the past,
his friend's face in the rictus of the evening,
the dark spots on the hillside
that are cows, pigs, the letters P.O.W.
darkening in the particulars of rain.
The rest is circumstantial, the sisters
streetwalking, the gloss on their lips
washing off with the rain from their hair.

Sometimes what we say is love, a kind of desperate love,
is just the mystery and melancholy of the streets.
Each night is a freedom, a black reflection.
I lift the tone arm over a record,
the disc turning without sound below the stylus
like the cars passing in the rain-streaked windows:
an aquarium that doesn't invite us
or drive us away.
I remember a night with another woman, the row of flannel
    shirts
that weren't mine lined up in the closet.
The helpless way without a light
I had to crawl along the walls to the bathroom.
The breath on the lip of the water glass

tasted of tobacco and peppermint.
I was a minor character
shot early in the novel
to create gratuitous tension
or one just not mentioned after a while.
The night you left it was raining.
The lamp and the Zenith Portable
were dripping on the hood of the car.
You didn't say any more, the headlights curving.
In certain Middle Eastern countries, I remember,
when a woman leaves a man
he ties a beetle by a string to a nail
and draws a circle on the ground
like an arena.
As the beetle crawls round and round
shortening its tether
she eventually comes back to him.

2.

Water is running through the drainpipe
and the gutters.
A bottle is tossed from a speeding car.
On nights like these
we'd drive into Cambridge for a movie
with very little plot, subtitles
and a labyrinth of personalities.
Tonight I can't sleep or walk off the separations
sex becomes, an ache
to fascinate us with ourselves.
Hours pass, come tumbling out of these cupped hands
that touch nothing, and before I know,
it's light, and I see the woman next door

standing on her porch,
breaking bubbles on the screen.
Then she comes out
inspecting the eaves of her house.
With her hand she stops the wind chimes
in the chinaberry
and feeds the birdhouse
three yellow biscuits.

Such splendid exactness!
It doesn't matter that it's summer,
that the cypresses along the avenue
press into the future.
Soon sailboats on the reservoir
will tack into a steady breeze

as she walks through her garden,
gathering strawberries in a demitasse
to surprise her husband
with the music their loss will make on his tongue.
Or maybe she'll want to make love
and afterwards they'll sit apart on the floor
like wrestlers breathing.
I'll write a letter,
read the newspaper.
The wind outside turns corners in the air
with a scrap of paper
as though I were the egress to a long and bitter meditation
and each of my neighbors
at the window, waiting, thoughtful,
pulled me through.

KATHA POLLITT

Dreaming about the Dead

You'd think they'd just been out for a casual stroll
and found themselves by chance on the old street,
the old key still in their pocket, the way

they're sitting at the kitchen table when you come in.
Don't you believe it. They've obviously spent hours
arranging for the light to fall with that

phony lambency,
and haven't you noticed how slyly
they look at you when they think you're not looking at them?

True, it seems strange that they would come so far
to warn you against the new girl in the office
or give you a recipe for worms on toast,

but try it, interrupt, say *mirror of ashes,*
moonless heart—they'll only
smile a little vaguely, start hunting for matches

and suddenly the black car's at the door.
Will you come back? you call out after them.
Oh, definitely, no problem here. Again

and again, until
you learn they will never say what you need them to:
My death was mine. It had nothing to do with you.

THOMAS BOLT

Unpolluted Creek

All day,
Iron flecks
Sprinkle from the shell
Of a galvanized bucket,
Its bottom gone,
The clean sides being slowly punctured.

If anything happens here
In the changing sun
Among the weeds and stripped metals,
It is only water
Picking through junk, gradually
Enlarging flaws.

Also, among disconnected hoses
In the speckled back
Of a gutted dishwasher,
The smooth paint
Being furred with white mold;
There is no hurry.

What is not important here
Is not important.

In the Park

You have forty-nine days between
death and rebirth if you're a Buddhist.
Even the smallest soul could swim
the English Channel in that time
or climb, like a ten-month-old child,
every step of the Washington Monument
to travel across, up, down, over or through
—you won't know till you get there which to do.

He laid on me for a few seconds
said Roscoe Black, who lived to tell
about his skirmish with a grizzly bear
in Glacier Park. *He laid on me*
not doing anything. I could feel
his heart beating against my heart.
Never mind *lie* and *lay*, the whole world
confuses them. For Roscoe Black you might say
all forty-nine days flew by.

I was raised on the Old Testament.
In it God talks to Moses, Noah,
Samuel, and they answer.
People confer with angels. Certain
animals converse with humans.
It's a simple world, full of crossovers.
Heaven's an airy Somewhere, and God
has a nasty temper when provoked,
but if there's a Hell, little is made of it.
No longtailed Devil, no eternal fire,

and no choosing what to come back as.
When the grizzly bear appears, he lies/lays down
on atheist and zealot. In the pitch-dark
each of us waits for him in Glacier Park.

CHRISTOPHER MERRILL

Cotillions 283

The ex-greenskeeper in his coat and tails
Plowed up the practice green one night, churning
The spiked and fertilized sod into a punch.
He twisted miniature flags, like swizzle sticks.
Shredded the plastic cups, then seeded the green
In timothy and clover, a mad farmer
Saving a field spent senselessly, like a coin
Lost in a jukebox, in the local diner
Where the couples steeped in gin are drinking coffee,
Arranging a foursome for Saturday.

.   .   .

A padlocked clubhouse, and stumps of porticoes
Sinking in cement, like palmprints. Quack grass
Raving through the addled and abandoned lawn,
Spreading its message underground: *Listen*
To me, you fools, to me! . . . Against the wall,
Ivy drops its handkerchiefs, and spindle
Trees unspool scarlet yarn, which will wind its way
Around these vacant grounds, soaking up the names
Of the pianist and singer, the chaperones
And guests, the waiters at the last cotillion.

.   .   .

This tennis court with its nets down, this sea
Of crushed shells lapping against the rusted fence,
This *en tous cas*, is not a poem stripped
Of its music and its meaning; for here are women
In bare feet and long skirts dancing with men
In dungarees, adrift in the green clay
Sparkling with salt, avoiding the white tapes
Nailed into place, like strings of floats, the service
And base lines, the alleys where their children are
Asleep, working the moon for all its light.

Down the Little Cahaba

Soundless sun, the river. Home in August
we float down the Little Cahaba, the three of us,
rubber inner tubes, hot laps, in water so slow
we hear the rapids moving upstream toward us,
the whispers coming loud.
                        Then the river bends,
the standing water at the lip, hover, hover,
the moment before orgasm, before the head emerges,
then over suddenly, and sound rushing
back from my ears.
                    The youngest caught in the rapids:
half-grown, he hasn't lived with me in years,
yet his head submerged at a scrape of rock pushes
pain through me, a streak inside my thighs,
vagina to knee.
                Swept to the outside curve,
the boys climb upstream to plunge down again.

I stand at the mud bank to pick up
shells, river mussels with iridescent inner skin,
with riverine scars from once-close flesh.

   Years back, at the beach, with piles of shells
   in our laps, with the first final separation on us,
   one asked: *How do we know you won't forget us?*

   I told them how they had moved in my womb: each
   distinct, the impatient older, the steady younger.
   I said: *I can never forget you. You moved inside me.*

I meant: *The sound of your blood crossed into mine.*

PETER SCHMITT

It sounds so much like joy,
the boisterous honking of the geese returning,
coming back to the lake.

It always catches us unprepared,
at our desk or in the garden,
like uninvited, but always welcome guests.

Moving to the window, or turning
to wipe a brow, we watch their long-held
chevron or arrowhead descend,

to take a triumphant lap around
the lake. The water will be stretched
like foil, the sun glinting gold into the trees.

We know this feeling ourselves,
arriving home after a long vacation,
and pushing the horn to nothing

but an empty house. So we pause
from our afternoon tasks and watch
this renewal of old intimacies,

the geese testing the water,
the dock, the small pebbly shore.
By the time we are standing

on the little beach, the honking
all around us now, we hope that,
in some way, they are glad to see us too.

But it doesn't matter. More
and more of them are sliding
out of the sky, coming back,

and all making noise, so that the joy
we feel is in ourselves—
standing by a lake in very late summer,

as another season
rounds the sun
perfectly on schedule.

JOHN DUVAL (Trans.)

The True Fable
by Carlo Alberto Salustri

Night is about to fall,
shadows are growing, objects are getting dimmer.
Grandmother and the little boy are working
beside the kitchen window.
The old woman holds the red yarn, feeding
it out to the boy, who winds it into a ball.
The thread goes out to him. The ball gets bigger.
"Granny, tell me a story."—"I'm sleepy, child."
—"About the goblin man that Grandaddy killed.
The goblin climbed up through
the window one night. You were inside, in bed.
Were you scared? What did he do to you?
Did it hurt? What's a goblin? Was he bad?
Was he ugly? Was his face all wrong?"
"He was handsome! He was young!"
the old woman whispers, and she knits her brow
as if to see him now;
"I can still hear the three creaks the knife made
when your Grandpa pulled out the blade."
The old woman is quiet. She lets out the yarn
to the little boy, who winds it into a ball.
Across the room, a shadow seems to fall.
It cuts the thread, then flees across the lawn. . . .

ROBERT FAGLES (Trans.)

· *Achilles Fights the River*
from *The Iliad* by Homer

Achilles the famous spearman, leaping down from the bluff,
plunged in the river's heart and the river charged against him,
churning, surging, all his rapids rising in white fury
and drove the mass of corpses choking tight his channel,
the ruck Achilles killed—Scamander heaved them up
and bellowing like a bull the river flung them out
on the dry land but saved the living, hiding them down
the fresh clear pools of his thundering whirling current
but thrashing over Achilles' shoulders raised a killer-wave—
the tremendous thrust of it slammed against his shield
and he staggered, lost his footing, his arms flung out
for a tall strong elm, he clung but out it came by the roots,
toppling down, ripping away the whole cliff, blocking the
      stream
with a tangled snarl of branches crashing into it full length
to dam the river bank to bank—Bursting up from a whirlpool
Achilles dashed for the plain, his feet flying in terror
but the great god would not let up, hurling against him,
Scamander looming into a murderous breaker, dark, over him,
dead set on stopping the brilliant Achilles' rampage here
and thrusting disaster off the struggling Trojan force—
But the hero sprang away, far as a hand-flung spear,
swooping fast as the black eagle, the fierce marauder,
both the strongest and swiftest bird that flies the sky—
on he streaked and the bronze rang out against his chest,
clashing grimly—slipping out from under the wave he fled
with the river rolling on behind him, roaring, huge . . .
As a farmhand runs a ditch from a dark spring, sluicing
the gushing stream through plants and gardens, swinging
his mattock to knock the clods out down the shoot
and the water rushes on, tearing the pebbles loose
and what began as a trickle hits a quick slope and
down it goes, outstripping the man who guides it—
so the relentless tide kept overtaking Achilles,
yes, for all his speed—gods are stronger than men.

Again and again the brilliant swift Achilles whirled,
trying to stand and fight the river man-to-man and see
if all the immortal gods who rule the vaulting skies
were after him, putting him to rout—again and again
the mighty crest of the river fed by the rains of Zeus
came battering down his shoulders, down from high above
but Achilles kept on leaping, higher, desperate now
as the river kept on dragging down his knees, lunging
under him, cutting the ground from under his legs . . .

The Candid Shot

In a photograph, it's been said before,
all fact becomes opinion. But just look
at these two! Being so much themselves
has frozen them into a polychromed emblem
to be taken out and frowned over, later.
As soon as the camera went up he stiffened,
she pulled her coat closer, and now here
she is, taut and talkative, coffee cup
steadied on a tanned knee. He looks over
(dark, hunched) with a smile pulled into place
by something easily missed—habit? Regret?
And what about the quiver around the mouth,
or the loathing purring in the heavy throat?
Even with a magnifying glass it's hard
to map the movement of that sidelong glance:
the eyes slide painfully to the right, knowing
what it is they'll rest upon, what it is
that wrenches them around in their bloody beds.

The background wall dissolves to a dim orange
as fast film annihilates every outline.
There, just visible in that momentous
failure of definition, is the signal
for great buildings to totter and crash down
when the earth slides right out from under them,
or to blow stupidly apart in the endless
versions of war that shock us awake, often.
Fear settles like smoke in the darkened room,
though dials and digitals keep quietly winking,
and the whirr of the illuminated fishtank
whispers your name. For all the mechanisms
you gather to yourself like limbs, like folds
of the quilt, the camera out there offers
no escape; the sunlit world takes aim.

DIANE ACKERMAN

Beija-Flor (Hummingbird)

When you kiss me, moths flutter in my mouth;
when you kiss me, leaf-cutting ants lift up
their small burdens and carry them along
corridors of scent; when you kiss me,
caymans slither down wet banks in moonlight,
jaws yawning open, eyes bright red lasers;
when you kiss me, my tiny fist conceals
the bleached skull of a sloth; when you kiss me,
the waters wed in my ribs, dark and pale
rivers exchange their potions—she gives him
love's power, he gives her love's lure;
when you kiss me, my heart, surfacing, steals
a small breath like a pink river dolphin;
when you kiss me, the rain falls thick as rubber,
sunset pours molasses down my spine
and, in my hips, the green wings of the jungle flutter;
when you kiss me, blooms explode like land mines
in trees loud with monkey muttering
and the kazooistry of birds; when you kiss me,
my flesh sambas like an iguana; when you kiss me,
the river-mirror reflects an unknown land,
eyes glitter in the foliage, ships pass
like traveling miracle plays, and coca sets
brush fires in my veins; when you kiss me,
the river wraps its wet thighs around a bend;
when you kiss me, my tongue unfolds its wings

and flies through shadows as a leaf-nosed bat,
a ventriloquist of the twilight shore
which hurls its voice against the tender world
and aches to hear its echo rushing back;
when you kiss me, anthuria send up
small telescopes, the vine-clad trees wear
pantaloons, a reasonably evitable moon
rises among a signature of clouds,
the sky fills with the pandemonium
of swamp monkeys, the aerial slither
and looping confetti of butterflies;
when you kiss me, time's caravan pauses
to sip from the rich tropic of the heart,
find shade in the oasis of a touch,
bathe in Nature carnal, mute and radiant;
you find me there trembling and overawed;
for, when you kiss me, I become the all
you love: a peddler on your luminous river,
whose salted-fish are words, daughter
of a dolphin; when you kiss me, I smell
of night-blooming orchids; when you kiss me,
my mouth softens into scarlet feathers—
an ibis with curved bill and small dark smile;
when you kiss me, jaguars lope through my knees;
when you kiss me, my lips quiver like bronze
violets; oh, when you kiss me . . .

ALLEN GROSSMAN

Mary Snorak the Cook, Skermo the Gardener, and Jack the Parts Man Provide Dinner for a
and Jack the Parts Man Provide Dinner for a
Wandering Stranger

There is as much holiness now as there ever was
And there is as much fire now as there ever was
And as many locusts in the desert and bees
But there is no hope for the oaks. The winds fall
From a greater height, a heavier burden on their streams.
And the day darkens. When it grows too dark to read,
The sun having set, we begin to write—for *that*
We do not need our eyes—and continue still
The history of the stranger, Mind, that spends
His force on the immortal seas in search of a companion
Who is like himself, and finds nothing like himself,
Island after island. Welcome him! Welcome him!
He is the only stone that can be solitary
In the universe: a man of stone on a sea of shadows,
Worthy of a history inscribed in the dark.
By day he reads the Book of the Wandering Stranger
To regulate desire, until the dark comes on,
Turning the dead leaves like a restless wind.
All through the afternoon, at ease among faint recognitions,
He pronounces the syllables. "The beauty of it,
The beauty of it all." By night he swims
On immortal seas and visits the world
(Temples, towns, seaports, ponds, and wells)
A man of stone, subject of histories,
And yet how changed, how fallen from what he was.
The Mind is fallen, and travels in a blind disguise
(Above him the maelstrom of the holy ocean
And beneath a storm of fire in the skies),

Companionless wanderer in the dark.—Welcome him!
An undistinguished fragment of the greater thought,
A common flower on a barren hill, or stone by chance
Discovered at the shore—for no clear reason
Carried home—and somehow lost—forgotten on the sill
Of a summer bedroom or given away to an indifferent guest—
And now witness to the Millennium:
A stone of witness to the one world that is.
—Who will make the dinner, then, for the man of stone
And who arrange his pastoral? How is it done?
The gardener supplies the food, the "wreckage" of his hoe,
A person almost mute, not a reader, name of Skermo.
The cook is cheerful, dressed in a printed sack
(*Pillsbury Flour*, 500 lbs.). Her name is Mary, Mary Snorak,
So fat she sneaks out *sidewise* through the doorway
When she wants a smoke. Mary is in love with Jack,
The parts man, who likes his dinner (in fact, the only guest),
Good for a joke. For after all the Mind must dine alone
And find nothing like, until dawn breaks with a crack
Against the seashore where he lies among the stones,
Dreaming of the immortal ocean, and reading in the afternoons
The Book of the Wandering Stranger written in the dark.
Holy, holy, holy is the lordly host
And holy is witness Mind, "historic traveller," and guest.
But holiest of all the fools who arrange the feast,
Skermo the gardener, the parts man Jack, and sidewise Mary
Snorak who loves him as he is, and can take a joke.

ERIC PANKEY

Abstraction

1.
The eyesore on the beach was torn down.
The charred half-rafter hanging over
The gutted, broken frame and rubble
Fell last, fell as it should have fallen,
Undercut by flames, unsupported,
First. In three swipes the crane's shovel drove
The house down and raised cold cinder smoke.
The seagulls, mewling their childlike cries,
Pulled themselves into lumbering flight,
Outward from the pilings and then back,
A haphazard, elliptical chart,
Outward from the pilings and then back.

2.
He wanted to know she wanted him.
He wanted her to want him, to know
She wanted him without his asking,
Without hinting or soliciting.
To be wanted was what he wanted.
The ruined formula of his want
Was that he wanted. How could he know
What influence, what small coercion
His expectation had on her want,
The purity of her missing want?
He believed it to be missing, although
In this somber farce, how could he know?

3.
This will be his home: the foundation,
The stairway, the framed-in walls open
For now on all sides. The rooms seem small,
The halls narrow, too narrow to pass
Through together. When the doors are hung,
Perhaps, when the drywall and clapboards
Are hammered into place, perhaps then
The space will not seem so closed. The plans
Denied limits: luminous white lines
Opened the field of blue they enclosed.
He prefers the abstract design to this:
A place to live, a room for each need.

ELAINE TERRANOVA

They've built an understanding
with their pillars and 2x4s
and the crushed stone that goes into cement,
a way of cutting the dark to fit.
Moths flicker on the shiny, lit surfaces.
There is a border of red and white tulips
and impetuous birds sing. She learns to cook
such things as floating island.
He calls it eggs in snow.

They watch the wind
catch up the narrow yellow leaves
and listen for the knuckle-cracking thunder.
Then great stones begin to roll.
Rain falls. On the side of the woods
it falls again just for them
from the trees, gladly repeating itself.

But one day he notices an orange fungus
twisting over a tree stump.
It reminds him of his childhood, stiff and unreal.
And at night something flings bark and acorns
at the door. The pool,
green with algae, is sinking out of sight.
They forget the bright tanager,
its one note sucked through a straw.
Then no step in her garden
makes anything grow. Then theirs
is not a ship sailing with the wind
but a house with its chimney blown away.

When they leave, boards are knocking,
swollen out of place. Raccoons scratch
in the attic. It is hot and moist
under the rubble of their lives,
ideal conditions for growing. That summer
new owners are moving themselves in.
Younger, quicker. You can see
the sweat on their foreheads.
The woman in her flip-flops shoots ahead.
What does she carry in her arms? Ah,
she is hurrying in to feed their enormous baby.

SUSAN WOOD

Fourth of July, Texas, 1956

The night was nothing we knew. We'd never seen
such stars, not even there, in Texas.
My mother held the sky maps and leaned
so far back she fell.
She wasn't hurt. Nothing can hurt her.

I thought, who didn't know, and aimed
my flashlight at the night, and shot.
A long way from here to there, years
and years for light to go, my cousin said.
We were little planets

hurled from stars, spinning
and falling. We lay in the grass
and watched the sky revolve
until the words put on their shapes.
High in the western dark, the Teapot tipped
its spout. The Scorpion crept along the floor
so close I lifted up my hand
to brush its tail. And then,

because it was summer and we were children,
we stood on the porch
while the uncles set off fireworks
in the field. My mother sang
their names out: *Clustering Bees,*
Southern Blue, Tower of Jewels, Willow Tree.
She laughed and caught me
in her arms. The sky was somebody's

house, lit from within and bursting, and the stars,
those thousand broken embers, stars
raining down all over us, us and the earth,
what the sky comes down to.

KATHRYN STRIPLING BYER

Weep-Willow

At night she watched the road
and sang. I'd sigh and settle on the floor
beside her. One song led
to one more song. Some unquiet grave.
A bed of stone. The ship that spun round
three times 'ere it sank,
near ninety verses full of grief.
She sang sad all night long

and smiled, as if she dared me
shed a tear. Sweet Lizzie Creek swung low
along the rocks, and dried beans rattled
in the wind. Sometimes her black dog howled
at fox or bear, but she'd not stop,
no, not for God Himself, not even if He came
astride a fine white horse and bore the Crown
of Glory in His hands. The dark was all
she had. And sometimes moonlight
on the ceaseless water. "Fill my cup,"

she'd say, and sip May moonshine
till her voice came back as strong as bullfrogs
in the sally grass. You whippoorwills
keep silent, and you lonesome owls go haunt
another woman's darkest hours. Clear,

clear back I hear her singing me to sleep.
"Come down," she trolls,
"Come down among the willow
shade and weep, you fair
and tender ladies left to lie alone,
the sheets so cold,
the nights so long."

NICHOLAS CHRISTOPHER

Outside Perpignan in Heavy Rain

The trees sway darkly
along the black wall with its vines.
For shelter, a cat squeezes
between the steel bars over a window.
This is where the caretaker lives,
catty-corner to the cemetery,
with a door the color of stone.

We've just descended the mountains,
windshield wipers slapping mud
while we talked about the acrobat
who was in the papers in Barcelona
yesterday: how he attempted
to perch blindfolded on the highest
steeple of the Gaudí cathedral.

Through the gate, in the first
row of gravestones, a statue
depicts a young woman
raising her hand to her face:
the mortuary sign for a suicide.
Is she about to touch her forehead?
to tear out her hair?
to dig her nails into her cheek?
to stifle a cry
or make the sign of the cross?

In this life which is the only life
it is a gesture we see every day.
You say someone in a position
to know told you it's easy
to learn about these things
without learning anything at all.
Without ever running out of questions.
When that acrobat fell in bright sunlight,
did all the women in the street raise
their hands to shield their eyes?

GREG GLAZNER

Fin de la Fiesta

Los Conquistadores, Horseback, The Burning of Zozobra, Streetdance,
Sea of Trinkets, Coronation, Procession, Candlelight, Choir

At the duskfallen end of it, there were graces.
Downhill, the mock-adobe storefronts faded
and finally darkened, the glittering
misery of traffic eased a little,
and the torchbearer stooped at the switchback,
his lips tensed to hold his cigarette. He must have
paused to let the falseness leave him,
pressing the torchhead to a stack of pine,
his arm against the waist-high fire
shined with sweat, his eyelids gold.
There was a choir behind us, high-pitched
in their sentimental verses, but the surrender
in their voices, the amateurish earnestness
and the firelight on the path were undeniable.

In the dark we could hear the torchbearer
rasping as he climbed, slouching and lighting up
entirely, and shuffling on, half-silhouette again.
Then he was gone, and his luminarias
were set adrift in the lateness.
In the distance San Miguel, the mission
of the pueblo slaves, was muted to a black
relief in hotel lights, and music
from a bell choir somewhere floated
through the murmuring, the small, habitual bitternesses,
houses downhill lit before the news, the adlight rolling
like a sea-blue love of sleep across the fixtures.

But in the dark wash of the air, there were voices,
clerestory windows, the shadowy gathering of faces
stripped of everything but the need
to send up lights and sing. The towers
full of tolling at the end of mass, the street,
the first ranks of celebrants. It wasn't history
they entered, their candles, hundreds,
rippling toward us. It wasn't force
or crucifix or greed between the federal offices
and the trinket shops stripped down to their little
eyes of incandescence. Such a flickering progression
in the blankness. Faceless. The flames a current there.

At the atonal confluence where we waited, bell choir
and mariachis, whispers, *mas cerca mi hita*,
closer. Listen. He was gone, with his gold
eyes and his branch flame. Just the disembodied hands
and for their moments, bodies sidelit on the path
as if they passed through islands of original light.
There were graces. The young flashing through
the rich senselessness, so many ascensions,
cupped candles, palms flickering,
woodsmoke, breath. The vacuum.
Each face flushed brilliantly against it. Then not.

JEFFREY HARRISON

A Shave by the Ganges

Sleepwalking from one ghat to the next,
I came to the place where the barbers
all hunkered down, their bony knees akimbo,
dhotis bunched around their loins like diapers,
the tools of their trade laid out on burlap mats:
straight razors, scissors, combs, battered brass bowls.

Not once in my life had I been shaved by a barber,
but I sat down then to wait my turn.
I'd come this far, I'd just seen a foot
twisting up like a flag from a cremation,
I wanted to be shaved in that holy city
as if I were part of a daily ritual.

So I was happy to pay my two rupees
and surrender my face to those dark skilled hands
that slapped the foam on with a shaving brush
and worked the razor quickly across my cheek.
Sitting there as he turned my head this way
and that, I saw the crowds of bathers

in the river below, the temple stupas
looming overhead, as if about to fall,
a skeletal umbrella, a legless beggar
lolling on a dolly—all at angles odd enough
to make me see them finally, and feel
the rusty razor's edge against my throat.

Identities

One searches roads receding, endlessly receding, receding.
The other opens all doors with the same key. Simple.

One's quick to wrath, the wronged, the righteous, the wroth
    kettledrum.
The other loafs by the river, idles and jiggles his line.

One conspires against statues on stilts, in his pocket
The plot that dooms the city. The other's a *good* son.

One proclaims he aims to put the first aardvark in space.
The other patiently toils, making saddles for horseless headmen.

One exults as he flexes the glees of his body, up-down,
    up-down.
The other's hawk-kite would sail, would soar—who has tied
    it to carrion and bones?

One's a Tom Fool about money—those pockets are his, with
    the holes.
At his touch, gold reverts to the base living substance.

The other's a genius, his holdings increase by binary fission—
Ownings beget their own earnings, dividend without end.

One clasps in a bundle and keens for the broken ten laws.
The other scratches in Ogham the covenant of a moral pagan.

One with alacrity answers to '121-45-3628?'—'Yes, *Sir!*' The
    other
Bends his knee, doffs cap, to no man living or dead. One

Does all his doings predetermined by diskette or disc.
The other draws his dreams through the eye of the moon.

WILLIAM LOGAN

The cold of winter is somehow colder here,
the trees bleaker, with their rags of Spanish moss,
the very air clipped and impatient.
You wouldn't realize that summer's forest,
so much like New England, grew in a mattress of marsh,
until the leaves were down. Beneath the second growth
lives a low fringe of starved palmettos
in short, childlike arcs, their palest greens
worn almost to the color of old dollar bills.
In the rye fields and feed lots,
amid the swaying, wheezing cattle
lost to their mute philosophies,
stalk our self-important tourists, the sandhill cranes—
Nature's aristocrats, eyes flared with red eye-shadow
(carelessly applied, as if without a mirror),
their jaunty icepick heads eager or greedy,
but their bodies gooselike and timid—
and delicately boned, like young ballerinas.
They high-step away in virginal unease.

Nothing repairs the indifference of their veering,
neither the storm casting its tattered cloak
over the sand pines, nor the egrets huddled
against the lake's border, folded up like origami paper,
nor the water, sullen as concrete, pocked and greasy,
a rusting tintype of our latent democratic vistas.
Like Ovid on the Black Sea, the restless stranger
might feel such cruel beauty monotonous.
The mud-headed turtle, patient as a land mine,
hopes that here the exotic will never be familiar.
But, inshore, a crusty alligator steams,
nosing into reeds to let off passengers
or take on canvas sacks of mail,
as if the weather had never once been tender
or required, like love, a moment of surrender.

Raven

She can't believe this jag-winged majesty
really wants a piece of her small cold life,
godless and cold, and yet it circles her
on shouldery black wings, blacker than dried blood,
now holding still against the sky like a slit
opening into somewhere else, now half-wheeling,
the charred remains of dark thoughts flown . . .

But not gone. It reappears and shadows her,
calling, calling her quick steps weak, weak
and bored and exposed for those of a woman
trying too hard to get lost in the woods,
clearing her throat as if for company,
snapping twigs, pretending to seek—to need—
what mitigated solace there may be
in the leatherish creak of new snow.

It's no use. She can't get lost,
can't even fear death with any decency,
seeing there the unmistakable glint
of sun off a window through the landscaped
brace of trees beyond these, these unplanned.
And because beneath her creaking boots
comes the unsoothing hum and wheeze
of not distant traffic, a muffled laughter
at the hungry anachronism overhead.

Oh, she'd like to believe she could die;
it would give her an edge,
a key to open the steely manmade gate
of reason's garden, let her into the wilderness
of fear and belief, where she could really freeze
to death and be eaten quickly by a big
black bird, and die consciously in the snow,
which would begin to feel delicious, like
a slow transfusion of warm *sake*,
and to taste unspeakably
like the saliva of a hungry god.

APRIL BERNARD

310   *Psalm: It Must Be*
            the Medication

So the hip rises, oh so slightly, in its golden socket,
and music continues despite the dawn

The lion threw his head back and sang two notes like a veery

Everywhere doubling, two acid drops on sugar,
two boiling drops on ice, close your eyes

And memory sound as a wooden bucket, more sound

Why fuss with innuendo, when
gold and russet fruit lie across the forest floor?

Here, the loon's vocal cascade, absolute,
for the moment without remove, write, "I can't stop laughing"

From a Chipped Cup

The Hopi say wherever there is mist
the gods are present: in fog
shrouded corn fields, in iron
kettle steam, in mesquite smoke
that hangs like a scrim.

But here in the prairie town
of northwest Ohio, naphtha
steam shoots from the blowhole.

An exhaust pipe points above
the alley, points at our house
for three generations.

A gray condensation has pitted
the timbers, and sickly mist
settles in doorways and windows.

There Mother's sweet potato vine
coils like a caduceus around
the kitchen sill. A fisted root
anchors the plant that feeds
on the swill in a chipped teacup.

Though the golden wreath has faded
from the hand-painted china,
the Red Dragon of Wales still
spans its scarlet wings.

With a raised front foot
it too is pointing—back
through the leafy glass
at the steam spitting bricks
of the drycleaning plant.

For wherever there is mist
the gods are present.

She was famous for kindness, Geneva.
And yet she could run down a hen
And chop off its head just like that.
"Macaroni!" I said, when I saw the insides,
And she crowed like a satisfied rooster.
I once watched her husband, the only man
I knew who had a mustache, string up
And slaughter a cow. I ran to Geneva
And buried my face in her lap. "Geneva,"
I said, "does it hurt?" "That old cow?"
Said Geneva. "Don't worry," she said.
"You don't feel a thing when you're dead."

Geneva giggled and taught me to piss
In the dark in a thunder jug.
I was from town and embarrassed,
But Geneva enjoyed that noise.
She taught me itchweed and outhouse.
She spanked me and wiped my ass.
She was a good one, Geneva.
The world was a joke, and everyone said:
"She's a real card, that Geneva."

She had warts and a nose, Geneva,
And a twisted smile with teeth,
But she also had beautiful daughters.
Hay and fresh faces and breasts.
They could cook. The kitchen had pails,
And everyone drank from the dipper.
I can taste the tang of the tin
And smell that slop-bucket stink
And the fragrance of bread on the table.
She was always baking, Geneva.

She taught me the stars, Geneva.
It was night. In the garden.
She was giving us something again:
Carrots, cucumbers, tomatoes, and such,
Everything cool and slick. "Chicken shit,"
Said Geneva. "That's the secret," she said.
My pants were all wet with the dew.
"Look at that," said Geneva
And showed me the star-spangled sky.
"It's a coloring book," said Geneva.
"It's all dot-to-dot. Don't you see?"
And I saw: The Sisters, The Hunter,
The Bull and The Bear, The Dipper
From which we all drank.

So I thank the stars for Geneva,
All of her muscles and fat, that
Quick chicken-killer, that ugly
She of the beautiful daughters
And prize-winning hogs, that woman
Of pickles and jam. Geneva,
She taught me the mud and the stars,
And when I am ready to die
She will come with her hatchet in hand
And her face like a kerosene lamp
And her dress all feathers and blood.

Song

A yellow coverlet
in the greenwood:
spread the corners wide to the dim, stoop-shouldered pines.
Let blank sky
be your canopy.
Fringe the bedspread with the wall of lapsing stones.
Here faith has cut
in upright granite
"Meet me in Heaven" at the grave of each child
lost the same year,
three, buried here,
a century ago. Roots and mosses hold
in the same bed
mother, daughter, dead
together, in one day. "Lord, remember the poor,"
their crumbling letters pray.
I turn away.
I shall meet you nowhere, in no transfigured hour.
On soft, matted soil
blueberry bushes crawl,
each separate berry a small, hot globe of tinctured sun.
Crushed on the tongue
it releases a pang
of flesh. Tender flesh, slipped from its skin,
preserves its blue heat
down my throat.

CYNTHIA ZARIN

Fire Lyric

Three flames
on a branched
candlestick.

One is Wick,
another
Tender,

the third
Pitch. Pitch
is gone.

Wick and
Tender are
two steamship

vents. Then
each in Alice
blue, two

can-can
dancers.
Then ghosts.

Tender's
out. Gold but
with a heart

of ash, Wick's
an owl on
a matchstick.

Feathers
singe in that
harsh hiss.

Topaz flares
two times
in the pier

glass—third eye
to find her
sisters there.

CYRUS CASSELLS

Soul Make a Path Through Shouting

for Elizabeth Eckford
Little Rock, Arkansas 1957

Thick at the schoolgate are the ones
Rage has twisted
Into minotaurs, harpies
Relentlessly swift;
So you must walk past the pincers,
The swaying horns,
Sister, sister,
Straight through the gusts
Of fear and fury,
Straight through:
Where are you going?

I'm just going to school.

Here we go to meet
The hydra-headed day,
Here we go to meet
The maelstrom—

Can my voice be an angel-on-the-spot,
An amen corner?
Can my voice take you there,
Gallant girl with a notebook,
Up, up from the shadows of gallows trees
To the other shore:
A globe bathed in light,
A chalkboard blooming with equations—

I have never seen the likes of you,
Pioneer in dark glasses:
You won't show the mob your eyes,
But I know your gaze,
Steady-on-the-North-Star, burning—

With their jerry-rigged faith,
Their spear of the American flag,
How could they dare to believe
You're someone sacred?:
Nigger, burr-headed girl,
Where are you going?

I'm just going to school.

AMY CLAMPITT

Syrinx

Like the foghorn that's all lung,
the wind chime that's all percussion,
like the wind itself, that's merely air
in a terrible fret, without so much
as a finger to articulate
what ails it, the aeolian
syrinx, that reed
in the throat of a bird,
when it comes to the shaping of
what we call consonants, is
too imprecise for consensus
about what it even seems to
be saying: is it *o-ka-lee*
or *con-ka-ree*, is it really *jug jug*,
is it *cuckoo* for that matter?—
much less whether a bird's call
means anything in
particular, or at all.

Syntax comes last, there can be
no doubt of it: came last,
can be thought of (is
thought of by some) as a
higher form of expression:
is, in extremity, first to
be jettisoned: as the diva
onstage, all soaring
pectoral breathwork,
takes off, pure vowel
breaking free of the dry,
the merely fricative
husk of the particular, rises
past saying anything, any
more than the wind in
the trees, waves breaking,
or Homer's gibbering
Thespesiae iachē:

those last-chance vestiges
above the threshold, the all-
but dispossessed of breath.

.

DAVID CLEWELL

A Long Way from the Starlight

Under hypnosis, UFO abductees often are able to recall the unsettling events that
occurred on board the craft during a period of what's usually no more than a few hours
they cannot account for in their waking lives. This aspect of the phenomenon is known
as Missing Time.

      —from a symposium, "UFOs in the '90s"

When it came to the Starlight Drive-In, everyone I knew
was willing to go to extremes: hunkering down in the back seat,
laying low, packed together in the dark of someone's trunk.
    We thought
so little of using up our lives, a couple of hours at a time,
in the washed-out glow of the Starlight
where feature after cheesy feature reeled off its bargain
    basement share
of the only intelligent life in the universe we wanted in on:
Teenagers from Space. Invaders from Mars. Catwomen of the Moon.

And like it or not, I remember them all without even trying.
Whatever I might have been thinking at the time, it turns out
that most things aren't nearly forgettable enough:
not the obligatory scientist's earnest and beautiful daughter
falling one more time for the cub reporter who can't believe
    his luck.
Not the sad, radiated creature growing to fifty times its
    natural size.
Not any hapless alien a long way from home who means us
no harm. Not any who does. Not another histrionic question mark
when we all finally make it to *The End?* Not the most inept
    Attack of . . .
nor the dumbest *Brain That. . . .* Not the smallest *Thing,* that
    misguided
piece of 1950s bad advice, *Watch the skies.* As if some grade-B
human vigilance might somehow be enough to guarantee
that whatever happened there that night surely would never
    happen again.

And I wish I could be one of those people who never stopped watching
but remember only under hypnosis what they saw, taking
   themselves seriously
back to that time they can't fathom any other way, to a place
where everything's strangely in focus for once, made up
of amazing circumstances that never occur to them otherwise:
   space ships,
examination tables, telepathy in the nude, vaguely biological
experimentation. Now they're lying down again, counting
   backwards
from 10, and in their deepest artificial sleep they can't stop
dreaming up story after story they've been chosen to star in.
They're covering that stretch of road again between where
   they were picked up
and where they were inevitably let down. Between the car
   stalling out
and the engine running again like a dream where nothing ever
   really came off
between the swagger at midnight and the cold sweat at 2 AM.
These days they pour their whole lives into filling the hole
in a day they didn't even know was there.
And I don't know where they find that kind of time.

Something like that should be harder to forget, especially in a world
so full of smaller oddball wonders it's impossible to stop
   recollecting:
the light in the attic of a childhood that went out
with no warning, freezing you in the sudden dark.
   Daydreaming through
Debbie Fuller's Brownie uniform while she carried on nobly
with a bad day's Show-and-Tell. How the school nurse
   smiled and swore
this would be the last shot of anything you'd ever need.
The capital of Wyoming, maps made out of soap, Avogadro's Number,
the Pythagorean Theorem, every explorer who sailed the rough seas

of 3rd-period History, no land where they served lunch in sight.
And later, the name of every bar you learned to spend long nights in,
trying to forget it all, remembering perfectly well
the number of the cab someone always calls for you, how it gets you
    miraculously home.

                    So is it asking too much of our abductees to
know by heart that beam of blue, immobilizing light that
    floated them on board?
The silvery suits and avocado heads of the alien crew?
The lasers and precision instruments that opened some
    private part of them
and for once it didn't hurt like they knew it would? The
    star-map
on the wall, with the usual red arrow: *Don't You Wish You
    Were Here?*
The number of light-years until the next rest stop and maybe
    at least
where they left the car, even if the goddamn keys they can't
    find
are lost by now in some deep pocket of space too unlikely
    to remember?

When we were young we never would have dreamed
of admitting that we hadn't seen anything yet. We were
    going around
in circles, all our precarious featherweight cargo stuffed into
the rusted-out Chevy of our lives. With a speaker still
hooked on the window so we wouldn't feel as alone: *Not of
    This Earth.*
The Man from Planet X. We couldn't help humming
right along through the static with the soundtrack's every
    flutter.
and wow. We were never too far from the Starlight.

The way these people tell it, we may never know what we're missing
until it's almost too late. They've been ruined or redeemed, depending
on which version needs believing most. That such a thing's actually
possible, either way, should be enough: that today anyone understands
in any case a little more than yesterday how some of us ended up
astonishingly here, dressed in these strange clothes, dazed
but remarkably ready to go, one more mysterious incision we can point to
in an arm, in a leg, in the thin skin of days
that more or less holds us together. Where something's been added
or taken away, if only we could go back over our arithmetic.

We weren't always quite this suggestible, taking whatever instructions
we think we can live with: when we wake up, we will remember nothing.
Or far too much. So often what comes back is sized to fit
no matter what we believe we've lost out on: a few minutes, a day,
a leap year, a lifetime. And sometimes we're so anxious to make that up,
we do. By now you've got to know the feeling.

You're barely aware of turning the key in the ignition, and
　　out of nowhere
it's you, emerging from the car way too many miles later
with no real idea where you were when the scenery changed.
　　You might think
on the one hand *I'm lucky to be alive*, but on the other, *every day*
is like this. Even though both hands on the wheel were yours,
　　steering
with an uncanny sense of direction.

　　　　　　　　　　　　　　We're all making it up
as we go along: how fast is too fast. When we noticed the sky
clouding over. What we should have said to the attendant at
　　the Starlight
shining his flashlight into our back seat, looking for the same
　　thing
we're still looking for today: a certain dark secret more-of-us
　　than ever
we can probably afford to own up to.
And some of us are not about to be stopped if we can help
　　it, not
this time, now that we're finally getting somewhere. Now
that those Starlight nights are behind us, when anything
　　forgettable
couldn't possibly hurt us beyond belief, and those hours we
　　wasted
hoping for once we'd get lucky during *The Day the Earth*
　　Stood Still
meant nothing to us, with all the time in the world.

Science

Then it was the future, though what's arrived
isn't what we had in mind, all chrome and
cybernetics, when we set up exhibits
in the cafeteria for the judges
to review what we'd made of our hypotheses.

The class skeptic (he later refused to sign
anyone's yearbook, calling it a sentimental
degradation of language) chloroformed mice,
weighing the bodies before and after
to catch the weight of the soul,

wanting to prove the invisible
real as a bagful of nails. A girl
who knew it all made cookies from euglena,
a one-celled compromise between animal and plant,
she had cultured in a flask.

We're smart enough, she concluded,
to survive our mistakes, showing photos of farmland,
poisoned, gouged, eroded. No one believed
he really had built it when a kid no one knew
showed up with an atom smasher, confirming that

the tiniest particles could be changed
into something even harder to break.
And one whose mother had cancer (hard to admit now,
it was me) distilled the tar of cigarettes
to paint it on the backs of shaven mice.

She wanted to know what it took,
a little vial of sure malignancy,
to prove a daily intake smaller
than a single aspirin could finish
something as large as a life. I thought of this

because, today, the dusky seaside sparrow
became extinct. It may never be as famous
as the pterodactyl or the dodo,
but the last one died today, a resident
of Walt Disney World where now its tissue samples

lie frozen, in case someday we learn to clone
one from a few cells. Like those instant dinosaurs
that come in a gelatin capsule—just add water
and they inflate. One other thing this
brings to mind. The euglena girl won first prize

both for science and, I think, in retrospect, for hope.

The Dream

Once, years after your death, I dreamt
you were alive and that I'd found you
living once more in the old apartment.
But I had taken a woman up there
to make love to in the empty rooms.
I was angry at you who'd borne and loved me
and because of whom I believe in heaven.
I regretted your return from the dead
and said to myself almost bitterly,
"For godsakes, what was the big rush,
couldn't she wait one more day?"

And just so daily somewhere Messiah
is shunned like a beggar at the door because
someone has something he wants to finish
or just something better to do, something
he prefers not to put off forever
—some little pleasure so deeply wished
that Heaven's coming has to seem bad luck
or worse, God's intruding selfishness!

But you always turned Messiah away
with a penny and a cake for his trouble
—because wash had to be done, because
who could let dinner boil over and burn,
because everything had to be festive for
your husband, your daughters, your son.

PETER GIZZI

Creeley Madrigal

I.

Where is the stamen she lost
as she has gone solo
as she discarded

or where is the stamen she seeks
as she gave up on
as she thought everything in

then living's flourish to be less
now she's absent without regard
empty space as she was

as open sky is everywhere
of/now the form's recognition
and animal cries animal hunger

II.

Where is the flourish he missed
as he became faint
as he distilled

or where is the flourish he sought
as he let go of
as he believed deliverance through

then thinking's alembic to be loose
now he's thin without regret
zero place as he is

as close ground is nowhere
of/now the verb's winnow
and foliate list foliate void

III.

Where is the alembic we ruined
as we have left astray
as we ignored

or where is the alembic we want
as we misplaced
as we sought an approach to

then faith's mystery to be blind
now we've seen without respect
untrodden path as we are

as actual garden is elsewhere
of/now the poem's meaning
and grammar land grammar world

IV.

Where is the mystery they glean
as they have pronouns
as they invoke

or where is the mystery they plumb
as they wander
as they make sacrifice for

then healing's balm to be soiled
now their ritual without reflex
open wound as they were

as crisp linen is closeted
of/now the world's stain
and lunar eyes lunar whirr

RICHARD HOWARD

Like Most Revelations
    after Morris Louis

It is the movement that incites the form,
discovered as a downward rapture—yes,
it is the movement that delights the form,
sustained by its own velocity. And yet

it is the movement that delays the form
while darkness slows and encumbers; in fact
it is the movement that betrays the form,
baffled in such toils of ease, until

it is the movement that deceives the form,
beguiling our attention—we supposed
it is the movement that achieves the form.
Were we mistaken? What does it matter if

it is the movement that negates the form?
Even though we give (give up) ourselves
to this mortal process of continuing,
it is the movement that creates the form.

What the Living Do

Johnny, the kitchen sink has been clogged for days, some utensil
    probably fell down there.
And the Drano won't work but smells dangerous, and the crusty
    dishes have piled up

waiting for the plumber I still haven't called. This is the
    everyday we spoke of.
It's winter again: the sky's a deep headstrong blue, and the
    sunlight pours through

the open living room windows because the heat's on too high
    in here and I can't turn it off.
For weeks now, driving, or dropping a bag of groceries in the
    street, the bag breaking,

I've been thinking: This is what the living do. And yesterday,
    hurrying along those
wobbly bricks in the Cambridge sidewalk, spilling my coffee
    down my wrist and sleeve,

I thought it again, and again later, when buying a hairbrush:
    This is it.
Parking. Slamming the car door shut in the cold. What you
    called *that yearning*.

What you finally gave up. We want the spring to come and the
    winter to pass. We want
whoever to call or not to call, a letter, a kiss—we want more
    and more and then more of it.

But there are moments, walking, when I catch a glimpse of
    myself in the window glass,
say the window of the corner video store, and I'm gripped by a
    cherishing so deep

for my own blowing hair, chapped face and unbuttoned coat
    that I'm speechless:
I am living. I remember you.

CAROLYN KIZER

On a Line from Valéry
(The Gulf War)

Tout le ciel vert se meurt
Le dernier arbre brûle.

The whole green sky is dying. The last tree flares
With a great burst of supernatural rose
Under a canopy of poisonous airs.

Could we imagine our return to prayers
To end in time before time's final throes,
The green sky dying as the last tree flares?

But we were young in judgement, old in years
Who could make peace; but it was war we chose,
To spread its canopy of poisoning airs.

Not all our children's pleas and women's fears
Could steer us from this hell. And now God knows
His whole green sky is dying as it flares.

Our crops of wheat have turned to fields of tares.
This dreadful century staggers to its close
And the sky dies for us, its poisoned heirs.

All rain was dust. Its granules were our tears.
Throats burst as universal winter rose
To kill the whole green sky, the last tree bare
Beneath its canopy of poisoned air.

MARY JO SALTER

Brownie Troop # 722 Visits
the Nursing Home

As if being eighty-five or ninety
and terrified and talked down to loudly
and pushed around in wheelchairs by the staff
all day weren't bad enough,

for tonight's entertainment the local Brownies
have come to sing Christmas carols. Nice
youngsters, all of them, but so off-
key that it could kill you off

just listening. Didn't they ever practice?
And for this they get a social service
badge . . . but not to worry. Most
of the audience is deaf as a post.

Afterward, the troop leader has
each girl belt out what she wants for Christmas.
"Ice skates? A kitten? A doll?" she repeats,
then turns (as she must) to ask, "What treats

would *you* like Santa to bring this year?"
A row of old faces with snow-white hair
stares back at her blankly. Another spring,
young woman; only to see the spring.

Eros

By rights one should experience holy dread
At the young woman gowned in black chiffon
Who, at a mirror, slightly turns her head,
Large eyes intent, and puts an earring on.
One should fear redwoods where the sun sinks shafts
Of glowing light through dust-revolving drafts
And where the cyclist slimly coasts through trees
As she leans forward, her arms long and brown,
And gives her brakes a moderating squeeze.

Yet the soul loves the braided rope of hair,
The sense of heat and light, the cheek's faint flush.
Time blurs; nights end; one climbs a narrow stair,
The studio's warm, the city is a hush
Of streetlamps and the snow that, all night, falls.
But later when one rises and recalls
How, in the dark, the spirit clings and melts,
It is as if the ardent, giddy rush
Had happened, somehow, to somebody else.

Gently to brush hair from the sleeping face,
To feel breath on the fingers, and to try
To check joy in that intimate, small place
Where joy's own joyousness can't satisfy—
This is pain. This is power that comes and goes.
This is as secret as the fresh clean snows
Which, destitute of traffic to confess,
Will serve at dawn as witness to a sky
Withdrawing to its high blue faultlessness.

CHRISTIANNE BALK

Envy the wild dog stalking on the snow's
   wavering path and his ice-imprinted steps.
      The water snake disappears. Her rope-looped
wake takes longer to erase, diminishing
   in ever-widening arcs. Falling always
      down, the rain is pulled towards the earth's iron
heart. A pair of hawks press their bellies, turn hooked heads,
   entangle talons, free-fall towards slate
      roofs. Sprung at the seam, each barely touching,
the Scot's Broom's pods burst open, twisting old
   husks in two. Swooping north over the slope
      in broad day, the short-eared owl embraces
the hill beyond the chainlink fence with the wide

      ovals of her flight. Hooped wings direct the air.
      Dark lines ellipse shoulders, face. Overhead,
the geese hurl their collective weight along
   triangulated necks. Does the milkweed
      doubt the wind? Held out like children's hands,
the hawthorne's leaves cup themselves,
   fastened to green limbs shooting up and down
      in a rush of yellow-red as bent as
water falling from a spring no one can
   see. A pheasant whirs her blustered feathers
      upwards. Another nests his ring-necked chest
in sable grass, parting wide with wasps. Yet
   somehow each is whole. Dear pale, displaced feet,
      abandoned! Envy them.

Mother Love

Who can forget the attitude of mothering?
       Toss me a baby and without bothering
to blink I'll catch her, sling him on a hip.
       Any woman knows the remedy for grief
is being needed: duty bugles and we'll
       climb out of exhaustion every time,
bare the nipple or tuck in the sheet,
       heat milk and hum at bedside until
they can dress themselves and rise, primed
       for Love or Glory—those one-way mirrors
girls peer into as their fledgling heroes slip
       through, storming the smoky battlefield.

So when this kind woman approached at the urging
       of her bouquet of daughters,
(one for each of the world's corners,
       one for each of the winds to scatter!)
and offered up her only male child for nursing
       (a smattering of flesh, noisy and ordinary),
I put aside the lavish trousseau of the mourner
       for the daintier comfort of pity:
I decided to save him. Each night
       I laid him on the smoldering embers,
sealing his juices in slowly so he might
       be cured to perfection. Oh, I know it
looked damning: at the hearth a muttering crone
       bent over a baby sizzling on a spit
as neat as a Virginia ham. Poor human—
       to scream like that, to make me remember.

Song

Listen: there was a goat's head hanging by ropes in a tree.
All night it hung there and sang. And those who heard it
Felt a hurt in their hearts and thought they were hearing
The song of a night bird. They sat up in their beds, and then
They lay back down again. In the night wind, the goat's head
Swayed back and forth, and from far off it shone faintly
The way the moonlight shone on the train track miles away
Beside which the goat's headless body lay. Some boys
Had hacked its head off. It was harder work than they had imagined.
The goat cried like a man and struggled hard. But they
Finished the job. They hung the bleeding head by the school
And then ran off into the darkness that seems to hide everything.
The head hung in the tree. The body lay by the tracks.
The head called to the body. The body to the head.
They missed each other. The missing grew large between them,
Until it pulled the heart right out of the body, until
The drawn heart flew toward the head, flew as a bird flies
Back to its cage and the familiar perch from which it trills.
Then the heart sang in the head, softly at first and then louder,
Sang long and low until the morning light came up over
The school and over the tree, and then the singing stopped . . . .
The goat had belonged to a small girl. She named
The goat Broken Thorn Sweet Blackberry, named it after
The night's bush of stars, because the goat's silky hair
Was dark as well water, because it had eyes like wild fruit.
The girl lived near a high railroad track. At night
She heard the trains passing, the sweet sound of the train's horn
Pouring softly over her bed, and each morning she woke
To give the bleating goat his pail of warm milk. She sang
Him songs about girls with ropes and cooks in boats.
She brushed him with a stiff brush. She dreamed daily
That he grew bigger, and he did. She thought her dreaming
Made it so. But one night the girl didn't hear the train's horn,
And the next morning she woke to an empty yard. The goat
Was gone. Everything looked strange. It was as if a storm

Had passed through while she slept, wind and stones, rain
Stripping the branches of fruit. She knew that someone
Had stolen the goat and that he had come to harm. She called
To him. All morning and into the afternoon, she called
And called. She walked and walked. In her chest a bad feeling
Like the feeling of the stones gouging the soft undersides
Of her bare feet. Then somebody found the goat's body
By the high tracks, the flies already filling their soft bottles
At the goat's torn neck. Then somebody found the head
Hanging in a tree by the school. They hurried to take
These things away so that the girl would not see them.
They hurried to raise money to buy the girl another goat.
They hurried to find the boys who had done this, to hear
Them say it was a joke, a joke, it was nothing but a joke. . . .
But listen: here is the point. The boys thought to have
Their fun and be done with it. It was harder work than they
Had imagined, this silly sacrifice, but they finished the job,
Whistling as they washed their large hands in the dark.
What they didn't know was that the goat's head was already
Singing behind them in the tree. What they didn't know
Was that the goat's head would go on singing, just for them,
Long after the ropes were down, and that they would learn to listen,
Pail after pail, stroke after patient stroke. They would
Wake in the night thinking they heard the wind in the trees
Or a night bird, but their hearts beating harder. There
Would be a whistle, a hum, a high murmur, and, at last, a song,
The low song a lost boy sings remembering his mother's call.
Not a cruel song, no, no, not cruel at all. This song
Is sweet. It is sweet. The heart dies of this sweetness.

Earth

You see a woman of a certain age,
not old, yet seeing every sign
of how the world will age her.
More and more, you'll find her in the garden
but not for onions or potatoes.
She wants blooms, color,
a breaking in the earth's disorder.
Swollen branch, the right bird—
they can make her cry. And the fussing
over moving this or that to the right location.
Learning to be alone,
she brings out ten varieties of rose,
armed against pest and blight
and the cutting northern cold
she fights with blankets of dirt.
Earliest spring will find her hovering
over the waxy perfection of tulips, the ones
closest to the thawing ground.
You'd think it's the opening she loves,
the loosening flower revealing
the meticulous still-life deep in the cup.
But what she needs is to see
those stiff-petaled, utterly still ones
rise out of the dirt.

The weather won't cooperate. She sinks
hundreds of bulbs in the rain,
mud on her hands, black smear on her neck.
For this birthing, all she pays
is stiff joints, and she knows again
the insistence of flowering.
Falling, she knows the flowers
fall to the season, and the seasons
to the great wheel. Fallen, she's learned
to prefer the fallen.

NAOMI SHIHAB NYE

Streets

A man leaves the world
and the streets he lived on
grow a little shorter.

One more window dark
in this city, the figs on his branches
will soften for birds.

If we stand quietly enough evenings
there grows a whole company of us
standing quietly together.
Overhead loud grackles are claiming their trees
and the sky which sews and sews, tirelessly sewing,
drops her purple hem.
Each thing in its time, in its place,
it would be nice to think the same about people.

Some people do. They sleep completely,
waking refreshed. Others live in two worlds,
the lost and remembered.
They sleep twice, once for the one who is gone,
once for themselves. They dream thickly,
dream double, they wake from a dream
into another one, they walk the short streets
calling out names, and then they answer.

At the head of this poem I have laid out
a boning knife a paring knife a wooden spoon a pair of tongs.
Oaken grain beneath them olive and rusty light
around them.
And you looming: This is not your scene
this is the first frame of a film
I have in mind to make: move on, get out.
And you here telling me: What will be done
with these four objects will be done
through my lens not your words.

The poet shrugs: I was only in the kitchen
looking at the chopping board. (Not the whole story.)
And you telling me: Awful is the scope
of what I have in mind, awful the music I shall deploy, most
awful the witness of the camera moving
out from the chopping board to the grains of snow
whirling against the windowglass to the rotating
searchlights of the tower. The humped snow-shrouded tanks
laboring toward the border. This is not your bookish art.

But say the poet picks up the boning knife and thinks *my bones*
if she touching the paring knife thinks *carrot, onion, celery*
if staring at the wooden spoon I see the wood is split
as if from five winters of war
when neither celery, onion, carrot could be found
or picking up the tongs I whisper *What this was for*

And did you say *get on, get out* or just *look out?*
Were you speaking from exhaustion from disaster from your last
    assignment were you afraid
for the vision in the kitchen, that it could not be saved
—no time to unload the heavy
cases to adjust
the sensitive equipment

to seize the olive rusty light to scan the hand that reaches
    hovering
over a boning knife a paring knife a wooden spoon a pair
    of tongs
to cull the snow before it blows away across the border's
    blacked-out sheds
and the moon swims in a bluish bubble dimmed
by the rotating searchlights of the tower? Here
it is in my shorthand, do what you have in mind.

JAN RICHMAN

Tourette's Journey

Shudder and sigh, fuck fuck fuck, stutter
and thwack the roof of the car, knuckles
calloused and winking, each tin pop a delight,
then swing to strike again, think of nothing
but the bright pang of your body knocked against
the rollicking world, eyes banged shut
like a doll set in motion, poke at your balls
till you feel the rush swerving off you like steam
off a fresh pile of shit.

Check the speedometer. Hands on the wheel.
Ask your wife if she's thought about dinner
or whether it matters your spare pair of glasses
lies bent by a heft of mail on the kitchen
counter. For her, the world is flat. Pat
her thigh. A margin of bottlebrush pitches by
on the right, blooming pinch-red bristles onto the
outside lane. You know this road so well
a river of shame wouldn't surprise, too
well, ice and eyes.

Her thighs are warm as kettles, your palms moist
as hiss, a calm discontent falls down
like a bucket from a balcony, luck and piss
and sweat and boil offer up most of their honey-
tongued tricks. Crack your window, slap the pane
that separates this chestnut hush from that
parenthetical strain. Shit it's good to brain
something, to be clashed and parried, pummeled
into a different meaning, shifted into distress,
breastplate gleaming, god damn, god fucking
damn, and god bless.

ANDREW SCHELLING

Writing in Darkness

I was jotting in a notebook
trees full of
      buzzards
cutting words on stone
a house known as
      writing in darkness

thought of
them crazy *antiguos*
all the maize it took to build up their
      cities
ruinous now
stelae eaten by water

Well here's our Hornitos and lime
our buildings also to crumble
we'll wedge rags
in the screen
      keep out mosquitoes
but who mucked up these
sheets

footprints all over the mattress?

dear Anne
to this room I've taken no other
      woman
let's call it
tracks on the bedsheets

let's call it
writing in darkness

      10 August 1993
      Tulum, Yucatan

EDWARD SNOW (Trans.)

The Spirit Ariel 347
    After reading Shakespeare's Tempest

by Rainer Maria Rilke

Once long ago somewhere you freed him
with that same jolt with which as a young man
you tore yourself toward greatness, away from all regard.
Then he grew willing, and ever since he serves,
after each deed poised for freedom.
And half imperiously, half almost ashamed,
you inform him that for this and that
you still require him, and, ah, must tell again
that story of how you helped him. And yet you feel, yourself,
how everything that you keep back through him
is missing from the air. How sweet and almost tempting:
to let him go—, and then, no longer conjuring,
enrolled in fate like all the others,
to know that his light friendship,
without strain now, nowhere any obligation,
a surplus to this breathing's space,
is at work in the element, thoughtlessly.
Henceforth dependent, no longer with that gift
to shape the dull mouth into that call
at which he came. Powerless, aging, poor
and yet breathing him like incomprehensibly far-flung
allotted fragrance by which alone the invisible
is made complete. Smiling, that you could
summon him so, in such great dealings
so easily at home. Perhaps weeping too,
when you remember how it loved you and
longed to leave, both, always the same urge.

(Have I let it go? Now this man frightens me,
who is becoming Duke again. How gently
he draws the wire through his own head and hangs
himself up with the other figures and begs
henceforth the play's indulgence. . . . What an epilogue
to lordship consummated. Mere naked standing-there
with nothing but his own strength: "which is most faint.")

JOHN YAU

Self-Portrait with Max Beckmann

One vision alone would be much simpler
but then it would not exist

Love in an animal sense is an illness
I am not a squirrel

though I have been told I eat like one
Everywhere attempts are being made

to lower our capacity for happiness
to the level of termites

To be sure it is a foolish undertaking
to try to put these ideas into words

Have you not sometimes been with me
in the deep hollow of a champagne glass

where red lobsters crawl around
and waiters serve flaming hats

mounted with pink and yellow flowers
Have you not given up searching

for a way out of the machine phantoms
Have you not observed the Law of Surface

in the poisonous splendor of the orchid
Did you not set out to build a crystal hut

because you wanted to forge
three corners into a circle

Perhaps we shall awaken one day
alone or together

Perhaps we will enjoy ourselves
in the forms we have been given

I am an acrobat climbing a ladder
a man in a tuxedo smoking a cigar

The clothes are a disguise
a small parcel I shall soon retract

To you
I am not a very nice man

who was lucky enough
to marry a beautiful woman from Graz

But to myself
I am a painter

who sleeps in a small room
adjacent to the long corridors

of a yellow night

GEORGE BRADLEY

The Fire Fetched Down

When they knew what he had given them,
This florid colossus with the sunrise in his eyes
And skin the color of perfectly ripened fruit,
Understood what he had done in the name of freedom,
Of self-esteem, their first thought was to give it back,
Who had been happy in their miserable condition,
Had been content each hour to kill or cringe,
Pleased to end their days in the detached mercy
Of stupent sense, the sweet shock that flesh is air to;
When they saw what he intended, this monstrous
Avatar wrapped in conceits of agony, of honor,
Their every instinct (before such brute reflex
Was blunted by the dull weight of the abstract)
Was to spurn the bounty, slay the bearer, to destroy
The visiting light, its unwanted complication.
After all, his differences had not been theirs,
His absurd dispute with the divine, his squabble
About a sacred ox and some celestial secret;
His ambition for their state was nothing they could grasp,
And they wished only to be as they had been, dying
To extinguish the moted mazy rays that floated
Like gleaming locks on his titanic head, to blot out
The subtle moonbeams that shone so as he smiled. . . .
But the fire he brought was beautiful, a jewel
Of countless facets, a spectrum infinitely broad,
An aetherial motion they never tired of looking on;
The flame was gorgeous, and they were human,
And they took that gift, reaching to accept
The ember of ideas, the conflagration of tongues,
And then his name was their name (*Forethought,
Premonition*, how the word had frightened them!),
And his pain became theirs, too,
Chained in the rational abyss and torn
Time and again by cruel and busy claws, raked
By the razor bill of what they could conclude.

ALFRED CORN

Lago di Como: The Cypresses

Cupressus lusitanica,
The species name, and factual
Probes in an old *Britannica*
Confirm it came from Portugal.

Greeks, too, arrived as immigrants
And planted the olive at its side,
A Mediterranean romance
Green long after Greek had died.

The drawback? Immobility,
But isn't the breezes' clear intention
To set the rooted captives free
With four fresh knots of intervention?—

Which bends each tree in a slow arc
As buried souls wake up again,
Fresh conscripts drawn out of the dark.
Tall, tapering, and midnight green,

They stand as cypress did for them,
Anonymous memorials
Disburdened of the flat pro tem,
In soil thought through by human skulls.

When the trees seem to tremble (much
As their Lisbon cousins would have done
In the great earthquake), only a Dutch
Painter would try to render one.

I'm satisfied to watch as light
Begins to slant and breezes fall.
In shade as dark as minor night,
They hear my tentative footfall,

And breathe a welcome neither Greek
Nor Portuguese, a country drawl
Seasoned without being antique:
"Come join these ranks for the long haul!

Of course there is an alternative
Less difficult than our endeavor,
Which only suits those who can give
Notice to time and change forever."

In the distance I see a small van go
Speeding away with passengers,
Who might say "We're not ready," though
What happens happens when it prefers.

Becalmed a moment, the trees will soon
Return to their colloquium,
Branches billowing toward the moon
Risen over Elysium.

MICHAEL CUDDIHY

An Old Pride   353

Doubleyou be Yeats, was it you wrote this
Or someone else, drunk, on pilgrimage to Sligo
A few summers ago?
> *dipsomania dim sum dimity dimwit*
> *doppelgänger diapason*

  This long white poem—
I wear it to bed like a white nightgown.
The purity of the eye, the ear, is not in question
But the words stumble, volleys of laughter
As they cross over into the park,
Hand in hand, each one.

      I hear them now,
The clamor of their wings on Coole Park Lake,
Creak of oarlocks, rustle of a dress—
The hand on his sleeve Maud Gonne's,
His heart rising like a trout.

      White swans,
Necks arched in the lily's matchless curve,
An old man dreaming of youth, that woman
He saw first in a canter at harriers
And again, at the Galway races, thoroughbreds
Galloping in an open field, flanks
Heaving, heaving his Ireland
With an English rider.

He has no heart—his patriot friends,
Helpless to move this slow, musing aristocrat,
Forehead pressed to the windowpane.
No dream he would celebrate
But their own fatalities, his tongue urgent with their names—
MacDonagh and MacBride and Connolly and Pearse—
Saying goodbye to an old pride as it slowly melted
Before that terrible beauty: schoolmaster, clerk, country
    gentleman
Come together: "Easter 1916,"
A flag planted in the heart, this poem
That sets a man crying.

JON DAVIS

The Modern Condition

In the drowse of the saxophone, in that bittersweet drama,
    roses on the nightstand, one shoulder bared.
Summer evenings, warm pavement underfoot, she would slip
    her hand into his pocket and jingle his change.
"What is love?" the "soulful" chanteuse sang, "flowers and
    champagne / a walk in the lane / oh, baby, ain't that
    love?"
When the narrative fractured, the vermilion sky darkened.
The alto was given to sweetness, but ideas about sweetness
    launched flights of discordant squawking.
The papers called this "The Modern Condition."
A certain motif presented itself and they all joined in.
The light changed and a ruckus ensued—Subarus, Porsches,
    Fleetsides, Stepsides, earnest bicyclists wobbling among
    the drainage and litter.
The lovers imagined the traffic noise was a waterfall.
The lovers imagined a great affection circulating along the
    Green Belt, among the placid waterfowl, the stream
    "coursing" through these natural settings.
That they were exempt from suffering was itself a kind of
    suffering.
The stockbrokers and magistrates, the mannered speeches and
    posturing glam-rockers; the cheerful and the winded; the
    sunset smearing its orange sentiments across the New
    England horizon.
Even the homeless have the flamboyance of rock stars—their
    assembled rags, hopeful speeches, the artful presentation
    of their desires.
Then the string quartet in the gazebo, a pleasant falseness they
    longed for when the muttering ducks surrounded them,
    their hungers upon them like the polyblend uniforms of
    the doomed.
Later, there would be frozen yogurt, light caresses, laughter,
    plotless fiction, ubiquitous music.

The Angel of the Little Utopia

Shall I move the flowers again?
Shall I put them further to the left
into the light?
Will that fix it, will that arrange the
thing?
Yellow sky.
Faint cricket in the dried-out bush.
As I approach, my footfall in the leaves
drowns out the cricket-chirping I was
coming close to hear . . .
Yellow sky with black leaves rearranging it.
Wind rearranging the black leaves in it.
But anyway I am indoors, of course, and this is a pane, here,
and I have arranged the flowers for you
again. Have taken the dead cordless ones, the yellow bits past
       apogee,
the faded cloth, the pollen-free abandoned marriage-hymn
back out, leaving the few crisp blooms to swagger, winglets,
       limpid debris. . . .
Shall I arrange these few remaining flowers?
Shall I rearrange these gossamer efficiencies?
Please don't touch me with your skin.
Please let the thing evaporate.
Please tell me clearly what it is.
The party is so loud downstairs, bristling with souvenirs.
It's a philosophy of life, of course,
drinks fluorescent, whips of syntax in the air
above the heads—how small they seem from here,
the bobbing universal heads, stuffing the void with eloquence,
and also tiny merciless darts
of truth. It's pulled on tight, the air they breathe and rip.

It's like a prize the way it's stretched-on tight
over the voices, keeping them intermingling, forcing the breaths
    to marry,
cunning little hermeneutic cupola,
dome of occasion in which the thoughts re-
group, the footprints stall and gnaw in tiny ruts,
the napkins wave, are waved, the honeycombing
thoughts are felt to *dialogue*, a form of self-
congratulation, no?, or is it suffering? I'm a bit
dizzy up here rearranging things,
they will come up here soon, and need a setting for their fears,
and loves, an architecture for their evolutionary
morphic needs—what will they *need* if I don't make the place?—
what will they know to miss?, what cry out for, what feel the
    bitter restless irritations
for? A bit dizzy from the altitude of everlastingness,
the tireless altitudes of the created place,
in which to make a life—a *liberty*—the hollow, fetishized,
    and starry place,
a bit gossamer with dream, a vortex of evaporations,
oh little dream, invisible city, invisible hill
I make here on the upper floors for you—
down there, where you are entertained, where you are passing
time, there's glass and moss on air,
there's the feeling of being numerous, mouths submitting to air,
    lips to protocol
and dreams of sense, tongues, hinges, forceps clicking
in anticipation of . . . as if the moment, freeze-burned by
    accuracies-of
could be thawed open into life again
by gladnesses, by rectitude—no, no—by the sinewy efforts at

358

sincerity—can't you feel it gliding round you,
mutating, yielding the effort-filled phrases of your talk to air,
compounding, stemming them, honeying-open the sheerest
        innuendoes, till
the rightness seems to root, in the air, in the compact indoor sky,
and the rest, all round, feels like desert, falls away,
and you have the sensation of muscular timeliness,
and you feel the calligraphic in you reach-out like a soul
into the midst of others, in conversation,
gloved by desire, into the tiny carnage
of opinions. . . . So dizzy. Life buzzing beneath me
though my feeling is the hive is gone, queen gone,
the continuum continuing beneath, busy, earnest, in con-
versation. Shall I prepare. Shall I put this further
to the left, shall I move the light, the point-of-view, the shades are
drawn, to cast a glow resembling disappearance, slightly red,
will that fix it, will that make clear the task, the trellised
        ongoingness
and all these tiny purposes, these parables, this marketplace
of tightening truths?
Oh knit me that am crumpled dust,
the heap is all dispersed. Knit me that *am*. Say *therefore*. Say
philosophy and mean by that the pane.
Let us look out again. The yellow sky.
With black leaves rearranging it. . . .

MARTIN GREENBERG (Trans.)

On the Drowned Girl
(Vom Ertrunkenen Mädchen)
by Bertolt Brecht

As she went under and drowned and floated down
The swift-running streams into the quieter river,
The heavens shone marvellously opaline
As if to appease and placate the cadaver.

Weeds and algae winding around her
Slowly added more and more weight to the body,
Fish brushed her leg coolly, swimming by her,
Fauna and flora burdened her final journey.

And the sky in the evening darkened to smoke,
And stars swung in the black with night's coming.
Yet it brightened above, again dawn broke,
For her there was still night and morning.

As her pale corpse decayed in the eddying water,
What happened was, very slowly, God forgot her,
First her white face, then her hands, and lastly her hair,
Till she was carrion with all the carrion in the river.

DEBORA GREGER

Adam's Daughter

Golden Transparent: by the light of an apple
I saw the earth, and it was green and good.
Under the dust it almost glowed. Gorged,
I lay in the back of the station wagon

between the boxes of apples my father had picked.
Golden Delicious: I had eaten of the fruit
of the knowledge of good and evil
but my eyes were not opened, I was no god.

No, I was a snake, well-fed,
crushed beneath the heel of the desert air
heavy with isotopes. I was none the wiser.
Brought forth in sorrow, I was the daughter

of a radiation monitor, entry level,
who would work his way up to "feasibility studies"
for reactors yet to be built. Once a month
he left two glass flasks of his urine in a leaden case

on the front porch. Oh, let him not be "hot."
By the unearthly glow of an apple—
no, by the faint, sainted blue of atomic decay,
uranium father to daughter, longing to be lead,

the cottonwoods of the shelterbelt shivered.
Leaves whispered rumors of nothing, nothing amiss.
A rattlesnake's lazy hiss turned on itself,
a cyclotron asleep in the dirt.

A train wailed like a prophet weary of wilderness.
In a lead-lined car, steel flasks of plutonium,
squeezed drop by drop from rock,
tried not to be shaken by the world

outside the reactor gates. But what did I know?
As if out there at the checkpoint
a seraph had lifted a fiery sword.

Nell

Not until my father had led her into the paddock
And driven her a month in circles and made
Her walk six weeks with the collar on her neck
And the bags of seeds on her back did he snap

The leather traces to the hames, for she was not
Green halter-broke when he took her that way,
Rearing and shying at each birdcall of shadow.
It would be another year in blinders before she

Began seeing how it would go from then on,
Moving not as herself alone but as one of a pair,
With the sorrel gelding of the same general
Conformation and breed shuffling beside her,

And between them only the split tongue
Of the wagon. As is often the case with couples,
He the subdued, philosophical one, and she
With the great spirit and the preternatural knack

Of opening gates, they had barely become a team
When their kind of beasts began vanishing from
The fields, and the fields, one by one, fell
Before the contagion of houses. Still, they

Were there for a long time after the first
Tractors and the testing of rockets, so you
Could see how it had been that way for years
With them, just the one motion again and again

Until at dusk when the harnesses were lifted,
The odor that rose seemed history itself,
And they bent to their feed in the light
That would be that way for the rest of their lives.

How I used to wish
watching out across the wet road bed's
black glide—the usual:
shell-shore of the first world
willed back in a blink,
ling cod, then, thickening the ocean like
Life with Time:
              No time, by God!
good night now licking
eyelids up in some immense, sleep-swimming
immemorial armored fish,
fusion mirrored there on that flat nerve,
novas and so forth, symmetries,
this smattering of energies,
G-force veering to the simple
solipsism of the born stars: sol
mating with himself himself in that fresh
electric swamp where further fetchlights
limn away all wavery and settling
long before nylon stockings ever
were or lunatic desire
seared us, just void,
volts and amps and the blue hiss
isn't it?—and then that's this.

PHILIP SCHULTZ

Alzheimer's

In the beginning it visits
your mother like a polite
but somewhat obtrusive stranger
whose silence, like the dripping
from every faucet, pots cracking
under burners, toast abandoned
like words in mid-sentence,
is vaguely disturbing. Then it's there
every time you visit; in the blinking
& shivering nods, in the way her fork
freezes in midair, inches & entire years
from her mouth; in the lizard's lash
of her tongue removing invisible crumbs.
One day it answers all your questions,
insisting you are her father, mother, brother,
smiling at you as if at any moment you might
ask her to dance & her life would begin again
at the beginning, long before you were someone
she could forget.

Now there is no present you can sit with her
upon like a sofa & discuss the world you shared
one small beautifully wrapped moment at a time;
that world has been lost like an old map in which
every street & neighborhood you loved her in
has faded into a memory of everything you believed
she was or was meant to be, all the dear good feeling
now floating past like cloud shadows crossing
her still bright smile one memory at a time . . .

Now—her dreamy knuckle clicking
on tables as if in answer to someone's knocking.
No one is ever at the door, of course, but you
want someone to be there, just once, knocking.

STEPHEN YENSER

Kerouacky

> *I want my Partotooty*
> *Sweetie backpie back*
>   —*Mexico City Blues*

Oh, where are those lovely early smogs,
Those sheer, cherry smazes of 1959
That jazzed up the evening sun
Before it went out for the orgasmic night
In crazy organzas of blushes and jacaranda blues.

In the old days, the bold, the bop days on the beach,
In the starry daze of those fried nights, those satyr days,
Skinny-dipping, cocky, nippled in the bud,
Hip and slaphappy, dripping moon and copping feels,
We promised that we'd leave no tern unstoned.

Riffs, we wanted, rough drafts, *the gist of poesy*, the jism,
Just drift and spin—and lowest tides got high with us,
Before we roach-clipped the kick sticks and, bushwhacked,
    lipstuck,
Hellbent, slabhappy now, laid some rubber, split
To crash, and to record some slipsticked Zs.

We never cried over spilt milk, spilt pot, spilt seed,
Back then, before the tarring of the feathery tribes
(So to speak), the greasing of palms, the rigging of the bay . . .
One night someone changed the sign to read:
"$50 FINE FOR LETTERING."

Back before that, we were still learning
How to treat in turn the nasty sewage badly,
And the city's sordes of insults rolled off the coast
Like water off a great merganser's back . . .
One morning it was thick crude.

So here's one more, one long, one wasted breath,
Axed out of that beat, beat, beat past
To weave into a blasted wreath
To float out over those blessed but bested wraiths,
Oiled, maybe, polluted, but far-out, man, way-out at last.

ACKNOWLEDGMENTS

Special thanks are due to the Chancellors of The Academy of American Poets, and particularly to Chancellor Richard Wilbur, for his kind preface; to Academy President Jonathan Galassi and Executive Director William Wadsworth, for advice and supervision throughout the preparation of the revised edition; and to Paul Gottlieb, President of Harry N. Abrams, Inc., whose imagination brought this book to be, and whose commitment has seen it through to its current incarnation.

The Academy would also like to acknowledge Edith Pavese and Margaret Rennolds Chace at Abrams, for their work on the previous edition; and on the Academy's own staff at the time, Henri Cole, Peter Batacan, Mary Busch, and Alexander Tulinsky, in preparing the original manuscript. Finally, the revised edition would not have been possible without Ellen Cohen's editorial foresight and the assistance of Rebecca Tucker.

CREDITS AND PERMISSIONS

Grateful acknowledgment is made for permission to reproduce the following poems:

"Grapes Making" from *Poems: A Selection* (Funk and Wagnalls Co.) by Léonie Adams, reprinted by permission of Léonie Adams. Copyright © 1954.

"Ice" from *Killing Floor* by Ai, reprinted by permission of Houghton Mifflin Company. Copyright © 1979 by Ai.

"Preludes for Memnon, II" from *Collected Poems*, Second Edition, by Conrad Aiken. Copyright © 1953, 1970 by Conrad Aiken; renewed 1981 by Mary Aiken. Reprinted by permission of Oxford University Press, Inc.

"For John Clare" from *The Double Dream of Spring* by John Ashbery, reprinted by permission of Ecco Press. Copyright © 1970 by John Ashbery.

"In Praise of Limestone" from *W.H. Auden: Collected Poems*, edited by Edward Mendelson. Reprinted by permission of Random House. Copyright © 1976 by W.H. Auden.

"Interval" from *Sunrise Trumpets* by Joseph Auslander. Copyright © 1924 by Harper & Row, Publishers, Inc.; renewed 1953 by Joseph Auslander. Reprinted by permission of Harper & Row Publishers, Inc.

"Flyfishermen in Wartime" from *Day of Fire* by Leonard Bacon. Copyright © 1943 by Oxford University Press, Inc.; Renewed 1971 by Martha Bacon Ballinger. Reprinted by permission of the publisher.

"The Guard at the Binh Thuy Bridge" from *After Our War* by John Balaban, reprinted by permission of University of Pittsburgh Press. Copyright © 1974 by John Balaban.

Marvin Bell, "These Green-Going-To-Yellow" from *These Green-Going-To-Yellow* copyright © 1981 by Marvin Bell. Reprinted with the permission of Atheneum Publishers, Inc. First appeared in *The New Yorker.*

"Jesse James" reprinted by permission of Dodd, Mead & Company, Inc. from *Golden Fleece* by William Rose Benét. Copyright 1933, 1935 by Dodd, Mead & Company. Copyright renewed.

"The Beautiful Ruined Orchard" from *Time Without Number* by Daniel Berrigan, S.J., reprinted by permission of the author. Copyright © 1957 by Daniel Berrigan.

"Dream Song #48" from *77 Dream Songs* by John Berryman, reprinted by permission of Farrar, Straus & Giroux, Inc. Copyright © 1964 by John Berryman.

"Poem" from *Geography III* by Elizabeth Bishop, reprinted by permission of Farrar, Straus & Giroux, Inc. Copyright © 1976 by Elizabeth Bishop.

"Evening in the Sanitarium" from *The Blue Estuaries: Poems 1923–1968* by Louise Bogan, reprinted by permission of Farrar, Straus & Giroux, Inc. Copyright © 1968 by Louise Bogan.

"Stove" from *Available Light* by Philip Booth. Copyright © 1976 by Philip Booth. Originally published in *The New Yorker*. Reprinted by permission of Viking Penguin Inc.

"In a U-Haul North of Damascus" from *In a U-Haul North of Damascus* by David Bottoms, reprinted by permission of William Morrow & Co., Inc. Copyright © 1983 by David Bottoms.

"Driftwood" from *Selected Poems* by Witter Bynner (Alfred A. Knopf), reprinted by permission of the Witter Bynner Foundation for Poetry. Copyright © 1963 by Witter Bynner.

"Transformation Scene" from *The Angled Road* by Constance Carrier (Swallow Press), reprinted by permission of Ohio University Press. Copyright © 1973 by Constance Carrier.

"At the Sign-Painter's" from *Work, for the Night Is Coming*; copyright © 1980 by Cheat Mountain Poets and reprinted by permission of Jared Carter.

"An Old Woman of the Roads" by Padraic Colum from *Wild Earth and Other Poems* (Henry Holt & Co., 1916), copyright by the Estate of Padraic Colum, reprinted by permission of Maire O'Sullivan.

"Rent" reprinted by permission of *Green House* and Anvil Press Poetry: London, from *Scaffolding: New and Selected Poems*. Copyright © 1984 by Jane Cooper.

370

"Night Thoughts" by Henri Coulette, from *The Iowa Review*, fall 1983, reprinted by permission of *The Iowa Review*. Copyright © 1983 by Henri Coulette.

"Nightsong" by Louis Coxe, from *The Yale Review*, summer, 1983, reprinted by permission of *The Yale Review*, copyright © Yale University.

"my father moved through dooms of love" Copyright 1940 by e.e. cummings; renewed 1968 by Marion Morehouse Cummings. Reprinted from *Complete Poems 1913–1962* by e.e. cummings by permission of Harcourt Brace Jovanovich, Inc.

"To Whom It May Concern" © J.V. Cunningham, 1983. From *Two Poems*, Chimera Broadsides, Series Two: Matrix Press, Palo Alto, California.

"The Money Cry" by Peter Davison, from *Poetry*, August 1982. Reprinted by permission of *Poetry*. Copyright © 1982 by Peter Davison.

"Earliness at the Cape" from *Collected Poems 1919–1962* by Babette Deutsch (Indiana University Press). Copyright © 1963 by Babette Deutsch. Reprinted by permission of Adam Yarmolinsky.

Stephen Dobyns, "The Delicate, Plummeting Bodies" from *Heat Death*. Copyright © 1980 by Stephen Dobyns. Reprinted with the permission of Atheneum Publishers. First appeared in *The New Yorker*.

"Animal" from *Poems of Five Decades*, copyright 1954 by Max Eastman, copyright renewed by Yvette Szekely Eastman 1982. All rights reserved.

"The Fury of Aerial Bombardment" from *Collected Poems 1930-1976* by Richard Eberhart. Copyright © 1960, 1976 by Richard Eberhart. Reprinted by permission of Oxford University Press, Inc.

Peter Everwine, "The Brother" from *Collecting The Animals*. Copyright © 1972 by Peter Everwine. Reprinted with the permission of Atheneum Publishers.

"Mae West" from *Stars in My Eyes* by Edward Field. Reprinted by permission of Sheep Meadow Press. Copyright © 1978 by Edward Field.

"Ya Se Van Los Pastores" by Dudley Fitts, from *Poems 1929–1936*, copyright 1937 by New Directions. Reprinted by permission of New Directions Publishing Corporation.

"History" by Robert Fitzgerald, from *Spring Shade, Poems 1931–1970*, copyright 1943 by Robert Fitzgerald. Reprinted by permission of New Directions Publishing Corporation.

"The Visitor" from *The Country Between Us* by Carolyn Forché. Copyright © 1979 by Carolyn Forché, reprinted by permission of Harper & Row, Publishers, Inc. First appeared in *The Atlantic Monthly*.

"Squash in Blossom," copyright © 1950, 1978 by Robert Francis, reprinted from *Robert Francis: Collected Poems, 1936–1976* (University of Massachusetts Press, 1976).

"Never Again Would Birds' Song Be the Same" from *The Poetry of Robert Frost* edited by Edward Connery Lathem. Copyright 1942 by Robert Frost. Copyright © 1969 by Holt, Rinehart and Winston. Copyright © 1970 by Lesley Frost Ballantine. Reprinted by permission of Holt, Rinehart and Winston, Publishers.

"October Elegy" from *Long Walks in the Afternoon* by Margaret Gibson, reprinted by permission of Louisiana State University Press. Copyright © 1982 by Margaret Gibson.

"Beginning by Example" by Christopher Gilbert reprinted by permission of the author. Copyright © 1981 by Christopher Gilbert. First appeared in *Tendril*, Summer 1981, No. 11.

"The Two-Headed Calf" by Laura Gilpin, Copyright © 1976 by Transatlantic Review, from *The Hocus-Pocus of the Universe* by Laura Gilpin. Reprinted by permission of Doubleday & Company, Inc.

"Anachronism" reprinted from *Collected Poems* by Oliver St. John Gogarty by permission of Devin Adair copyright 1954, renewed 1982.

"Elegy and Flame" from *Another Look* by Horace Gregory. Copyright © 1973, 1974, 1975, 1976 by Horace Gregory. Reprinted by permission of Holt, Rinehart and Winston, Publishers.

"La Fontaine de Vaucluse" from *Taking Notice* by Marilyn Hacker. Reprinted by permission of Alfred A. Knopf. Copyright © 1980 by Marilyn Hacker.

"Ox Cart Man" from *Kicking the Leaves* by Donald Hall (Harper & Row, 1978), reprinted by permission of the author. Originally appeared in *The New Yorker*. © 1978 by Donald Hall.

"Lighting the Night Sky" reprinted from *Lighting the Night Sky* by Kenneth O. Hanson with the permission of Breitenbush Publications. Copyright © 1983 by Kenneth O. Hanson.

"A Dawn Horse" from *One Long Poem* by William Harmon, reprinted by permission of Louisiana State University Press. Copyright © 1982 by William Harmon.

"Locus" is reprinted from *Angel of Ascent, New and Selected Poems* by Robert Hayden, by permission of Liveright Publishing Corporation. Copyright © 1975, 1972, 1970, 1966 by Robert Hayden.

"The Transparent Man" by Anthony Hecht first appeared in *The New England Review*, Winter 1980. Reprinted by permission of the author.

"Nocturne" from *Collected Poems* by Robert Hillyer. Reprinted by permission of Alfred A. Knopf. Copyright © 1961 by Robert Hillyer.

"For the Sleepwalkers" from *For the Sleepwalkers* by Edward Hirsch. Reprinted by permission of Alfred A. Knopf. Copyright © 1961 by Robert Hillyer.

"Plans for Altering the River" is reprinted from *Making Certain It Goes On, The Collected Poems of Richard Hugo*, with the permission of W.W. Norton & Co., Inc. Copyright © 1984 by the Estate of Richard Hugo.

"The Offering of the Heart" from *The Wind of Time* (Charles Scribner's Sons) by Rolfe Humphries. Copyright © 1949 by Rolfe Humphries. Reprinted by permission of the Trustees of Amherst College.

"90 North" from *The Complete Poems* by Randall Jarrell, reprinted by permission of Farrar, Straus & Giroux, Inc. Copyright © 1941 and renewed in 1968 by Mrs. Randall Jarrell.

"Hurt Hawks" from *The Selected Poetry of Robinson Jeffers*. Reprinted by permission of Random House. Copyright © 1965 by Robinson Jeffers.

"Bus Stop" Copyright © 1966 by Donald Justice reprinted from *Night Light* by permission of Wesleyan University Press.

"In a Prominent Bar in Secaucus One Day" from *Nude Descending a Staircase* by X.J. Kennedy (Doubleday), reprinted by permission of the author and Curtis Brown Ltd. Copyright © 1961 by X.J. Kennedy.

"Saint Francis and the Sow" from *Mortal Acts, Mortal Words* by Galway Kinnell. Copyright © 1980 by Galway Kinnell. Reprinted by permission of Houghton Mifflin Company.

"The Testing Tree" from *The Poems of Stanley Kunitz 1928–1978*, reprinted by permission of Little, Brown and Company. Copyright 1978 by Stanley Kunitz. First appeared in *The New York Review of Books*.

"Report from a Planet" from *Poems from Three Decades* by Richmond Lattimore (Charles Scribner's Sons). Reprinted by permission of Alice Lattimore. Copyright © 1972 by Richmond Lattimore.

"Angel" from *Hundreds of Fireflies* by Brad Leithauser. Reprinted by permission of Alfred A. Knopf. Copyright © 1982 by Brad Leithauser.

"Degli Sposi" from *Etruscan Things* by Rika Lesser, reprinted by permission of George Braziller, Inc. Copyright © 1983 by Rika Lesser.

Philip Levine, "On My Own" from *One For the Rose*. Copyright © 1981 by Philip Levine. Reprinted with the permission of Atheneum Publishers, Inc.

"For Zbigniew Herbert, Summer, 1971, Los Angeles" from *The Dollmaker's Ghost* by Larry Levis, reprinted by permission of E.P. Dutton. Copyright© 1981 by Larry Levis.

"For the Union Dead" from *For the Union Dead* by Robert Lowell, reprinted by permission of Farrar, Straus & Giroux, Inc. Copyright© 1964 by Robert Lowell.

"After Tempest" by Percy MacKaye from *My Dear Lady Arise* published by MacMillan Company Copyright© 1940.

"You, Andrew Marvell" from *New and Collected Poems 1917–1976* by Archibald MacLeish. Copyright© 1976 by Archibald MacLeish. Reprinted by permission of Houghton Mifflin Company.

"The Third Wonder" from *New Poems: Eighty Songs at Eighty* by Edwin Markham, reprinted by permission of Doubleday & Company, Inc. Copyright© 1932 by Edwin Markham.

"The Hill" from *Spoon River Anthology* by Edgar Lee Masters (Macmillan), reprinted by permission of Ellen C. Masters. Copyright© 1962 by Edgar Lee Masters.

"A Winter Without Snow" from *Scenes from Another Life* by J.D. McClatchy, reprinted by permission of George Braziller, Inc. Copyright© 1981 by J.D. McClatchy.

"Parents" from *The Cheer* by William Meredith, reprinted by permission of Alfred A. Knopf. Copyright© 1980 by William Meredith. First appeared in *The New Yorker*.

James Merrill, "Lost in Translation" from *Divine Comedies*. Copyright© 1980 by James Merrill. Reprinted with the permission of Atheneum Publishers, Inc. First appeared in *The New Yorker*.

W.S. Merwin, "Yesterday" from *Opening the Hand*, Copyright© 1983 by W.S. Merwin. Reprinted with the permission of Atheneum Publishers, Inc.

"Couplets, XX" from *Couplets* by Robert Mezey (Westigan Press), reprinted by permission of the author. Copyright© 1977 by Robert Mezey.

"Family" from *To All Appearances* by Josephine Miles. Reprinted by permission of the University of Illinois Press. Copyright© 1974 by Josephine Miles. First appeared in *The New Yorker*.

"The Cameo" from *Collected Poems* by Edna St. Vincent Millay (Harper & Row), reprinted by permission of Norma Millay. Copyright© 1956 by Edna St. Vincent Millay.

"The Jerboa" from *Collected Poems* by Marianne Moore, reprinted by permission of Macmillan Publishing Co., Inc. Copyright 1935 by Marianne Moore, renewed 1963 by Marianne Moore and T.S. Eliot.

"Monet Refuses the Operation" by Lisel Mueller, from *The Paris Review*, summer, 1982, reprinted by permission of the author. Copyright© 1982 by Lisel Mueller.

"Now Blue October" by Robert Nathan, from *The Green Leaf* (Alfred A. Knopf), reprinted by permission of the author. Copyright© 1950 by Robert Nathan.

From *The Song of Jed Smith* by John G. Neihardt, copyright John G. Neihardt, published by the University of Nebraska Press.

"The Makers" from *Sentences* by Howard Nemerov (University of Chicago Press) reprinted by permission of the author. Copyright© 1980 by Howard Nemerov.

"Cigar Smoke, Sunday, After Dinner" from *Collected Poems* by Louise Townsend Nicholl, reprinted by permission of E.P. Dutton. Copyright© 1953 by Louise Townsend Nicholl.

"Tide Turning" from *The Kiss: A Jambalaya* by John Frederick Nims. Copyright© 1982 by John Frederick Nims. Reprinted by permission of Houghton Mifflin Company. First appeared in *The Atlantic Monthly*.

"The Kiss" from *The Night of the Hammer*© 1959, by Ned O'Gorman. Reprinted by permission of Harcourt Brace Jovanovich, Inc.

"First Love" by Sharon Olds, from *The American Poetry Review*, volume 12, number 3, reprinted by permission of the author. Copyright© 1983 by Sharon Olds.

"Jurgis Petraskas, the Workers' Angel, Organizes the First Miners' Strike in Exeter, Pennsylvania" from *Jurgis Petraskas* by Anthony Petrosky, reprinted by permission of Louisiana State University Press. Copyright © 1983 by Anthony Petrosky.

"Last Words" from *The Collected Poems of Sylvia Plath* edited by Ted Hughes. Copyright© 1961 by Ted Hughes. Reprinted by permission of Harper & Row, Publishers, Inc.

"Villanelle: The Psychological Hour" by Ezra Pound, from *Personae*, copyright© 1926 by Ezra Pound. Reprinted by permission of New Directions Publishing Corporation.

"Judith of Bethulia" from *Selected Poems, Third Edition, Revised and Enlarged*, by John Crowe Ransom. Reprinted by permission of Alfred A. Knopf. Copyright 1945 by John Crowe Ransom.

"Strength Through Joy" by Kenneth Rexroth, from *Collected Shorter Poems of Kenneth Rexroth*, copyright 1944 by New Directions. Reprinted by permission of New Directions Publishing Corporation.

"Singing Death" from *Some Lamb* by Stan Rice, reprinted by permission of The Figures. Copyright© 1975 by Stan Rice.

"Lost on a September Trail, 1967" from *Whispering to Fool the Wind* by Alberto Ríos. Reprinted by permission of Sheep Meadow Press. Copyright© 1982 by Alberto Ríos.

Edwin Arlington Robinson, "For a Dead Lady" from *The Town Down the River*. Copyright 1910 Charles Scribner's Sons. Copyright renewed 1938 Ruth Nivison. Reprinted with the permission of Charles Scribner's Sons.

"Effort at Speech Between Two People" from *Waterlily Fire* by Muriel Rukeyser (Macmillan) reprinted by permission of International Creative Management, Inc. Copyright© 1935 and 1962 by Muriel Rukeyser.

"The People, Yes," section 11, from *The People, Yes* by Carl Sandburg, copyright 1936 by Harcourt Brace Jovanovich, Inc.; renewed 1964 by Carl Sandburg. Reprinted by permission of the publisher.

"The Fifth Season" from *Essay on Air* by Reg Saner, reprinted by permission of Ohio Review Books. Copyright 1984 by Reg Saner.

"The Living Room" from *Portraits and Elegies* by Gjertrud Schnackenberg. Copyright© 1982 by Gjertrud Schnackenberg. Reprinted by permission of David R. Godine, Publisher, Inc.

"Salute" from *Freely Espousing* by James Schuyler (Doubleday), reprinted by permission of the author. Copyright© 1969 by James Schuyler.

"What is Poetry" from *Apollo Helmet* by James Scully (Curbstone Press), reprinted by permission of the author. Copyright © 1983 by James Scully.

"A Dimpled Cloud" by Frederick Seidel, from *Raritan*, winter, 1983, reprinted by permission of the author. Copyright © 1983 by Frederick Seidel.

"Definition" by Lauren Shakely, from *Sulfur #5*, reprinted by permission of the author. Copyright© 1982 by Lauren Shakely.

"Old Mountain Road" from *Austerities* by Charles Simic, reprinted by permission of George Braziller, Inc. Copyright © 1982 by Charles Simic.

"Old Apple Trees" from *If Birds Build With Your Hair* by W.D. Snodgrass, reprinted by permission of Nadja Press. Copyright © 1979 by W.D. Snodgrass. First appeared in *The New Yorker*.

"Gifts" from *Outsiders* by Karen Snow, by permission of The Countryman Press Copyright© 1983 by Karen Snow.

"Swans" from *Slow Wall: Poems (Together With) Nor Without Music and Further Poems*, by Leonora Speyer. Reprinted by permission of Alfred A. Knopf. Copyright © 1939 by Leonora Speyer.

374

"Spell Against Spelling" from *The Argot Merchant Disaster* by George Starbuck, copyright © 1980 by George Starbuck. First appeared in *The Atlantic Monthly*. By permission of Little, Brown and Company in association with the Atlantic Monthly Press.

"I Remember Galileo" from *The Red Coal* by Gerald Stern, reprinted by permission of Houghton Mifflin Company. Copyright © 1981 by Gerald Stern.

"Ants and Others" from *Heroes, Advise Us* (Charles Scribner's Sons) reprinted by permission of Curtis Brown Ltd. Copyright © 1964 by Adrien Stoutenberg.

Mark Strand, "My Mother on an Evening in Late Summer" from *Selected Poems*. Copyright © 1980 by Mark Strand. Reprinted with the permission of Atheneum Publishers, Inc. First appeared in *The New Yorker*.

"Speaks the Whispering Grass" from *Album of Destiny* by Jesse Stuart (E.P. Dutton), reprinted by permission of The Jesse Stuart Foundation, Judy B. Daily, Chair, P.O. Box 391, Ashland, Kentucky 41114. Copyright © 1944.

"Some Small Shells from the Windward Islands" from *Half Sun Half Sleep* by May Swenson (Charles Scribner's Sons), reprinted by permission of the author. Copyright © 1966 by May Swenson. First appeared in *The New Yorker*.

"Aeneas at Washington" from *Selected Poems* by Allen Tate (Charles Scribner's Sons), reprinted by permission of Farrar, Straus & Giroux, Inc. Copyright © 1937, 1977 by Allen Tate.

"Adam's Dying" from *Poems* by Ridgely Torrence, by permission of Macmillan Publishing Co., Inc. Copyright 1941, 1952, 1980 by Macmillan Publishing Co., Inc.

"Telephone Poles" from *Telephone Poles and Other Poems* by John Updike. Reprinted by permission of Alfred A. Knopf. Copyright © 1963 by John Updike.

"The Seven Sleepers" from *100 Poems* by Mark Van Doren, reprinted by permission of Hill & Wang, a division of Farrar, Straus & Giroux, Inc. Copyright © 1967 by Mark Van Doren.

Mona Van Duyn, "Letters from a Father" from *Letters from a Father*. Copyright © 1982 by Mona Van Duyn. Reprinted with the permission of Atheneum Publishers.

"Driving into Enid" from *More Trouble with the Obvious* by Michael Van Walleghen. Reprinted by permission of the University of Illinois Press. Copyright © 1981 by Michael Van Walleghen.

"The Shooting of John Dillinger Outside the Biograph Theater, July 22, 1934" from *Collected Poems 1956–1976* by David Wagoner, reprinted by permission of Indiana University Press. Copyright © 1976 by David Wagoner.

"American Portrait: Old Style" from *Now and Then: Poems 1976–1978* by Robert Penn Warren. Reprinted by permission of Random House. Copyright © 1978 by Robert Penn Warren.

John Hall Wheelock, "Hippopotamothalamium" from *The Gardener and Other Poems* copyright © 1961 by John Hall Wheelock. Reprinted with the permission of Charles Scribner's Sons.

"Advice to a Prophet" copyright © 1959 by Richard Wilbur. Reprinted from his volume *Advice to a Prophet and Other Poems* by permission of Harcourt Brace Jovanovich, Inc.

"The Mental Hospital Garden" by William Carlos Williams, from *Pictures from Brueghel*, copyright 1954 by William Carlos Williams. Reprinted by permission of New Directions Publishing Corporation.

"Two Stories" reprinted from *The Other Side of the River* by Charles Wright, by permission of Random House. Copyright © 1984 by Charles Wright. First appeared in *The New Yorker*.

"The Minneapolis Poem" copyright © 1966 by James Wright. Reprinted from *James Wright: Collected Poems* by permission of Wesleyan University Press.

"Text" copyright © 1934, 1935 by Audrey Wurdemann. Reprinted from *Bright Ambush* (The John Day Co., Inc.) by permission of Harper & Row, Publishers, Inc.

For the Expanded Edition:

"Beija-Flor" from *Jaguar of Sweet Laughter* by Diane Ackerman, reprinted by permission of Random House, Inc. Copyright © 1991 by Diane Ackerman.

"Shadow Roses Shadow" and "Hôtel de la Paix" from *In the Storm of Roses*, translated by Mark Anderson, reprinted by permission of the author. Copyright © 1986 by Mark Anderson.

"The Storm" from *The Storm and Other Things*, translated by William Arrowsmith, reprinted by permission of W. W. Norton, Inc. Copyright © 1986 by William Arrowsmith.

"The Wild Dog's Steps" from *Desiring Flight* by Christianne Balk, reprinted by permission of Purdue University Press. Copyright © 1995 by Christianne Balk.

"Thirty-six Poets" from *The Weight of Numbers* by Judith Baumel, reprinted by permission of Wesleyan University Press. First published in *The Paris Review*. Copyright © 1988 by Judith Baumel.

"Psalm: It Must Be the Medication" from *Psalms*, by April Bernard, reprinted by permission of W. W. Norton, Inc. Copyright © 1993 by April Bernard.

"Garments" from *Against Romance* by Michael Blumenthal. Copyright © 1987 by Michael Blumenthal. Used by permission of Viking Penguin, a division of Penguin Books USA Inc.

"Unpolluted Creek" from *Out of the Woods* by Thomas Bolt, reprinted by permission of Yale University Press. Copyright © 1989 by Thomas Bolt.

"The Fire Fetched Down" from *The Fire Fetched Down* by George Bradley, reprinted by permission of Alfred A. Knopf, Inc. Copyright © 1996 by George Bradley.

"Down the Little Cahaba" from *Crime Against Nature* by Minnie Bruce Pratt, reprinted by permission of Firebrand Books. Copyright © 1989 by Minnie Bruce Pratt.

"Weep-Willow" from *Wildwood Flower* by Kathryn Stripling Byer, reprinted by permission of Louisiana State University Press. Copyright © 1992 by Kathryn Stripling Byer.

"Soul Make a Path Through Shouting" from *Soul Make a Path Through Shouting* by Cyrus Cassells, reprinted by permission of Copper Canyon Press. Copyright © 1994 by Cyrus Cassells.

"Outside Perpignan in Heavy Rain" from *In the Year of the Comet* by Nicholas Christopher. Copyright © 1992 by Nicholas Christopher. Used by permission of Viking Penguin, a division of Penguin Books USA Inc.

"Syrinx" from *A Silence Opens* by Amy Clampitt, reprinted by permission of Alfred A. Knopf, Inc. Copyright © 1994 by Amy Clampitt.

"A Long Way from the Starlight" from *Now We're Getting Somewhere* by David Clewell, reprinted by permission of The University of Wisconsin Press. Copyright © 1994 by David Clewell.

"Science" from *Science and Other Poems* by Alison Hawthorne Deming, reprinted by permission of Louisiana State University Press. Copyright © 1994 by Alison Hawthorne Deming.

"Mother Love" from *Mother Love* by Rita Dove, reprinted by permission of Alfred A. Knopf, Inc. Copyright © 1995 by Rita Dove.

"The True Fable" from *Tales of Trilussa* by John DuVal, reprinted by permission of The University of Arkansas Press. Copyright © 1990 by John DuVal.

"Crows in a Strong Wind" from *Victims of the Latest Dance Craze* by Cornelius Eady, reprinted by permission of the Ommation Press. Copyright © 1996 by Cornelius Eady.

"Achilles Fights the River" from *The Iliad*, translated by Robert Fagles. Copyright © 1990 by Robert Fagles. Used by permission of Viking Penguin, a division of Penguin Books USA Inc.

"The Dream" from *The Life and Letters* by Irving Feldman, reprinted by permission of the author. Copyright © 1994 by Irving Feldman.

"A Night-Time River Road" from *Strangers* by David Ferry, reprinted by permission of the author. Copyright © 1983 by David Ferry.

"Creeley Madrigal" by Peter Gizzi was first published in a limited edition for the Materials Press. Copyright © 1994 by Peter Gizzi.

"Adam's Daughter" by Debora Greger, from *The Nation* (February 12, 1996) Copyright © 1996 The Nation Company, Inc.

"Fin de la Fiesta" from *From the Iron Chair* by Greg Glazner, reprinted by permssion of W. W. Norton, Inc. Copyright © 1992 by Greg Glazner.

"Valentine's Day, 1916" from *The Squanicook Eclogues* by Melissa Green, reprinted by permission of W. W. Norton, Inc. Copyright © 1987 by Melissa Green.

"Mary Snorak the Cook, Skermo the Gardener..." from *The Ether Dome* by Allen Grossman, reprinted by permission of New Directions Press. Copyright © 1991 by Allen Grossman.

"Mother's Visit No. 29" by Peter Hargitai was first published in *California Quarterly* (1986). Copyright © 1986 by Peter Hargitai.

"A Shave by the Ganges" by Jeffrey Harrison, first published in *The New Yorker* (August 31, 1992), and reprinted with permission. Copyright © 1992 by Jeffrey Harrison.

"Gauguin's White Horse" from *In the Absense of Horses* by Vicki Hearne, reprinted by permission of the author. Copyright © 1983 by Vicki Hearne.

"Identities" by Daniel Hoffman, from *The Best American Poetry 1992*. Copyright © 1992 by Daniel Hoffman. First published in *Boulevard* literary magazine.

"The Mad Potter" from *Harp Lake* by John Hollander, reprinted by permission of Alfred A. Knopf, Inc. Copyright © 1988 by John Hollander.

"The Candid Shot" from *Game of Statues* by Martha Hollander, reprinted by permission of Atlantic Monthly Press. Copyright © 1990 by Martha Hollander.

"Volcano House" from *The River of Heaven* by Garrett Hongo, reprinted by permission of Alfred A. Knopf, Inc. Copyright © 1988 by Garrett Hongo.

"Like Most Revelations" from *Like Most Revelations* by Richard Howard, reprinted by permission of Pantheon Books. Copyright © 1994 by Richard Howard.

"The Chinese Insomniacs" from *The Chinese Insomniacs* by Josephine Jacobsen, reprinted by permission of University of Pennsylvania Press. Copyright © 1981 by Josephine Jacobsen.

"Nell" by Rodney Jones was first published in *The Georgia Review*, and forthcoming in *Things That Happen Once* (Houghton Mifflin, 1996). Copyright © 1996 by Rodney Jones.

Brigit Pegeen Kelly: "Song" copyright © 1995 by Brigit Pegeen Kelly. Reprinted from *Song*, by Brigit Pegeen Kelly, with the permission of BOA Editions, Ltd,. 92 Park Ave., Brockport, NY 14420.

"On a Line from Valéry" by Carolyn Kizer, reprinted from the *Princeton University Library Chronicle*, Vol. 55, no. 3 (Spring 1994). Copyright © 1994 by Carolyn Kizer.

"In the Park" by Maxine Kumin from *Nurture*, reprinted by permission of the author. Copyright © 1989 by Maxine Kumin.

Li-Young Lee: "From Blossoms" copyright © 1986 by Li-Young Lee. Reprinted from *Rose*, by Li-Young Lee, with the permission of BOA Editions, Ltd., 92 Park Ave., Brockport, NY 14420.

"From a Chipped Cup" from *Steam Dummy & Fragments from the Fire* by Chris Llewellyn, reprinted by permission of Bottom Dog Press. Copyright © 1993 by Chris Llewellyn.

"Florida in January" by William Logan first appeared in the *Southwest Review* (Spring/Summer 1992), and is reprinted by permission of the author. Copyright © 1992 by William Logan.

"At the Window" form *These Modern Nights* by Richard Lyons, reprinted by permission of the University of Missouri Press. Copyright © 1988 by Richard Lyons.

"Earth" from *Guardian* by Cleopatra Mathis, reprinted by permission of Sheep Meadow Press. Copyright © 1995 by Cleopatra Mathis.

"Cotillions" from *Watch Fire* by Christopher Merrill, reprinted by permission of White Pine Press, 10 Village Square, Fredonia, NY 14063. Copyright © 1994 by Christopher Merrill.

"Evening" from *The Selected Poetry of Rainer Maria Rilke*, translated by Stephen Mitchell and reprinted by permission of Random House, Inc. Copyright © 1984 by Stephen Mitchell.

"Hansel and Gretel" by Harold Moss from *A Swim off the Rocks*, Copyright © 1976 by Howard Moss. Reprinted by permission of the Estate of Howard Moss.

"Streets" from *Words under the Words* by Naomi Shihab Nye, reprinted by permission of Far Corner Books. Copyright © 1995 by Naomi Shihab Nye.

"Abstraction" from *Apocrypha* by Eric Pankey, reprinted by permission of Alfred A. Knopf, Inc. Copyright © 1991 by Eric Pankey.

"Take" from *Dark Fields of the Republic* by Adrienne Rich, reprinted by permission of W. W. Norton, Inc. Copyright © 1995 by Adrienne Rich.

"Dreaming about the Dead" by Katha Pollitt, first published in *The New Yorker* (October 3, 1988), and reprinted with permission. Copyright © 1988 by Katha Pollitt.

"Tourette's Journey" from *Because the Brain Can Be Talked into Anything* by Jan Richman, reprinted by permission of Louisiana State University Press. Copyright © 1995 by Jan Richman.

"Raven" by J. Allyn Rosser first appeared in *Poetry* (October 1992), and is reprinted by permission of Helen Klaviter. Copyright © 1992 by The Modern Poetry Association.

"Brownie Troop #722 Visits the Nursing Home" from *Sunday Skater* by Mary Jo Salter, reprinted by permission of Alfred A. Knopf, Inc. Copyright © 1994 by Mary Jo Salter.

"Writing in Darkness" from *Old Growth* by Andrew Schelling, reprinted by permission of Rodent Press. Copyright © 1995 by Andrew Schelling.

"Homecoming" from *Country Airport* by Peter Schmitt, reprinted by permission of Copper Beech Press. Copyright © 1989 by Peter Schmitt.

"A Luna Moth" from *The Minute Hand* by Jane Shore, reprinted by permission of University of Massachusetts Press. Copyright © 1986 by Jane Shore.

"The Spirit Ariel" from *Rainer Maria Rilke: Uncollected Poems*, translated by Edward Snow and reprinted by permission of Farrar, Straus & Giroux. Copyright © 1995 by Edward Snow.

"Eros" from *The Color Wheel* by Timothy Steele, reprinted by permission of The Johns Hopkins University Press. Copyright © 1994 by Timothy Steele.

Barton Sutter: "Geneva" copyright © 1993 by Barton Sutter. Reprinted from *The Book of Names*, by Barton Sutter, with the permission of BOA Editions, Ltd., 92 Park Ave., Brockport, NY 14420.

"Their House" by Elaine Terranova, first published in *The New Yorker* (June 10, 1991), and reprinted with permission. Copyright © 1991 Elaine Terranova.

"Feverish Propositions" from *The Reproduction of Profiles* by Rosmarie Waldrop, reprinted by permission of New Directions Press. Copyright © 1987 by Rosmarie Waldrop.

"Song" from *Stained Glass* by Rosanna Warren, reprinted by permission of W. W. Norton, Inc. Copyright © 1993 by Rosanna Warren.

"For a Girl Walking the Fields of Michigan in Mourning" from *The Unlovely Child* by Norman Williams, reprinted by permission of Alfred A. Knopf, Inc. Copyright © 1985 by Norman Williams.

"Fourth of July, Texas, 1956" from *Campo Santo* by Susan Wood, reprinted by permission of Louisiana State University Press. Copyright © 1991 by Susan Wood.

"Self-Portrait with Max Beckmann" from *Berlin Dyptichon*, Poems by John Yau, Photographs by Bill Barrette, text © John Yau 1995. Reprinted by permission of Timken Publishers.

"Kerouacky" by Stephen Yenser is forthcoming in the *Partisan Review* (1996). Copyright © 1996 by Stephen Yenser.

"Fire Lyric" from *Fire Lyric* by Cynthia Zarin, reprinted by permission of Alfred A. Knopf, Inc. Copyright © 1993 by Cynthia Zarin.

The Academy of American Poets
Chancellors, Fellows, and Award Winners Since 1934

Peter Gizzi (1959–), Peter I.B. Lavan Younger Poets Award, 1994.
Page 329.

Greg Glazner (1958–), Walt Whitman Award, 1991. Page 303.

Oliver St. John Gogarty (1878–1957), Fellow, 1954. Page 53.

Jorie Graham (1951–), Peter I.B. Lavan Younger Poets Award, 1990.
Page 356.

Melissa Green (1954–), Peter I.B. Lavan Younger Poets Award, 1989.
Page 267.

Martin Greenberg (1918–), Landon Translation Award, 1989.
Page 359.

Debora Greger (1949–), Peter I.B. Lavan Younger Poets Award, 1987.
Page 360.

Horace Gregory (1898–1982), Fellow, 1961. Page 149.

Allen Grossman (1932–), Bassine Prize, 1989. Page 293.

Marilyn Hacker (1942–), Lamont Poetry Selection, 1973. Page 182.

Donald Hall (1928–), Lamont Poetry Selection, 1955. Page 162.

Kenneth O. Hanson (1922–), Lamont Poetry Selection, 1966.
Page 226.

Peter Hargitai (1947–), Landon Translation Award, 1988. Page 261.

William Harmon (1938–), Lamont Poetry Selection, 1970. Page 201.

Jeffrey Harrison (1957–), Peter I.B. Lavan Younger Poets Award, 1989.
Page 305.

Robert Hayden (1913–1980), Fellow, 1975. Page 132.

Vicki Hearne (1946–), Peter I.B. Lavan Younger Poets Award, 1984.
Page 254.

Anthony Hecht (1923–), Chancellor, 1971–present; Fellow, 1969.
Page 177.

Robert Hillyer (1895–1961), Chancellor, 1949–1961; Sponsor.
Page 105.

Edward Hirsch (1950–), Peter I.B. Lavan Younger Poets Award, 1983.
Page 190.

Daniel Hoffman (1923–), Chancellor, 1972–present. Page 306.

John Hollander (1929–), Chancellor, 1981–present; James A. Michener
Series Abroad, 1984. Page 272.

Martha Hollander (1959–), Walt Whitman Award, 1989. Page 289.

Garrett Kaoru Hongo (1951–), Lamont Poetry Selection, 1987.
Page 276.

Richard Howard (1929–), Chancellor, 1991–present; Fellow, 1989.
Page 331.

Marie Howe (1950–), Peter I.B. Lavan Younger Poets Award, 1988.
Page 332.

Richard Hugo (1923–1982), Fellow, 1981. Page 143.

Rolfe Humphries (1894–1969), Fellow, 1955. Page 91.

Josephine Jacobsen (1908–), Fellow, 1987. Page 252.

Randall Jarrell (1914–1965), Chancellor, 1956–1965. Page 81.

Robinson Jeffers (1887–1962), Chancellor, 1946–1956; Fellow, 1958; Sponsor; Commemorative Stamp Issued, 1973. Page 51.

Rodney Jones (1950–), Peter I.B. Lavan Younger Poets Award, 1986. Page 362.

Donald Justice (1925–), Lamont Poetry Selection, 1959; Fellow, 1988. Page 123.

Brigit Pegeen Kelly (1951–), Lamont Poetry Selection, 1994. Page 339.

X.J. Kennedy (1929–), Lamont Poetry Selection, 1961. Page 109.

Richard Kenney (1948–), Peter I.B. Lavan Younger Poets Award, 1985. Page 363.

Galway Kinnell (1927–), Landon Translation Award, 1978; James A. Michener Series Abroad, 1984. Page 172.

Carolyn Kizer (1925–), Chancellor, 1995–present. Page 334.

Maxine Kumin (1925–), Chancellor, 1995–present; Fellow, 1985. Page 282.

Stanley Kunitz (1905–), Chancellor, 1970–present; Fellow, 1968. Page 134.

Richmond Lattimore (1906–1984), Fellow, 1984. Page 139.

Li-Young Lee (1957–), Lamont Poetry Selection, 1990; Peter I.B. Lavan Younger Poets Award, 1994. Page 262.

Brad Leithauser (1953–), Peter I.B. Lavan Younger Poets Award, 1983. Page 198.

Rika Lesser (1953–), Landon Translation Award, 1982. Page 229.

Philip Levine (1928–), James A. Michener Series Abroad, 1984. Page 191.

Larry Levis (1946–), Lamont Poetry Selection, 1976. Page 193.

Chris Llewellyn (1942–), Walt Whitman Award, 1986. Page 311.

William Logan (1950–), Peter I.B. Lavan Younger Poets Award, 1989. Page 307.

Robert Lowell (1917–1977), Chancellor, 1962–1977; Copernicus Award, 1974. Page 115.

Richard Lyons (1951–), Peter I.B. Lavan Younger Poets Award, 1992. Page 277.

Percy MacKaye (1875–1956), Fellow, 1948. Page 70.

Archibald MacLeish (1892–1982), Chancellor, 1946–1949; Fellow, 1966; Special Honorary Fellow, 1974. Page 54.

Edwin Markham (1852–1940), Fellow, 1937; Sponsor. Page 58.

Edgar Lee Masters (1868–1950), Fellow, 1946; Commemorative Stamp Issued, 1969. Page 38.

Cleopatra Mathis (1947–), Peter I.B. Lavan Younger Poets Award, 1984. Page 341.

J.D. McClatchy (1945–), Chancellor, 1996–present; James A. Michener Series Abroad, 1983; Fellow, 1991. Page 231.

William Meredith (1919–), Chancellor, 1963–1987; Fellow, 1990. Page 185.

Christopher Merrill (1957–), Peter I.B. Lavan Younger Poets Award, 1993. Page 283.

James Merrill (1926–1995), Chancellor, 1979–1995. Page 151.

W.S. Merwin (1927–), Chancellor, 1988–present; Fellow, 1973. Page 233.

Robert Mezey (1935–), Lamont Poetry Selection, 1960; Bassine Prize, 1988. Page 160.

Josephine Miles (1911–1985), Fellow, 1978. Page 142.

Edna St. Vincent Millay (1892–1950), elected a Fellow, declined, 1949; Commemorative Stamp Issued, 1981. Page 52.

Stephen Mitchell (1943–), Landon Translation Award, 1984, 1990. Page 256.

Marianne Moore (1887–1972), Chancellor, 1952–1964; Fellow, 1965. Page 60.

Howard Moss (1922–1987), Chancellor, 1987; Fellow, 1986. Page 251.

Lisel Mueller (1924–), Lamont Poetry Selection, 1975. Page 203.

Robert Nathan (1894–1985), Chancellor, 1951–1968; Honorary Fellow, 1974. Page 93.

John G. Neihardt (1881–1973), Chancellor, 1951–1967; Special Honorary Fellow, 1974. Page 76.

Howard Nemerov (1920–1991), Chancellor, 1976–1991; Fellow, 1970. Page 181.

Louise Townsend Nicholl (1890–1981), Fellow, 1954. Page 95.

John Frederick Nims (1913–), Fellow, 1982. Page 205.

Naomi Shihab Nye (1952–), Peter I.B. Lavan Younger Poets Award, 1988. Page 342.

Ned O'Gorman (1929–), Lamont Poetry Selection, 1958. Page 106.

Sharon Olds (1942–), Lamont Poetry Selection, 1983. Page 237.

Eric Pankey (1959–), Walt Whitman Award, 1984. Page 295.

Anthony Petrosky (1948–), Walt Whitman Award, 1982. Page 230.

Sylvia Plath (1932–1963), College Prize Award, 1955. Page 133.

Katha Pollitt (1949–), Peter I.B. Lavan Younger Poets Award, 1984. Page 280.

Ezra Pound (1885–1972), Fellow, 1963. Page 40.

Minnie Bruce Pratt (1946–), Lamont Poetry Selection, 1989. Page 284.

John Crowe Ransom (1888–1974), Fellow, 1962. Page 45.

Kenneth Rexroth (1905–1982), Copernicus Award, 1975. Page 84.

Stan Rice (1942–), Edgar Allan Poe Award, 1977. Page 144.

Adrienne Rich (1929–), Fellow, 1992. Page 343.

Jan Richman (1960–), Walt Whitman Award, 1994. Page 345.

Alberto Ríos (1953–), Walt Whitman Award, 1981. Page 208.

Edwin Arlington Robinson (1869–1935), Founder; Advisor.
Page 37.

J. Allyn Rosser (1957–), Peter I.B. Lavan Younger Poets Award, 1991.
Page 308.

Muriel Rukeyser (1913–1980), Copernicus Award, 1977. Page 65.

Mary Jo Salter (1954–), Lamont Poetry Selection, 1988; Peter I.B.
Lavan Younger Poets Award, 1990. Page 335.

Carl Sandburg (1878–1967), Sponsor. Page 67.

Reg Saner (1931–), Walt Whitman Award, 1975. Page 235.

Andrew Schelling (1953–), Landon Translation Award, 1992.
Page 346.

Peter Schmitt (1958–), Peter I.B. Lavan Younger Poets Award, 1991.
Page 285.

Gjertrud Schnackenberg (1953–), Peter I.B. Lavan Younger Poets
Award, 1983. Page 211.

Philip Schultz (1945–), Lamont Poetry Selection, 1984. Page 364.

James Schuyler (1923–1991), Fellow, 1983. Page 129.

James Scully (1937–), Lamont Poetry Selection, 1967. Page 238.

Frederick Seidel (1936–), Lamont Poetry Selection, 1979. Page 245.

Lauren Shakely (1948–), Walt Whitman Award, 1977. Page 207.

Jane Shore (1947–), Lamont Poetry Selection, 1986. Page 263.

Charles Simic (1938–), Edgar Allan Poe Award, 1975; James A.
Michener Series Abroad, 1983; Landon Translation Award, 1993.
Page 213.

W.D. Snodgrass (1926–), Fellow, 1972. Page 170.

Edward Snow (1941–), Landon Translation Award, 1985. Page 347.

Karen Snow (1923–), Walt Whitman Award, 1978. Page 241.

Leonora Speyer (1872–1956), Chancellor, 1948–1951; Sponsor.
Page 71.

George Starbuck (1931–), James A. Michener Series Abroad, 1982.
Page 214.

Timothy Steele (1948–), Peter I.B. Lavan Younger Poets Award, 1986.
Page 336.

Gerald Stern (1925–), Lamont Poetry Selection, 1977; Fellow, 1993.
Page 194.

Adrien Stoutenberg (1916–1982), Lamont Poetry Selection, 1964.
Page 118.

Mark Strand (1934–), Chancellor, 1996–present; Edgar Allan Poe
Award, 1974; Fellow, 1979. Page 186.

Jesse Stuart (1907–1984), Fellow, 1960. Page 86.

Barton Sutter (1949–), Bassine Prize, 1986. Page 312.

May Swenson (1919–1990), Chancellor, 1980–1990; Fellow, 1979.
Page 124.

Allen Tate (1899–1979), Chancellor, 1966–1979; Fellow, 1963.
Page 56.

Elaine Terranova (1939–), Walt Whitman Award, 1990. Page 297.

Ridgely Torrence (1875–1950), Founder; Chancellor, 1950; Fellow,
1947; Sponsor. Page 78.

John Updike (1932–), Sponsor. Page 113.

Mark Van Doren (1894–1972), Chancellor, 1949–1952; Fellow, 1967;
Sponsor. Page 87.

Mona Van Duyn (1921–), Chancellor, 1985–present; Fellow, 1980.
Page 217.

Michael Van Walleghen (1938–), Lamont Poetry Selection, 1980.
Page 195.

David Wagoner (1926–), Chancellor, 1978–present. Page 119.

Rosmarie Waldrop (1935–), Landon Translation Award, 1994.
Page 269.

Robert Penn Warren (1905–1989), Chancellor, 1972–1988; Copernicus
Award, 1976; James A. Michener Series Abroad, 1982. Page 163.

Rosanna Warren (1953–), Peter I.B. Lavan Younger Poets Award, 1992;
Lamont Poetry Selection, 1993. Page 314.

John Hall Wheelock (1886–1978), Chancellor, 1947–1971; Special
Honorary Fellow, 1974. Page 111.

Richard Wilbur (1921–), Chancellor, 1961–1995. Page 107.

Norman Williams (1952–), Peter I.B. Lavan Younger Poets Award,
1987. Page 257.

William Carlos Williams (1883–1963), Fellow, 1956. Page 97.

Susan Wood (1946–), Lamont Poetry Selection, 1991. Page 299.

Charles Wright (1935–), Edgar Allan Poe Award, 1976. Page 248.

James Wright (1927–1980), Fellow, 1971. Page 126.

Audrey Wurdemann (1911–1960), Founder; Sponsor. Page 59.

Jon Yau (1950–), Peter I.B. Lavan Younger Poets Award, 1988.
Page 348.

Stephen Yenser (1941–), Walt Whitman Award, 1992. Page 366.

Cynthia Zarin (1959–), Peter I.B. Lavan Younger Poets Award, 1994.
Page 315.